A WOMEN'S
Berlin

A WOMEN'S
Berlin

Building the Modern City

Despina Stratigakos

UNIVERSITY OF MINNESOTA PRESS

MINNEAPOLIS • LONDON

This book is supported by a grant from the Graham Foundation for
Advanced Studies in the Fine Arts.

Published by the University of Minnesota Press
111 Third Avenue South, Suite 290
Minneapolis, MN 55401-2520
http://www.upress.umn.edu

Library of Congress Cataloging-in-Publication Data

Stratigakos, Despina.
A women's Berlin : building the modern city / Despina Stratigakos.
p. cm.
Includes bibliographical references and index.
ISBN 978-0-8166-5322-5 (hc : alk. paper)—ISBN 978-0-8166-5323-2 (pb : alk. paper)
1. Architecture and women—Germany—Berlin. 2. Space (Architecture)—Germany—
Berlin. 3. Berlin (Germany)—Social conditions—19th century. 4. Berlin (Germany)—
Social conditions—20th century. I. Title.
NA2543.W65S77 2008
720.82′0943155—dc22
2008010012

15 14 13 12 11 10 09 08   10 9 8 7 6 5 4 3 2 1

CONTENTS

ACKNOWLEDGMENTS

Guidance, sustenance, and encouragement for this book have come from many quarters. My visits to Berlin archives over the years yielded not only research materials but also friendship and counsel that enriched and shaped the book. Adriane Feustel at the Alice-Salomon-Archiv, Sabine Sander at the archive of the Pestalozzi-Fröbel-Haus, Andreas Matschenz at the Landesarchiv Berlin, Laurie Stein at the Werkbund-Archiv, Jörg Limberg at the Amt für Denkmalpflege in Potsdam, Gabriele Kirchner at the Zentrum für Berlin-Studien, and Sonja Miltenberger at the Heimatmuseum Charlottenburg-Wilmersdorf have generously offered their time and expertise. Numerous librarians at the Staatsbibliothek zu Berlin and the Kunstbibliothek helped track down the obscure books, pamphlets, and journals that put flesh on the bones of this history.

The Sanders Research Fellowship at the Taubman College of Architecture and Urban Planning at the University of Michigan, the Office of the Dean of Harvard College, and the Whiting Postdoctoral Fellowship in the Humanities at Bryn Mawr College facilitated travel to archives and libraries as well as giving me the time and space to write. Grants from the Graham Foundation for Advanced Studies in the Fine Arts and the Center for Research on Learning and Teaching at the University of Michigan defrayed publication expenses. I am also grateful to the Committee on Degrees in Studies of Women, Gender, and Sexuality at Harvard University for supporting the leave needed to complete the book.

Along the path from archival discoveries to finished text, I benefited enormously from the opportunity to present my ideas to audiences in Europe and North America. For their challenging and thoughtful responses to conference papers and lectures, I thank Gülsüm Baydar, Amy Bingaman, Elizabeth Bolman, Zeynep Çelik, Marie Frank, Simon Gunn, Hilde Heynen, Gregor Kalas, Steven Nelson, Alastair Owens, Kimberly Rhodes, Lise Sanders, Judith Vega, Margrith Wilke, Catherine Zipf, and Rebecca Zorach. To Eve Blau, Margaret Crawford, Ed Dimendberg, Paul

Jaskot, Linda Kerber, Nancy Levinson, Nancy Stieber, and John Stuart, I owe a substantial debt for advice and support in the early phases of writing.

Four scholars read the manuscript from beginning to end, and I am deeply grateful for their help in producing a richer, more nuanced history: Ann Taylor Allen,
Marta Gutman, Susan Henderson, and Leslie Topp. Barbara Miller Lane contributed her expertise and guidance to an early version of the text. For generously sharing their research with me, I am indebted to James Albisetti, Nicola Gordon Bowe,
Grace Brockington, Cornelia Carstens, Winfried Görg, Erika Rappaport, Dorothy
Rowe, and Lora Wildenthal. As the book neared completion, Didem Ekici gathered
elusive images, and Robin Whitaker lent a polishing hand to the text. I have been
especially fortunate to work with Pieter Martin at the University of Minnesota
Press, whose encouragement and belief in the project have never faltered.

Finally, I thank my family and friends for the proximity and warmth of their
hearts and for teaching me how to leave the past behind and emerge, breathing, into
the present.

INTRODUCTION

A Forgotten Metropolis

I F HISTORIES OF BERLIN MENTION WOMEN AND BUILDING, they usually refer to the *Trümmerfrauen*, or rubble women, who after 1945 literally put the city back together again. Berlin's town hall was reassembled largely by female hands and has honored women's labor with a bronze *Trümmerfrau*, who stands today at its entrance. Although portrayed as a heroic figure, she is an accidental builder who salvages rather than constructs. Accounts of women as intentional and even visionary builders in Berlin are difficult to find. Without such stories, evidence of their presence, which still lingers in the city, cannot be integrated into our mental geography of the place.[1] The professional female builder photographed in 1910 while balancing on a ladder above the town hall thus remains suspended in a narrative vacuum (Figure I.1): We lack the means to explain her appearance on the city's rooftops or describe her relationship to the urban landscape below. Similarly, a 1913 woman's guidebook to the German capital fits uneasily in the conventional framework of urban narratives. It reveals a metropolis seen through the lens of the modern woman, who challenged the gendered perimeters of urban life.[2] Old maps disclose her mark on the urban terrain and point us to a surprising number of buildings created by and for women in the years leading up to the First World War, some of which still stand today. Overlooked by architectural historians and unconnected to a broader context, these structures nevertheless persist as stubborn but mute monuments to an alien world. What (and where) is this unknown place that is glimpsed unexpectedly in such images, texts, and physical artifacts? This book retraces a largely forgotten city, a site of both dreams and real spaces, that I call a women's Berlin.

Around the turn of the twentieth century, women began to claim Berlin as their own, expressing a vision of the German capital that embraced their feminine modernity. They did so partly in terms of physical interventions in the built environment, erecting structures, creating spaces, and occupying terrains. From residences to restaurants, a visible network of women's spaces arose to accommodate changing patterns of life and work. Alongside these material transformations emerged a visionary encounter: In words and images, female residents reconceived the metropolis in search of an urban experience that acknowledged and supported their evolving identities. Female journalists, artists, political activists, and social reformers portrayed women as influential actors on the urban scene, encouraging female audiences to view their relationship to the city in a radically different light. Connecting the imaginary to the physical, dreams to asphalt, women remapped Berlin as the birthplace of a new female subject.

Four important factors coincided in the imperial period (1871–1918) to give rise to this experiment and, in particular, to its physical dimensions. The first of these involved money. By the end of the nineteenth century, the bourgeois women's

FIGURE I.1. A woman builder making repairs to the roof of Berlin's town hall, 1910. From *Illustrierte Frauenzeitung* 38, no. 2 (1910): 17.

movement in Germany had coalesced into a strong and dynamic (if not entirely unified) force for social change.[3] Among its achievements, it counted the entry of bourgeois women into higher education and professional careers, a change that held the potential to revolutionize conventional gender and family roles. The emergence of independent women, an unprecedented social type, produced new architectural needs as women broke away from the domestic spaces that had defined the traditional orbit of their lives. As individuals, they lacked offices and studios, dining rooms that made a lone woman feel welcome, places to entertain clients or relax with friends, and, at the end of the day, a place to call home. Collectively, they also needed schools, clubhouses, exhibition venues, and commercial spaces—indeed, a whole architectural infrastructure to sustain an emerging urban culture of "emancipated" women. Women devised a variety of strategies to finance building projects, which also received the committed support of wealthy female patrons, including some of Berlin's richest widows. The increasing economic clout of the women's movement, moreover, coincided with shifts in German financial institutions, particularly cooperatives, which further empowered women's groups as architectural patrons (see chapter 1). Thus, women's increasing wealth and the development of legal structures that enabled mutual aid provided the means to intervene in Berlin's built environment, which required a level of capital far in excess of the moderate resources available to most individual women.

Yet the ability to build does not explain why women would choose to do so. Evolving gender roles, as noted above, provoked a desire for architectural innovation. The often monumental scale of women's building projects in Berlin, however, suggests that more than functional necessity was at stake. Architecture also fulfilled a new representational concern among women, which they shared with other emerging urban constituencies. The imperial period witnessed Berlin's debut as a global capital, accompanied by an acute self-consciousness among its residents of living in an era of unrivaled industrial and commercial growth. From German unification in 1871 to the end of the nineteenth century, Berlin's population rose from 826,000 to 3 million (including the suburbs).[4] Its boundaries expanded apace, rivaling London as the largest city in Europe. By 1914, the nation had also acquired territories in Africa, Asia, and the Pacific, making Berlin the metropole of a vast colonial empire. To its detractors and champions alike, Berlin epitomized the tempo, processes, and appearance of modernity. This was perhaps nowhere as visible as in the frenzied construction and development that seemed to overtake the capital, leading long-term residents to complain that they barely recognized their own city.[5] Berlin appeared to transform almost overnight from a provincial backwater into a crowded metropolis boasting "immense and palatial buildings" and "magnificent" thoroughfares.[6] Like other groups struggling to make their presence felt in a rapidly transforming urban landscape, middle-class women grasped the importance of spatial capital. With the city sprawling in all directions and new buildings going up at an over-whelming pace, women understood that their claim to urban power rested in part on being able to express it visibly in physical form.

In addition to the financial resources of the women's movement and the pressure to build in the German capital, the integration of the design professions repre-sented a third contributing factor to the creation of a women's Berlin. In the first decade of the twentieth century, when many of the women's building projects dis-cussed in this book were conceived, women earned the right to matriculate in the architecture programs of Germany's technical colleges. In the same period, some government-run applied art schools began to admit female students, supplementing the design training available to women in segregated private institutions.[7] Berlin, offering economic and cultural opportunities difficult to find elsewhere, as well as a supportive community of professional women, became a center for female archi-tects and designers. In 1907, Emilie Winkelmann opened her office in the city's fash-ionable West End, establishing the first architectural firm owned by a woman in Germany. Highly successful, her office expanded to fifteen employees, including junior female architects.[8] While her firm remained a rarity, interior design businesses headed by women artists blossomed in Berlin before the First World War.[9] Although men were also hired to design women's spaces, a significant number of such com-missions went to their female colleagues (and to Winkelmann in particular). Female patrons called on women architects and designers to help them define and articulate their architectural needs. Many of the projects analyzed in the following chapters represent a collaborative effort uniting female patrons, architects, and designers to explore the nature of female aesthetics and spaces. This creative process might have occurred without female design professionals, but their presence in the city appears to have pushed women toward a more extensive engagement with built form.

Finally, the appearance of a sizable population of single independent women in Berlin provided an identifiable clientele for architectural experimentation, as well as a strong stimulus to rethink women's relationship to their urban environment. This is not to say that married women did not also actively participate in the creation of a women's Berlin. Embracing the challenges of modernity as housewives and moth-ers, married women contributed to reordering the urban spaces of female subjec-tivity on both an intellectual and a material basis. Nevertheless, single independent women—and a public awareness of them as a new and needy urban constituency—represented a critical driving force in many of the built projects featured in this book. By the 1890s, increasing access to higher education produced a group of middle-class women with the capacity to leave the parlor for a more public life centered on work, friends, and the rich life of the metropolis. Many of these women did not marry, either by choice or by necessity. Following the example of other German states, the Prussian government imposed a celibacy clause on female teachers, the largest group of women in the free professions. Unlike their male colleagues, who could wed and retain their positions, female teachers were expected to model their lives on those of nuns.[10] In general, Wilhelmine Germans tended to dismiss the possibility of women combining marriage and career, and Prussian law gave husbands the right to terminate their wives' employment contracts.[11] Thus, many women who strove for a professional life either could not or would not marry. As these growing contingents of educated single women explored their new urban identities, they articulated the desire for a built environment responsive to their changing lifestyles. Despite often meager salaries, their ability to pool resources along with the generosity of wealthy patrons furnished sufficient capital to realize this dream in part. Working-class women living on their own in Berlin, who far outnumbered self-supporting bourgeois women, did not enjoy the resources to reshape the urban built environment in a comparable manner. Their uses and appropriation of urban space thus remain largely outside the parameters of this study, which focuses on women's architectural interventions. Nonetheless, chapter 5 examines an area in which working- and middle-class women collided in the struggle to control urban space: specifically, in the architecture of social work.

Class remains, however, a dominant theme of the book, for the new freedom enjoyed by bourgeois women depended, in large measure, on their class status, and the architecture they created for themselves showcased their identities as members of an increasingly influential urban bourgeoisie. The vision of a women's Berlin was thoroughly and deeply inflected by class. Chapter 1, which focuses on the 1913 women's guidebook to the city, reveals a mental map of the city predicated on a certain level of social and economic entitlement. Chapter 2, on the Lyceum Club, a women's professional organization, illustrates how members in Berlin contributed to middle-class debates on luxury by using their clubhouse to reform the image of women as aesthetic spendthrifts. Other chapters explore the intersection of architecture and class values from the point of view of domesticity (chapter 3), exhibition design (chapter 4), and social welfare (chapter 5). Through their architecture, bourgeois women distinguished their urban identities not only from those of men but also, and importantly, from those of other women. Gender was never the only variable in the construction of the modern woman.

Beyond class, age and professional status further united or divided women in their search for meaningful architectural form. Experiments in housing the single woman, explored in chapter 3, redefined domesticity around personal relationships based on the bonds of youth, old age, or professional identity. For example, female teachers in Berlin, tired of living in rented rooms among strangers, hired the architect Paul

Mebes to design an apartment block reserved exclusively for women in their profession. By contrast, many of the projects discussed in this book are notable for
their efforts to forge connections among women from different walks of life. The
women's clubs discussed in chapters 2 and 5 advertised themselves as class-bridging
organizations seeking to lessen the impact of Berlin's rigid social hierarchies. They
also welcomed members across religious lines, uniting the city's Jewish, Protestant,
and Catholic women. As a tool for empowerment, architecture could be used to
foster identity politics that emphasized or downplayed differences.

   In a period of rampant German imperialism, it is not surprising to find that
efforts to define women's spaces were bound up with issues of national identity.
Chapter 2 recounts the painful growing struggles of the Berlin branch of the Lyceum
Club, headquartered in London, as it attempted to shed its image as a British trans-
plant in Berlin and create an architectural style worthy of its German members.
In tracing the evolution of its clubhouse from "English" ostentation to "German"
simplicity, this chapter underscores the importance of local and national contexts
in determining how women intervened in the urban built environment. Although
the phenomenon of women claiming urban space was widespread at the turn of
the twentieth century and manifested itself in cities as diverse as Dallas and Paris,
methods varied according to local conditions.[12] In the case of the clubhouse, architectural strategies that successfully enabled women to appropriate space in London
proved disastrous in Berlin. At the same time, this chapter reveals the importance of
transnational dialogues among women seeking to reshape the modern city. Female
builders in Berlin looked to parallel developments in Western cities, particularly
London, for inspiration. Women's magazines and newspapers in Germany maintained a competitive eye on other countries, reporting on the creation of a women's
hotel in New York, for example, or a women's center on the Champs-Elysées, in
Paris.[13] The articulation of women's spaces thus represented a convergence of transnational conversations, involving a shared exploration of gendered public space, with
local and national discourses. In the book, I have attempted to remain attentive to
this broader picture while emphasizing the importance of specificity in the vision
of a women's Berlin.

   Among Western cities, Berlin represents an especially important case study
because of the concentration of women's building projects before the First World
War, due to the factors listed above, which produced a more fully realized conception of an alternative metropolis. Berlin, furthermore, is unusual not only because
of the copiousness of such construction but also for the involvement of women
architects and designers. To date, most accounts of women's claims to urban space
have been written by scholars of urban literature and social historians.[14] The topic
has been broached rarely by architectural historians, with the result that buildings

have largely dropped out of consideration in analyzing how women created a public presence for themselves in the modern city. This book seeks to refocus attention on the built environment, particularly on the importance of architectural language, in the gendered appropriation of urban spaces. Paying close attention to the choices made by builders and patrons, I demonstrate how women in Berlin employed architectural language to create specific and meaningful identities for themselves as public citizens. Architecture became a medium through which women expressed contested notions of modernity in a language shared and understood by Berliners. By reading the buildings as carefully coded texts, I hope to make apparent the significance of visual and spatial representations to marginal urban populations seeking a metropolis that recognized and accommodated difference.

Architecture does more than signify, however, and I am equally concerned with understanding how it reshaped gendered experiences, particularly the experience of the public sphere. I pay special attention to monumental projects, such as the Victoria Studienhaus, a residential center for university women that was designed by Winkelmann and created a new model for the German academic experience (see chapter 3). Scholars of vernacular architecture, decrying the limitations of mainstream architectural history, have rightly emphasized the importance of structures usually considered too humble or derivative for the canon. As they point out, such a narrow view excludes the vast majority of building, sharply distorting our historical perception.[15] Historians of women's architecture have made similar arguments for the significance of the vernacular, including interstitial and temporary sites.[16] I would argue that a balanced picture also depends on a consideration of how women used monumentality—with its associations of power and permanence—for their own purposes. Although women had fewer resources than men to build on a large scale, the following chapters make clear that they dreamed big and fought hard to realize their visions. Moreover, Berlin does not represent an anomaly among Western cities. In 1893, for example, women in New York endorsed the design of a giant clubhouse that would shelter the city's women's clubs. Fourteen stories high, the palazzo-style building would offer members luxurious facilities, including meeting rooms, a banquet hall, a gymnasium, Turkish baths, a library, a theater, and a museum, as well as shops and workspaces.[17] Although this scheme failed to leave the drawing board, other similarly grand projects reached completion, such as the Woman's Temple, a "state-of-the-art skyscraper" erected in 1892 in downtown Chicago by the Woman's Christian Temperance Union.[18] Such projects do not appear in architectural history books, for having assumed that women did not build skyscrapers or other "big" things, we have failed to look for them.

Monumentality challenged cultural precepts that forbade "respectable" women to be visible in the city. Big buildings constituted an explicitly disruptive urban presence, boldly refuting traditional conceptions of women's proper place. Their monumentality declared that women would not be contained but would instead expand upward and outward into the public spaces of urban life. This desire to express one's modern identity through buildings also suggests a very different strategy from that adopted by the *flâneur*. The phenomenon of women building their modernity into the very fabric of the city underscores, as sociologist Janet Wolff has argued about literature, the insufficiency of notions of subjectivity that emphasize disembodied engagement or ephemerality as a universal response to the experience of modernity, a position exemplified in the writings of urban commentators such as Georg Simmel, Karl Scheffler, and Hans Ostwald.[19] These male critics, lamenting the instability of modern life, voiced one reaction—to be sure, shared by many Wilhelmine Germans—to the capital's unruliness. Not all Berliners, however, took a pessimistic view of urban dislocation.[20] Seeing the familiar landscape of the city vanish under the onslaught of industrial urbanization, many middle-class women glimpsed their liberation and joined the fray, helping to construct the new Berlin with the zeal of the converted. "We must all adapt to the lively new tempo," wrote a contributor to the 1913 women's guidebook, "or like Epimenides, sleep through the entire boom."[21]

As visionary builders constructing an alternative way of being in the city, Berlin women rejected a homogenizing view of modernity and defined their experiences in relation to the concept of difference. This book seeks to understand how they marked difference in spatial and architectural terms. Surprisingly, the rise of a more explicitly gendered landscape undermined the fixity of separate spheres for men and women, a model that historians and political theorists reject as simplistic and misleading.[22] Instead of presenting us with a clear and deep divide, a women's Berlin proves both more permeable and edgier: Women pressed against traditional boundaries, crossing over into a "man's" world, while also erecting new barriers that protected and nurtured their evolving urban identities. The Victoria Studienhaus, which allowed women to participate more fully in German academic life, but on their own terms, is an apt example. Such architectural interventions pursued neither integration nor separation but something more fluid and dynamic. They also reveal bourgeois women to be more radical than we might expect on the basis of either the chief ideology of the women's movement at the time or its subsequent histories. Leaders of the bourgeois women's movement emphasized "spiritual motherhood," a seemingly more conciliatory stance toward the problem of women's rights.[23] Against the adversarial politics and violent protests of English suffragettes, who, insisting on equality with men, hurled bricks through store windows and stormed Parliament, German feminist reformers such as Henriette Goldschmidt and Alice Salomon maintained that women would better effect profound social and cultural change by honing maternal qualities specific to their gender and introducing these gently into German culture, primarily by raising their children to become more peaceable citizens and by participating in social service. This strategy allowed German men and women to understand the struggle for women's emancipation as a more palatable quest for national improvement and fostered certain assumptions, reinforced by some historians, about the docility of German feminists vis-à-vis the London militants, suggesting a temperamental divide between Teutonic and Anglo-Saxon women.[24] While not displacing the ideological centrality of "spiritual motherhood" in the German bourgeois women's movement, which indubitably shaped women's attitudes toward the built environment (such as in the campaign for female housing inspectors, discussed in chapter 5), a focus on architecture suggests a more complex and, in some cases, contradictory picture of gendered politics on the ground. Berlin's bourgeois women emerge as bolder and more explicitly confrontational and aggressive than we have come to expect; they, too, used bricks to fight exclusions, but by combining them with mortar rather than launching them through glass.

A city reimagined and reshaped by women is too vast an entity to be contained in a single book. In selecting themes, buildings, and narratives, I have concentrated on those that highlight an awareness of the role of the urban built environment in the creation of a modern female identity. While I believe the resulting picture is representative, it is by no means exhaustive. More work remains to be done, particularly in understanding women's physical imprint on the urban fabric. For lack of space, I have excluded institutions and structures worthy of attention, such as the Association of Berlin Female Artists and the impressive building they erected in 1911 to house their classes and exhibitions, and have barely touched on other significant projects, such as a hospital designed by Winkelmann for female doctors and patients.[25] I hope this study itself acts as a guidebook, sufficiently intriguing readers to prompt further explorations in archives and books and on the city's streets.

The Berlin that emerges in the following chapters is at once familiar and strange: We recognize the street names, but the maps look different. Place and gender intersect to produce fresh accounts of the city and new meanings in the contested process of modernity. In 1910, Scheffler, alienated by the ceaseless pace of change in the German capital, declared that Berlin was condemned forever to become and never to be.[26] We can and should expect no less of its history, and the story of a women's Berlin, which interweaves architectural and gendered struggles, encourages us to look anew at the complex making and remaking of a modern metropolis.

I Remapping Berlin

A Modern Woman's Guidebook to the City

IN 1913, A NOVELTY APPEARED IN BERLIN BOOKSTORES. *Was die Frau von Berlin wissen muss* (What a Woman Must Know about Berlin) was a guide to the city written by and for women (Figure 1.1). After two centuries of housewifery manuals that instructed women on their duties to family and home, this book encouraged women to look outward—to find their lives and identities in the streets and institutions of the modern city. Led by the reassuring voices of female experts, readers embarked on a voyage to the terra incognita of an anatomy classroom, political assemblies, and newspaper offices, among other traditionally male realms. Alongside these incursions, the book described the rise of a visibly different gendered landscape as female patrons and builders began to define and construct architectural spaces for women. Mapping the capital from a female perspective, the guidebook equated the modernity of urban living (Berlin's "American pulse," according to one of its authors) with a new kind of energetic and outgoing woman who embraced the metropolis as her own.[1]

Why did the city's female residents need such a book? Its editor, Eliza Ichenhaeuser, a prominent suffragette, promised readers an "intellectually, artistically, and socially profound guide through Berlin." This was no Baedeker, satisfying the tourist's superficial curiosity or desire to get from one site of amusement to another. Instead, the book presented itself as a compass to navigate the city's essential core. Its audience was envisioned as middle-class women, both long-term residents and recent arrivals to Berlin, who hungered for a deep and serious engagement with their urban milieu. In twenty-five essays, penned by women touted as "capable guides," the book offered readers a view of Berlin from an "artistic, scientific, literary, political, theatrical, musical, and social standpoint" while also encouraging them to become actively involved.[2] Dr. Rhoda Erdmann, a pioneer cellular biologist, outlined a woman's options for scientific study and the facilities available to her, including anatomical theaters segregated by gender (to avoid the embarrassment,

and potential moral danger, of young men and women studying naked bodies together).[3] Design critic Jarno Jessen, surveying the capital's thriving applied arts institutions and industries, noted applied arts schools where talented female students
received instruction from the city's best teachers, exhibitions and showrooms featuring women's design work, and the acclaim earned by female decorators producing Berlin's most stylish shop windows.[4] Even urban poverty and crime represented
new frontiers for reform-minded women. Dr. Alice Salomon, a preeminent social
work educator, emphasized professional opportunities in the city's welfare organizations, many of them founded and run by women.[5] Yet the guide was not all work
and no play. An essay on sports considered the mortal perils of traversing Berlin's

FIGURE 1.1. The cover
of *What a Woman Must
Know about Berlin*, 1913.
The image of a mirror
frame promised the
female reader a
glimpse of her own
urban reflection.

busy streets on bicycles and roller skates, while another on local excursions promoted the pleasures of hiking through Grunewald, the city's green lung.[6]

Conventional Berlin guidebooks aimed at the tourist typically structured their
contents around particular sightseeing areas. The section "Unter den Linden" in the
1912 English edition of Baedeker, for example, conducted the reader from the Bran-
denburg Gate past the Kaiser-Galerie, the royal library, the monument of Frederick
the Great, the university, and the opera house, ending at Schinkel's royal guard house
and the arsenal (Zeughaus).[7] This microtopographical method imparted a sense of
direction and control to the visitor, who might otherwise have been overwhelmed
by the vastness of the unknown. *What a Woman Must Know about Berlin* adopted a notably different approach. Rather than develop a narrow sense of mastery over a specific place, its thematically based chapters covered whole fields of activity that cut
across city districts. A chapter on Berlin fashion, for example, did not simply list the
names and addresses of linen drapers, furriers, and milliners in the shopping areas
around Leipziger Strasse, as we find in the Baedeker. Instead, fashion editor Frieda
Grünert affirmed the relationship between capitalism and the fashion industry and,
into the discussion of mass production, fashion trends, and international markets,
sprinkled the names and locations of particular commercial establishments where
one might shop, having understood how one's actions and choices fit within a larger
economic system.[8] Although the women's guidebook, like the Baedeker, also imparted
topical information needed to navigate the city at a local level, such as in a chapter
on public transportation, the actual physicality of the urban landscape remained
rather abstract. Against Baedeker's linear and grounded trajectories, geared to walk
the visitor from point A to point B, the women's guidebook gave the impression of
floating its readers through the more diffuse and complex spheres of a new world.
While carefully delineating spaces and organizations for women, authors situated
these within a broader, citywide constellation of industries, agencies, and institutions. A woman reading the chapter on Berlin as a city of music thus learned about
the struggles of a newly formed orchestra composed entirely of female musicians
("down to the double bass"), the pleasures of hearing Richard Strauss conduct the
court opera, a charitable foundation that supported poor female singers, the city's
prestigious conservatories, male music critics' exclusive hold on Berlin newspapers,
the cultivation of young talent in the semiprivate realm of salons (hosted by women),
and even the cost of renting a recital hall, among other things.[9] This rich but nebu-
lous mixture captured the vitality of a panurban music scene that, if not without
boundaries for women, contained layers and slippages that defied neat and tidy categories, whether gendered or geographical. The guidebook thus embraced the concept of the city writ large, a complex whole and expansive landscape that encouraged
interventions on the broadest scale.

Across the chapters, an image unfolded of the widening scope of women's urban lives. There was no longer one exclusive site for female activity (the home), but a network of spaces spanning the city. Inserting herself into the pages of the book, a reader might imagine studying at the university, working as a doctor at the Royal Charité Hospital, socializing and forging professional alliances at the Lyceum Club, and strengthening her body in tandem with other members of the Wannsee Ladies' Rowing Club (founded because women could not join the older Berlin Rowing Club). These possibilities undoubtedly thrilled and bewildered, and the guidebook can be interpreted as a quest for orientation in a global sense, an attempt to gain one's bearings in a city with rapidly expanding horizons for women.

The phenomenon of brave new vistas appearing before women was succinctly captured in two extraordinary photographs taken in 1910, a few years before the guidebook's publication. In the first, a female builder repairs the roof of Berlin's town hall (see Figure I.1). Balanced on a ladder high atop the city, this young woman physically intervenes in the urban built environment with her hands and tools. In the second image (Figure I.2), a female photographer stands daringly on the cage railing of a crane being used to construct the Stadthaus, a domed municipal building, as she records the cityscape below her. (Town Hall, the perch of the female builder, appears to the right, partly obscured by two smokestacks.) She, too, enacts mastery over the urban topography, this time through the gaze. Although the creator of these images is unknown, his or her intent appears to have been to document women in male professions. In both, the ascent of women to new occupations is associated with the vertical rise of Berlin, linking female modernity directly to that of the city itself.

Readers of the *Illustrierte Frauenzeitung,* a popular Berlin fashion magazine, encountered the striking image of the female builder amid pages devoted to elegant hats and dresses. The accompanying text introduced her as the first woman to undertake the demanding practical training required for this profession and emphasized the "great deal of courage and self-confidence it takes to stand on a ladder at this height in female clothing and, at the same time, perform a difficult task; in any case, however, this activity should be recommended only to vertigo-free ladies."[10] While depicting the new horizons opening up to women, then, the magazine's editors conveyed a sense of danger pertaining to the female body and its clothing. If her skirt did not snag, the subtext seemed to say, plunging a woman to her death hundreds of feet below, her mental instability (the supposed female tendency to swoon) might lead to a similar ruin. This message, a warning to "lesser" women not to follow in the path of exceptional (and perhaps aberrant) pioneers, was at variance with the calm assurance displayed by the builder, an attitude also manifested by the authors of the Berlin guidebook.

Indeed, the absence of tales of danger in *What a Woman Must Know about Berlin* stood in sharp contrast to the contemporary discourse on women and the city produced by German sociologists, sexologists, and other urban commentators. Such writings, intended for academic and popular audiences, burgeoned at the turn of the century. Many authors focused on working-class women and prostitution, linking deviant female sexuality to the moral depravity of modern urban life.[11] Those sympathetic to the plight of prostitutes portrayed them as victims who, out of naïveté or misfortune, had fallen prey to the corrupting influences of the metropolis. Others depicted them as urban predators, carriers of a diseased and excessive sexuality that destroyed the fabric of moral life. Most writers (and readers) assumed that "respectable ladies" were immune to such dangers. The 1905 publication of *Tagebuch einer Verlorenen* (Diary of a Lost Woman), which purported to be a firsthand account of the fatal descent of a "good" bourgeois daughter into Berlin's underworld, thus scandalized Wilhelmine society. Nonetheless, the diary (in actuality, a fictional work by writer Margarete Böhme) remained an anomaly in this period.[12] The more common view presented prostitution's threat to middle-class women in indirect terms, particularly as it entailed the risk of mistaken identity and the need

FIGURE 1.2. A female photographer high above Berlin, c. 1910. Bildarchiv Preussischer Kulturbesitz/Art Resource, New York.

to be ever-vigilant of one's reputation when venturing out alone in public. In Berlin and other German cities, prostitutes ignored police regulations that attempted to restrict them to certain areas and instead plied their trade along busy thorough-fares and in fashionable restaurants and cafés. Their presence in such places and the inability to distinguish them from "innocent" bystanders prompted acute concern. Male writers complained about the breach of urban boundaries and the risk of exposing their wives and daughters to abuse from prostitutes and their procurers.[13] Conversely, female commentators dreaded the leering glances and obscene remarks of "respectable" men who presumed their sexual availability. They also feared police harassment, behavior that seemed designed to keep all unaccompanied women, whether prostitutes or not, off the streets.[14]

Other narratives of urban danger cast the middle-class woman as their primary victim. Journalists and economists writing on kleptomania, for example, warned of the seductive power of the modern department store over its well-to-do female clientele. Berliners both lauded and condemned the appearance of retailing giants such as Wertheim and Tietz at the end of the nineteenth century, which marked their city as a world-class capital comparable to Paris yet also symbolized the ascendancy of a threatening form of capitalism. Identifying the pernicious effects of the department store, German critics pointed to shoplifting, a new form of urban crime associated with female customers. Émile Zola's *Au bonheur des dames*, published in 1883, exposed popular audiences to this phenomenon in Paris, and by the late 1890s, department store thefts were being widely reported in German newspapers. Alarmed observers noted that many offenders lived in material comfort, a finding that incited volumes of popular and scientific analysis of the conditions provoking wealthy women to steal. Defenders of smaller merchants accused the shopping palaces, with their copiously displayed luxury goods, of destroying bourgeois virtue by arousing women's sensual and impulsive nature. Sexologists, on the other hand, exonerated the department stores and pinned the crime on women's sexual frustrations.[15] In either case, and as with prostitution, urban vice and female sexuality were intertwined in this erotically charged vision of the metropolis.

Social critic Hans Ostwald did much to popularize the sexual image of urban modernity. Between 1904 and 1908, he edited and published a series of pamphlets, *Die Grossstadt-Dokumente* (Big City Documents), dedicated in part to exploring the forms and topography of sexual deviance in the metropolis. Authored by Ostwald and dozens of contributors, the fifty volumes covered topics ranging from lesbianism to banking, and many focused on Berlin. Aimed at a popular audience and sold cheaply, the *Documents* went through as many as fifteen editions in the first few years, with one or two titles remaining in print today.[16] The first pamphlet, *Dunkle Winkel in Berlin* (Dark Corners in Berlin), written by Ostwald, set the tone for much of the series with its vivid tableaux of obscure and highly sexualized urban spaces described from the perspective of the urban *flâneur*. Although Ostwald adopted a disinterested stance toward his subjects, art historian Dorothy Rowe persuasively argues that the *Documents* could be read "as moral indictments of many aspects of Grossstadt living." At the core of this urban corruption lurked the female prostitute, a recurring figure in the texts, who threatened physical and spiritual contagion with her ability to transgress "all of the boundaries that were set up to contain her."[17] The correlation of the "swollen metropolis" (to use Ostwald's term) with excessive female sexuality was certainly not limited to German discourses. Victorian writers, as historian Judith Walkowitz demonstrates, characterized London as a "dark labyrinth" haunted by monstrous female bodies. Particularly in the publicity surrounding the murders of Jack the Ripper, newspapers sensationalized the city's violent and uncontrollable dangers, evoking women's base animality (as embodied by the prostitute) as both the source and the target of crime.[18]

In a marked reversal of this perspective, *What a Woman Must Know about Berlin* portrayed the city's female residents as immanently rational, and Berlin itself as transparent and progressive. "Dark corners" vanish in this account. That is not to say that its authors viewed the German capital through rose-colored glasses. At a time when most public space was defined as insistently masculine and unattached women occupying this realm were presumed to be morally questionable, women faced real and serious problems in asserting their urban presence. Rather than perpetuate discouraging stories of entrenched moral or sexual danger, however, the Berlin guidebook addressed practical hassles that could be negotiated and overcome. In place of rowdy prostitutes and thieving ladies, contributors worried about finding inexpensive apartments and decently paying jobs. Moreover, such difficulties were presented to female readers as reasons not to avoid the public realm—as suggested by cautionary tales of the city's dangers—but rather, if anything, to fight back.

The guidebook's different narrative strategy and approach to female agency are nowhere more pronounced than in a short, and rare, passage that directly touched on the violation of women's bodies. It concerned a political event, overlooked by historians, that epitomized the highly contested boundaries between government authority and female bodies. In the fall of 1911, newspaper notices announcing the new Prussian cremation law caught the astonished eye of female readers. Buried at the end of a paragraph on reporting procedures to be followed by the coroner in cases of natural (that is, not violent) death, a provision mandated that female corpses be examined to ascertain virginity. Not surprisingly, Berlin women erupted with outrage at this seemingly nonsensical and aggressive act on the part of an all-male parliament—a decree that one female doctor described as "a slap in the face" to all women. According to Anna Pappritz, the outspoken leader of the Berlin branch of the International Abolitionist Federation, experts could not produce a valid reason to justify the need for such information. For years, Pappritz and her organization had opposed state regulation of prostitution, and she interpreted the cremation law as yet another government attempt to control the most intimate, private aspects of a woman's life. In this case, the victim, being dead, was wholly unable to resist the invasion, nor could she defend her reputation from the grave, should it be ruined by the coroner's report. Under the auspices of the IAF, Pappritz organized an emergency public meeting, for women only, to protest the new law. The massive turnout, followed by petitions, forced Prussia's secretary of the interior to repeal the virginity clause by early January.[19] Despite the victory, the autopsy scandal prompted calls in the women's press for a broader intervention, namely, female representation in parliament.[20]

Avoiding lurid detail, Anna Plothow, a prominent Berlin editor and feminist, mentioned the cremation law in her guidebook chapter on the women's movement and its organizations. She spoke of the hated provision and its defeat as a collective memory, shared by readers, of effective resistance to oppression.[21] In her account, women's public presence, in the form of a rally, implied something quite different from its usual depiction in mainstream narratives: Rather than expose women to danger, visibility became the vehicle through which they protected the female body and asserted political might. Plothow evoked this landmark of female defiance in a section outlining the campaigns led by middle- and upper-class women against the double standard of morality that permitted prostitution to flourish. In her vision of the German capital, Berlin's streets emerged as a terrain of power contested between men and women.

If city streets and meeting halls could be recuperated as sites of resistance, so, too, could female bodies occupying those (and other) places. Indeed, women's claims to greater authority over the urban environment coincided with efforts to control the contours of their own bodies. It is not surprising that the idea for *What a Woman Must Know about Berlin* originated with Gunda Beeg, a leader in the dress reform movement who died shortly before the guidebook's publication.[22] Dress reformers such as she combined an interest in female emancipation with an awareness of space and movement that shifted easily from the clothing enveloping a woman's body to her broader architectural environment. Fia Wille (also a contributor to the guidebook) and Else Oppler-Legband, both of whom designed and wore reform dresses, played key roles in some of the architectural projects discussed later in this book.[23] Decrying the corset's mutilating structure, reformers promoted loosely cut garments that allowed the female body to expand into space and move freely (Figure 1.3).[24] As middle-class women entered the workforce, some came to view the corseted body as a docile, constraining form of femininity counter to their own dynamic modernity. Women's rights advocates mined the political potential of dress reform as a symbol of liberated female bodies, implications that were not lost on antifeminists, who equated the corset's restraining features with the maintenance of civil order. A 1902–3 *Simplicissimus* cartoon by the artist Thomas Theodor Heine depicts burly policemen forcing a group of "unfeminine" suffragettes, stripped down to their baggy reform underwear, into corsets (Figure 1.4). A decade later, emancipating fashions remained controversial, and the appearance of women in radical clothes on Berlin's streets constituted a newsworthy event. In 1911, the weekly illustrated magazine *Die Welt* published a photograph of four women in bloomers out for a stroll in the Tiergarten, surrounded by a crowd of curious onlookers (Figure 1.5). According to the caption, the trousered ladies caused "a sensation."[25]

Attempts to control and discipline unruly women, whether through corsets or posthumous body searches, arose in a period of backlash against the New Woman, a novel urban type who symbolized a profound and disturbing challenge to social norms. From Chicago through London and Paris to Berlin, "a new female lifestyle became evident in the last decades of the nineteenth century as the marriage age increased and middle-class women began to gain entry into the universities and the workplace, therefore living away from the family home."[26] Their pursuit of "a life beyond the parlor" threatened the ideology of separate spheres.[27] As workers and consumers, they became increasingly visible in the urban landscape, confusing the assumed correlation between public women and prostitutes. Despite their relatively low numbers, the high profile of such women, combined with their unorthodox

FIGURE 1.3. A dress reform party in Berlin. From *Körperkultur* (1906–7): 386.

FIGURE 1.4. Thomas Theodor Heine, "Women's Rights at the Police Station," 1902–3.
From *Simplicissimus* 7, no. 36 (1902–3): 288. Bildarchiv Preussischer Kulturbesitz/Art Resource,
New York. Copyright 2008 Artists Rights Society (ARS), New York/VG Bild-Kunst, Bonn.

ambitions and lifestyles, prompted widespread debate and condemnation. "As a result, the New Woman, a social phenomenon and a literary type of the 1880s and 1890s, became a dominant preoccupation for writers of novels, essays, and popular journalism, propounded in her stereotypical form by satirical publications such as *Punch*."[28] With a combination of jocularity and anxiety, she was variously caricatured as a sexual rebel, a cigarette-smoking lesbian, an "emancipated bundle of nerves" (Thomas Hardy), a bookish frump, a fashionable cyclist, and a man-hating suffragette.[29]

Undoubtedly because of such associations, contributors to the Berlin guidebook avoided the term *New Woman*, alluding instead to "the thinking woman," "the modern woman," "the educated woman," or "the professional woman," among other labels. In most cases, they dispensed with modifiers altogether, simply referring to "women." This choice underscores the intended inclusiveness of the book, which was produced by and for both married and single women. By adopting a broader perspective, the guidebook positioned all of its readers, in their desire to engage with the modernity of the metropolis, as new women. Nonetheless, a significant portion of the book's content addressed the unmarried woman's education, career, housing, and social life. The vision that emerged of competent and intelligent single women

FIGURE 1.5. Four women in bloomers draw crowds in the Tiergarten, 1911. From "Eine Sensation im Berliner Tiergarten: Vier Damen im Hosenrock," *Die Welt* 23, no. 1 (1911): 5.

occupying Berlin's spaces of work and leisure challenged negative stereotypes of the New Woman, such as her self-defeating naïveté, which abounded in contemporary German-language novels, social and scientific tracts, and popular magazines.[30]

If the feminist New Woman often provoked ridicule and rage, another variation, the New Woman as stylish consumer, proved far more popular.[31] Money lay at the heart of her appeal and distinguished her from the parasitic old maid, who was traditionally defined, and reviled, as an unproductive member of society, both in terms of her corporeal infertility and her redundancy in the household economy. In Gabriele Reuter's 1895 novel, *From a Good Family*, spinster Agathe Heidling is dependent on her family for financial support and, lacking even a small allowance to call her own, cannot buy the books for which she desperately yearns.[32] Restricted by her family's sense of propriety and genteel poverty, Agathe lives in a tightly circumscribed world, as delineated by her physical surroundings and imagination. After the turn of the century, social commentators noted the disappearance of such women. "The creature that we used to call an 'old maid' has ceased to exist," exclaimed Bertha von Bülow (writing under a male pseudonym) in 1912.[33] Especially in the women's press, this "creature" was increasingly replaced by a dynamic version of the financially independent urban woman.[34] Among other things, this shift altered the representation of the spinster's domestic spaces (the concrete realization of which is the focus of chapter 3). Whereas the old maid seemed to fade into the obscurity of backrooms, the nascent architectural expression of the New Woman mimicked her public confidence. Recognizing the potential for a new clientele, architects published designs of modern and glamorous spaces for the self-supporting professional woman. Unlike the physical gloominess and discomfort associated with the old maid's room, captured in Reuter's novel, such projects echoed, in their bright and vibrant decoration, their inhabitants' energy and modern elegance.[35] Architects thereby introduced the public to a novel form of urban space in response to the appearance of a new urban type. Writing in the family journal *Daheim*, a male architect addressed the special domestic needs of the New Woman and his efforts to create a spatial "framework" for her lifestyle and personality. Although he emphasized the necessity for "decorous forms," his bedroom design contains a hint of eroticism in the fur rug by the bed (of which we glimpse, tantalizingly, only the foot) and in the frilly, and transparent, skirt on the dressing table (Figure 1.6). Gray, green, and violet silks decorated the room.[36] This was a far cry from the image of the frigid old maid and her equally cold surroundings.

As symbols of the New Woman's economic clout, lavish boudoirs or bicycles paled in comparison to the Women's Bank, which opened in 1910 in the Wilmersdorf district of Berlin as the first institution of its kind in Europe—a cooperative credit union managed by and for women (Figure 1.7).[37] Asserting that money is power, it promoted female emancipation through economic influence and initially envisioned its clientele as single independent women. Its appeal proved much broader, however, and membership grew to include women of all civil and social classes.[38] All of them shared the disadvantages created by a whole apparatus of state laws that reduced women to financial servitude. In its advertising materials, "the bank emphasizes the fact that 9,000,000 German women are engaged in trade and industry, and that if even a percentage of them band together for financial purposes they would represent a great capitalistic power."[39] Wealth talked to politicians, the bank claimed, more effectively than the "desperado politics" of the English suffragettes.[40] By 1914, the bank seemed on the path to success with fifteen hundred members and solid dividends.[41] In the same year, it launched the first financial weekly for women, *Frauenkapital—eine werdende Macht* (Women's Capital—a Power in the Making), a title that reinforced the message of women's financial enfranchisement. The bank portrayed itself as an instrument of the women's movement, offering loans and

FIGURE 1.6. "An Independent Lady's Dwelling," 1916. From "Diplomingenieur Dieter," "Die Wohnung einer selbständigen Dame," *Daheim* 52, no. 32 (1916): 23.

other financial services to women's groups. In so doing, it promoted the model of self-help over charity.

Demanding access for women to the realms of public finance, the new institution received a cool welcome from the banking establishment. A proposal made by *Women's Capital* in early 1914, that female representatives of the Women's Bank be admitted to the floor of the stock exchange, which then barred "women, children, idiots, bankrupts, criminals, and persons afflicted with contagious diseases," was mocked as "a premature April fool's joke" by the *National-Zeitung,* a powerful organ of the financial community.[42] (The London and New York stock exchanges similarly excluded women.)[43] From its inception, the bank had been subject to attacks in the press, particularly from the antifeminist right wing, which accused it of dismantling the German family by enabling the independence of women and children.[44] Unlike other German banks, the Women's Bank permitted its members to open accounts without the consent of fathers or husbands and accepted jewelry and furniture (often the only capital women possessed) as collateral for loans.[45] By the summer of 1914, the bank faced more widespread allegations of questionable practices, and women were warned to take their money elsewhere. Its "uncommon" business methods also brought it into conflict with government authorities.[46] In a police raid conducted on April 24, 1915, and reported on the front page of the *New*

FIGURE 1.7. Showing the money: the Independent Women's Credit Union (later renamed the Women's Bank) in Berlin. From "Die erste Frauen-Bank der Welt," *Deutsche Frauenzeitung* (1911): 623.

York Times, the bank's books were seized as part of a criminal case brought by the crown prosecutor, alleging "fraud and misuse of deposits."[47] In 1916, the bank collapsed under these and other pressures (including the war). Although short-lived, the institution represented a bold, and clearly threatening, attempt to enter the public world of finance and to institute the kind of structural changes necessary for women to amass capital.

Through its efforts to mobilize female economic power in the German capital, the projects discussed in its newspaper, and its physical presence in the city, the Women's Bank encouraged Berlin's female residents to reconceptualize the scope of their intervention in the urban built environment. Fostering self-help initiatives, the bank worked closely with the Women's Apartment Cooperative, a limited liability organization devoted to designing and building residences for the New Woman. Small-scale cooperatives of this sort, although less visible than the Women's Bank, formed a particularly important vehicle for challenging the gendered boundaries of space. Like the bank, they pooled women's economic resources for collective action but focused on specific projects. *What a Woman Must Know about Berlin* recorded the mushrooming variety of these mutual-aid societies, dedicated to ambitious goals as diverse as planning garden cities for single women and constructing a hospital solely for female doctors and patients.[48] Limited liability cooperatives of all types proliferated in Germany around the turn of the century, following an 1889 law that regulated their structure and operation.[49] The building cooperative proved especially popular among the middle classes, for it allowed them to combine their resources to address architectural needs neglected by Berlin's speculative market.

By documenting women's collaborative ventures, the Berlin guidebook once again challenged prevailing notions of female identity in the modern metropolis. Popular literature endorsed the vulnerability of the lone woman, who, lacking male protection, easily succumbed to big-city vices or fell victim to murder.[50] Rejecting this defeatist image, the guidebook offered a mental map of Berlin that bolstered the vulnerable "I" with a more formidable "we." From sculling crews on the idyllic Wannsee to philanthropic clubs in the city's polluted factory districts, the guide cataloged hundreds of female organizations that claimed an ever-increasing range of urban territory for middle-class women pulling together toward new goals. It thus promoted the concept of a female body politic in the city—an aggregate force with a significant social, political, and *physical* impact. Moreover, buildings such as women's clubhouses and residences enabled a woman to imagine and experience herself as part of an urban female collective by creating tangible symbols of female unity in the urban landscape and by physically gathering women in a common space. Mass meetings, such as the protest over the cremation law, also helped individuals visualize their incorporation into a larger female entity. Events of this sort had long been hampered by the Prussian Law of Association, in effect from 1850 to 1908, which prohibited women from belonging to organizations deemed political or attending meetings at which "political matters," defined in vague terms, were discussed.[51] By the time of the guidebook's publication in 1913, female collaboratives and alliances (both political and nonpolitical in nature) were flourishing. Through its encyclopedic effort, the book exposed its readers to the astonishing scope of female cooperation, constructing a powerful vision of Berlin as a place for collective female identity and action.

What a Woman Must Know about Berlin represented a cartography of female agency in the industrial metropolis. In clear, concise language, the guidebook mapped out the city of the modern woman, who, whether single or married, acting alone or in a group, defined herself by her interest in and engagement with her urban milieu. Hers was not, significantly, the detached curiosity of the *flâneur*, exemplified by Ostwald's manner of rambling through Berlin's underworld, discreetly observing the actions and speech of its inhabitants and distilling his experience into colorful vignettes, which the reader enjoyed from the comfort of an armchair. As historian Peter Fritzsche compellingly argues, Ostwald's narrative technique attempted to capture the fleeting sensations of a city perceived as provisional and fragmentary.[52] It also defined the narrator's modern identity as elusive and transitory, a fitting style for someone who had earlier written an autobiographical novel about his vagabonding days. While the women's guidebook shared in a larger project of modernity, it differed in intention and style. Its authors concerned themselves less with conveying impressions than with providing information that readers could put to immediate use. Although the book undoubtedly encouraged its readers to dream of unexplored terrains, it also expected them to act, to follow in the authors' footsteps, in contrast to Ostwald's audience, who (presumably) consumed an alien world voyeuristically through his gaze. Each chapter in the guidebook offered a brief but comprehensive survey of its topic. Assuming the authoritative voice of the expert, contributors recorded histories, analyzed new frontiers, and cataloged resources. Beyond serving a functional purpose, this cogent and orderly style expressed the confident rationality of the modern woman. Unlike Ostwald's narrator, she was not fugitive and becoming; rather, she had arrived.

2 From Piccadilly to Potsdamer Strasse
The Politics of Clubhouse Architecture

THE LYCEUM CLUB WAS NOT A TROJAN HORSE. Writing in November 1905, Gabriele Reuter appealed to readers of *Der Tag* to keep an open mind about the newest women's club in the city.[1] She knew that some of her fellow citizens looked askance at such clubs, the latest apparition in the rise of female strongholds in the city. When the first of these, the posh German Women's Club (Deutscher Frauenklub), opened its doors in 1898, its smoking room for ladies provoked an uproar in the Berlin press.[2] A few years later, journalist Leopold Katscher authored a pamphlet for Hans Ostwald's *Big City Documents* that portrayed women's clubs as the lair of the trousered lesbian, who indulged her desires free of the male gaze.[3] The discomfort elicited by exclusionary public female spaces, where women assembled beyond the scope of male supervision, was not limited to Berlin. By the end of the nineteenth century, clubs and commercial establishments catering to a female bourgeoisie—who, as workers and consumers, demanded their own places of rest and leisure in the city—were spreading rapidly in London, New York, and other Western cities. Alarmed social observers warned that these enterprises freed women from male authority and encouraged them to neglect domestic duties in pursuit of dangerous passions.[4] A *New York Times* reporter, sensing something amiss in ladies' tearooms, which he described as ersatz clubhouses that abetted "the modern woman's invasion of man's sphere," enlisted a female informant to expose their dirty secret: teapots filled with whiskey.[5] More concerned with politics than prohibition, an English novelist vilified female clubs in London "as a nursery for man-haters and rebels, and the nucleus of the new order of feminine supremacy."[6] Katscher was hardly alone, then, in suggesting that more went on in these female spaces than met the eye. Despite the moral suspicion of women's clubs in Berlin, however, Reuter took up her pen to counter libel of a different nature. A Trojan horse is a gift that deceives, and Reuter's task was to assure the German public that the Lyceum Club—imported from England, the nation's arch economic rival—was not about to unleash financial and cultural destruction on the city.

For an organization thought capable of foreign sabotage, the club had begun innocently enough. The idea originated in London as a response to the excitement and pathos of the "modern girl," who lived independently and supported herself through a profession. Constance Smedley, a young writer privileged by wealth and an indulgent family, felt compelled to help her less fortunate female colleagues. Personally working only for pocket money, she worried about daughters from "respectable" homes, who, unsheltered and alone, faced innumerable difficulties in earning a living without losing their reputations. Smedley thus directed her concern to educated middle-class women, whose numbers in the English workforce had risen sharply in the last decades of the nineteenth century.[7] As she stated in her autobiography, their entry into the professions yielded them meager salaries that barely covered room and board. One of her journalist friends skimped on food to pay for clothes that displayed gentility and thereby commanded respect. Social snobbery necessitated such sacrifices. As Smedley wrote: "The difference of the treatment accorded in newspaper offices to women who looked shabby and wretched and those who looked prosperous and insouciant was so great that it infuriated me." Often unable to rent more than a single room, professional women lacked a place to meet with employers or clients. Crucially important social connections also depended on the ability to return invitations with a comparable "impressive hospitality." In class-conscious London society, "the girls felt the need of a substantial and dignified *milieu* where women could meet editors and other employers and discuss matters as men did in their professional clubs: above all, in surroundings that did not suggest poverty."[8] Far from being incidental, architecture had a central role to play in gender equality.

Smedley and a group of friends dreamed of a grand clubhouse that would unite struggling professional women under one roof. In 1904, one year after the Lyceum Club was established with the help of sympathetic and powerful backers, "this Clubhouse in the air" became a reality in the heart of male clubland.[9] The building at 128 Piccadilly formerly housed the Imperial Service Club, a bastion of masculine empire. By taking over the site intact (complete with all the furnishings), the Lyceum Club instantly acquired a home that rivaled "in splendour of appearance and vastness of accommodation many of the London Clubs whose names have become household words" (Figures 2.1–2.3).[10] In these surroundings, women could compete with men on a more level playing field for advancement in the professions. Indeed, Smedley considered the inheritance (to use her term) of a masculine environment, complete with "masculine furniture," particularly advantageous for helping male visitors feel "at home." As the first women's club to enter Piccadilly, and the only one to hold its ground there for the next quarter century, the Lyceum Club excited great curiosity: "The presence of women on the Club balconies and in the great bow-windows created a general stir: the passengers on every bus craned their necks as they passed" (Figure 2.4). The English press, too, took note: "We never spent a cent on publicity," Smedley wrote; "we were merely interesting."[11]

Word of the new institution spread quickly. Within a year of opening its doors, the club had two thousand members, despite turning away scores of applicants on account of insufficient qualifications.[12] Membership was "limited to women of any nationality who have published (a) any original work in literature, journalism, science, art, or music; (b) who have University qualifications; (c) who are wives or daughters of men distinguished in any of the branches of work already referred to."[13] Although those in the last category lacked professional accomplishments of their own, Smedley realized the value of having members with access to powerful male networks.[14] Given the pecuniary difficulties of many professional women, the club attempted to accommodate small budgets, offering, for example, differently priced menus in its restaurant. Nonetheless, fees and membership dues were far from negligible and certainly beyond the range of the working classes, a group elided, in any case, in the Lyceum Club's understanding of the "modern worker."[15] At the same time, the inclusion of all nationalities (across racial categories) was truly extraordinary for a British club of this period.[16]

FIGURE 2.1. Lyceum clubhouse at 128 Piccadilly, London, c. 1905. Postcard, Noble collection C24 P19, Guildhall Library.

FIGURE 2.2. Hall of the London Lyceum Club. From "The Lyceum Club of London: An Organization of Women Engaged in Literary, Artistic, and Scientific Pursuits," *Critic* 46, no. 2 (1905): 136.

For their money, members received goods and services that made the club highly attractive. The club presented itself as a labor union for female "brain workers," aggressively pursuing international markets for their creative work. Promoting a form of gendered free trade, the club promised English women new opportunities to sell their work abroad and foreign members access to domestic markets.[17] To this end, a specially staffed bureau assisted members in their various occupations. It compiled information on publishers, art galleries, and schools and facilitated access to art collections and libraries both at home and abroad. In a more directly managerial role, it organized exhibitions (at the club's own gallery or at external venues), brokered the sale of art, arranged public performances of composers' music, negotiated publication deals for authors, and commissioned translations.[18] The point was not only to promote members' work but also, by rigorous means of selection, to improve its professional caliber.[19] Indeed, an early mission statement published in the club's journal, *The Lyceum*, emphasized the collective effort "to lift the onus of inferiority from women's work and to raise it by a strenuous effort and rigid self-denial to the high plane of man's achievement."[20] Smedley claimed that by elevating

FIGURE 2.3. Dining room at the London Lyceum Club. From "The Lyceum Club of London," 135.

FIGURE 2.4. Women taking tea on the balcony of the London Lyceum clubhouse. From Dora D'Espaigne Chapman, "The Lyceum Club: An International Club for Women," *Girl's Own Paper* 26, no. 1312 (1905): 323.

"the standard of work," the club would thereby raise "the standard of pay," erasing the difference between what men and women earned.[21] Also in the vein of self-improvement, the club encouraged the development of new skills, such as public speaking.[22] Events and speakers hosted by the club provided further opportunities for learning. Members enjoyed access to an in-house library, restaurant, and short-term accommodations. Most important, members benefited from one anothers' company, specifically the opportunity to network and socialize among a group of educated and often powerful women.

Despite similarities to elite men's clubs in London—namely, exclusivity, conspicuous luxury, and sociability—the Lyceum Club presented itself as a different sort of institution. Whereas the hallmark of gentlemen's club culture was aristocratic leisure, the Lyceum Club defined itself around the bourgeois values of professional advancement and self-improvement. Moreover, these elite clubwomen framed their intentions in decisively public terms, in opposition to the rhetoric of privacy articulated by male clubs.[23] This difference is revealing. As architectural historian Jane Rendell argues, "Existing simultaneously as both a public and a private space, the 'club' collapses the separate spheres ideology of two distinct spaces, the male, public city and the female, private home." Clubs, whether for men or for women, were public institutions inasmuch as they enabled people to gather for conversation or entertainment. At the same time, exclusionary membership and other policies, such as forbidding outsiders from entering the premises, asserted club privacy and secrecy. Clubhouses were modeled on domestic dwellings to symbolize their role as a second home, a refuge from the heterogeneous publics of London, and, in the case of men, a place to escape wives and children.[24] Clubs also performed domestic functions for their members, such as providing meals and overnight accommodations. And yet, if clubs blurred the separation between the male, public city and the female, private home, as Rendell maintains, the very different ways in which men and women occupied those realms structured the position of their clubs vis-à-vis broader society. Despite their attention to leisure, male clubs also represented sites of power where some of the nation's most important business was conducted "off the record" by an old boys' network. In this sense, gentlemen's clubs domesticated public matters. The Lyceum Club operated in the opposite direction, pushing from the domestic toward the public. Thus, in a speech delivered at the first anniversary celebration, club president Lady Frances Balfour referred to the clubhouse in Piccadilly as the realization, in a larger sphere, of the same moral values on which women had built British homes, "a city set on a hill among the clubs of our weaker brethren."[25] This metaphor, drawn from the Sermon on the Mount, emphasized the redemptive power of female, domestic virtues for urban life.

To a large extent, the desire for a public presence was true of all women's clubs established in London during this period. By the time the Lyceum Club opened its doors in Piccadilly, a separate "female clubland" had grown up around Dover Street, nicknamed "Petticoat Lane," in close proximity to the men's club district.[26] As historian Erika Rappaport demonstrates, these clubs enabled women to enter more fully into the public life of the city as consumers and citizens. The Lyceum Club's breach of male clubland marked a radical turn, for "nothing so palpably represented masculine power and dominance of the public sphere as the clubhouses that lined Pall Mall, Piccadilly, and St. James's."[27] The perceived threat to male privilege was captured by a journalist on the Lyceum Club's opening day, when

> from the windows of the eleven other clubs on Piccadilly men looked out with shocked faces, and in Pall Mall and St. James' Street there was a shaking of bald heads and a gloomy rustling of *The Times* newspaper. First Dover Street, now Piccadilly. What would the women conquer next?[28]

As Rappaport observes, Piccadilly was celebrated as a particularly masculine street, entrenched in the history and glory of empire.[29] By "conquering" Piccadilly, the Lyceum Club created female public space that literally overlapped with that of men and made explicit, in geographical terms, the founders' intention to gain access to the nation's centers of power. The architectural splendor of the clubhouse physically underscored that claim. Smedley and her friends understood the visible signs of privilege deployed by male clubhouses. By appropriating the latter's majesty and opulence, the Lyceum clubhouse threatened those visual markers of difference. Smedley's comment on the public's shock at seeing women in bow windows is of particular relevance here: This architectural feature was famously associated with the most exclusive gentlemen's clubs in London. "The bow window provided a place for viewing the street, but also allowed the occupants of the club to display their 'conspicuous consumption' or their dress and leisure time to the public."[30] Women's appropriation of such spaces, which put them on display in the city not as potential victims of the street but rather as its masters, thus constituted a highly charged architectural act. Beyond geography and architecture, the activities taking place within the clubhouse reinforced women's claim to public life as artists, intellectuals, and professionals. As much as Lyceum Club members inhabited male clubland, however, they were not of it. At least, not yet. If it did not quite achieve integration, the club attained a proximity to the male public sphere—an ideological space more pervasive and difficult to penetrate than physical male space—that clearly made men uncomfortable.

The Lyceum Club set its sights far beyond male clubland, even beyond England's borders. As Smedley noted in her autobiography, travel to foreign cities posed difficulties for women with limited financial resources or social connections. From the beginning, Smedley and her friends conceived the club as an international network, with "a chain of Clubhouses" uniting the urban centers of Europe and the New World.[31] Like embassies, they would create a welcoming home for the clubwoman abroad, offering inexpensive accommodations and entry into influential circles. The model for what became the International Association of Lyceum Clubs was the self-governing European social clubs established throughout the empire in the nineteenth century to foster Britishness in the colonies.[32] In place of their imperial nationalism, however, the Lyceum Club sought to establish a commonwealth of clubwomen. Judging from the list of foreign women who joined the Lyceum Club in its first year, which included Jane Addams (director of Hull House in Chicago) and M. Carey Thomas (president of Bryn Mawr College), the idea of an empire of female public space resonated strongly across national borders.[33] Indeed, by the late 1920s, the Lyceum Club nearly circumvented the globe, with twenty-eight branches in thirteen countries and on three continents, reaching from London to as far as China and Australia.[34]

Even before the clubhouse in London had opened, Smedley embarked on this expansionist phase, traveling abroad to promote the Lyceum Club mission. By 1908, sister clubs were established in Germany, France, and Italy, and preparations for others were under way in Holland and the United States. Smedley's letters home from Berlin, written in June 1904, describe a relentless circuit of introductions, meetings, and negotiations on behalf of the club. While there, she also attended the International Congress of Women, an event that brought women's rights activists from around the world to the German capital and fostered enthusiasm among local women for Smedley's vision of a global association.[35] Although Smedley felt discouraged by what she perceived as the isolation of female intellectuals from other women as well as by the cult of the "Hausfrau" among German men, Berlin ultimately proved to be fertile ground for her ideas.[36] In 1905, it became the site of the first continental clubhouse.

Of the women's institutions discussed in this book, the Lyceum Club in Berlin ranks among the most tenacious, still functioning today, long after others were swept away by political changes and more than seventy years after the London club was forced into bankruptcy.[37] But this longevity could not have been predicted in its early years. Soon after its founding, tensions between the London and Berlin clubs caused a secession. These struggles reveal a great deal about the importance of cultural differences in the creation of women's urban space and, more particularly, the role of visual signs in articulating those claims, which, like any other language, did not always translate well across national divides. Ultimately, the strategies that worked so effectively to assert a public presence for British women in London threatened to undermine the very same endeavor in Berlin.

The volatile mixture of globalization and local politics that prompted the rupture had already been stirred before the Berlin club existed. Art historian Grace Brockington places the Lyceum clubs in the context of a broad peace movement that opposed the increasing militarism and nationalism of Europe's major powers and spawned the proliferation of international organizations at the end of the nineteenth century. Smedley's efforts to build a global sisterhood centered on modern art, which she believed capable of surmounting human differences.[38] Among her other activities to spur the formation of a Berlin chapter, she coordinated two exhibitions to introduce the work of British Lyceum Club members to German audiences and to sow the seeds for further artistic exchange. The first show, devoted to the arts and crafts, opened in January 1905 in the new Modern Living Spaces gallery of the Wertheim department store (Figures 2.5 and 2.6); the second, featuring

FIGURE 2.5. Arts and crafts exhibition of the London Lyceum Club held in the Modern Living Spaces gallery of the Wertheim department store, Berlin, 1905. From Curt Stoeving, "Ausstellung des Londoner Lyceum-Club in Berlin," *Deutsche Kunst und Dekoration* 16 (1905): 510.

painting, was planned for later that spring at the prestigious Galerie Schulte. (It is unclear whether it took place.) True to Smedley's desire to remove the stigma of dilettantism from women's artistic production, the Wertheim exhibition was juried by prominent male artists in England, including C. R. Ashbee and Walter Crane, who sent along examples of their own work to "chaperone" the ladies' consignment on its travels.[39] The use of male judges, which became standard practice at both the London and Berlin clubs, sent the message that women artists had received the most stringent seal of approval—that of their male colleagues.

Curt Stoeving, artistic director of the new Wertheim gallery, published a favorable review of the show in *Deutsche Kunst und Dekoration,* an influential organ of the design reform movement in Germany. Stoeving acknowledged the "flood of artistic products from neighboring countries" conquering the nation's markets, an imbalance he blamed in part on the receptiveness of the German public to foreign goods

FIGURE 2.6. Objects by London Lyceum Club members on display at the Wertheim exhibition, 1905. From Stoeving, "Ausstellung des Londoner Lyceum-Club in Berlin," 511.

and styles.[40] Indeed, the exhibition attracted not only large crowds but also eager buyers.[41] Cultural organizations founded during this period, such as the German Werkbund, sought to lessen foreign artistic influences through public education and to stanch the flow of imports by raising the quality of German-made goods. England, a giant in industry and design reform, represented both a model and a for-midable competitor. It was to quell such anxieties that Reuter dismissed the threat of a Trojan horse: Drawing on the rhetoric of the peace movement, she assured her readers that the Lyceum clubhouse in Berlin was a symbol of friendship and coop-eration, not "a stronghold of Englishism" that would unleash "dangerous compe-tition" and "a flood" of English products.[42] This stance suggests that by attracting attention to the new channels she forged for British art in the German capital, Smedley both raised the profile of the Berlin club and put it on the defensive. Ger-man women in artistic professions already faced resistance from male colleagues who feared overproduction.[43] The Wertheim exhibition, which rolled out the red carpet for British craftswomen (and straight into one of the capital's most visible commercial venues), must have further angered those who, as Reuter reported, believed that the markets were already oversaturated with women's creative output. Women designers who joined the Lyceum Club in Berlin, many of whom were active in design reform circles, thus had a difficult position to negotiate, forging new opportunities for themselves through international collaboration while avoiding burning their bridges at home.

As Berliners flocked to buy the British wares on display at Wertheim, the Ger-man chapter of the Lyceum Club was preparing to launch its own public debut with the opening of its clubhouse on Potsdamer Strasse, not far from the luxury depart-ment store (Figure 2.7). Unlike London, Berlin did not have an established club dis-trict on par with St. James's or one ripe for "invasion."[44] With few exceptions, men's clubs in Berlin were modest compared with those in London and did not boast the palatial clubhouses or luxurious comforts familiar to the English.[45] The majority were gambling venues, and only a handful would have been recognizable as clubs in the English sense.[46] The Lyceum Club in Berlin thus was a foreign type trans-planted to German soil. By situating itself in close proximity to two other women's clubs on Potsdamer Strasse, moreover, it imitated the pattern of contiguity typical of London clubs.[47] More broadly, the choice of location reveals the club founders' intention to create, as in London, a public presence for women. Potsdamer Strasse was a busy commercial thoroughfare, lined with drapers, milliners, and other shops that catered to the affluent bourgeois women whom Ernst Ludwig Kirchner, work-ing a decade later, captured in his representations of Potsdamer Platz (Figure 2.8). Through its milieu, the Lyceum Club implicitly united the modernity of its mem-bers with the commercial vitality of the city.

FIGURE 2.7. View of Potsdamer Strasse (taken from the Potsdamer bridge looking toward Lützowstrasse) in the vicinity of the Lyceum clubhouse, 1900. Landesarchiv Berlin.

FIGURE 2.8. Ernst Ludwig Kirchner, *Frauen am Potsdamer Platz,* woodcut, 1914. Bildarchiv Preussischer Kulturbesitz/Art Resource, New York. Copyright by Ingeborg and Dr. Wolfgang Henze-Ketterer, Wichtrach/Bern.

Set amid the shops, the Lyceum clubhouse could be seen to offer Kirchner's women—looking quite vulnerable on their traffic island, encircled by men—a haven from an exciting but also stressful commercial environment. Rappaport describes how London retailers regarded women's clubs as a complement to shopping, institutions that encouraged consumerism by providing for the physical needs of weary shoppers.[48] Early promotional material for the Berlin club, however, suggests a radically different intention: namely, to transform women from consumers into producers or from objects in the city (note how Kirchner's women, with their finery, are on display to men) into its subjects.[49] Reuter, a founding member and leader of the club, was quite clear about this goal in the publicity piece she wrote for *Der Tag*. If "elegant ladies" shopping in town decided to take their tea at the clubhouse, that was all well and good, but it was beside the point, which, bluntly stated, was bolstering productivity and creating markets for members' goods.[50] Like Smedley, Reuter presented the club as a women's "trade union."[51] A club brochure from 1905 identified the "most important feature of the Lyceum Club," not as the shelter of the clubhouse or the comfort of its tearoom, but rather as the bureau that helped women to produce their work and distribute it in local and global markets.[52] Although the bureau was not original to the Lyceum Club in Berlin, being modeled on the one in London, its prominence in this recruitment document suggests an even greater emphasis on professionalization as a club goal.

This shift is confirmed in the Berlin club's stricter admission policy. Different membership categories, with unequal privileges, introduced a new hierarchy based on professionalism. At the top, women either with a university degree or recognized accomplishments in literature, journalism, science, and the fine or applied arts could become regular members. For the latter group, qualifying standards were higher than those set by the English club: For example, a woman artist was required to have exhibited her work not only publicly but also in a venue other than an all-female show (which, presumably, was less discriminating). Those who did not meet these criteria but whose interest and activity in the above fields made them desirable members could join at the associate level. So, too, could the wives and daughters of men—or the daughters of women—prominent in public life, literature, art, or the sciences. As in England, then, the club made provisions to include powerful and engaged women who, if not professionally distinguished, had a vital role to play as patrons.[53] When the German club became independent in 1906, entrance qualifications rose again. According to the new regulations, a professional woman seeking full membership had to demonstrate outstanding achievement in her field. For a female artist, this meant having exhibited in a major exhibition, not just a mixed one. The bar for university graduates also shot upward: Candidates had to possess a doctorate or, in the case of professional degrees, have passed civil exams, both of which were tremendously difficult for women in this period. Even associate members faced more stringent criteria. Significantly, women could no longer claim membership on the laurels of their mothers, husbands, or fathers.[54] As a result, the Lyceum Club in Berlin became a highly exclusive institution. The club roster represented a who's who of the city's female artists, writers, doctors, political leaders, and social reformers. It included Gertrud Bäumer, Lily Braun, Minna Cauer, Käthe Kollwitz, Helene Lange, Marie-Elisabeth Lüders, Anna Muthesius, and Alice Salomon, to name but a few of its better-known members.

The higher status of professionals as well as the rigorous standards for admission based solely on personal accomplishment reveal the influence of Germany's *Bildungsbürgerinnen* (women of the educated middle class) on the character of the club.[55] Although noblewomen also joined, and a number occupied important positions in the club, members were overwhelmingly drawn from the *Bildungsbürgertum,* and they remained deeply committed to the ethics of their class: hard work, self-discipline, outward simplicity, and inner growth. Even the club's royal patron, Queen Elisabeth of Romania (Carmen Sylva), earned this honor, according to Reuter, on the basis of her literary achievements, not her title.[56] These same class values also emerged as a determining factor in the club's architectural self-presentation and contributed to the abandonment of the new clubhouse a mere two years after it opened.

In their public pronouncements, club members delighted in their sumptuous quarters. Jarno Jessen, a Lyceum Club member and design critic with strong ties to England (as Berlin correspondent for the *Studio*), equated grandeur with contentment: Inside their "truly imposing" home, executed on a "grand scale . . . after the London model," Lyceum clubwomen basked in the realization, "We now have what we need."[57] Without doubt, the premises were impressive: The clubhouse occupied the entire building at 118b Potsdamer Strasse, which rose five stories above the street and was crowned by an onion dome (Figure 2.9).[58] The large and luxurious apartment house dated to 1883, when the street was being developed as a fashionable residential and commercial district. Following extensive renovations to the interior, the new clubhouse opened to much fanfare on November 4, 1905.[59] Passing through the doorway of the rusticated sandstone façade and climbing a flight of stairs, members entered a grand foyer (Figure 2.10). Proceeding inward, a stunning sequence of spatial riches unfolded: exhibition spaces, an auditorium with a stage, a grand restaurant, and a tearoom, as well as common rooms, such as a reading room filled with newspapers and magazines, a music room, a library, and rooms for smoking, writing, and playing billiards. About thirty guest rooms were located in the upper stories. As in London, these rooms were intended for traveling members from other clubs or, more commonly, women living at a distance from the city's center. On the ground floor, accessible through its own street entrance, commercial and managerial

FIGURE 2.9. Lyceum clubhouse at 118b Potsdamer Strasse, Berlin, 1905. From "Der Lyzeumklub," *Die Frau* 12, no. 12 (1905): 752.

rooms included a shop for the sale of applied arts by club members. At the rear of the edifice, an Italianate façade overlooked a secluded garden, where members dined in the summer months (Figure 2.11). Jessen credited these splendors to the English club tradition, pointing to the parallels between the London club and its sister institution.[60]

Glittering appearances, however, disguised another story. In her memoirs, Hedwig Heyl, who served as president of the German club from 1905 to 1920, looked back in unconcealed anger at the experience of setting up the clubhouse on Potsdamer Strasse.[61] Despite Smedley's stated commitment to the independence of the Lyceum Club's foreign branches, English authority over the Berlin clubhouse soon eroded the illusion of mutual cooperation. In London, Smedley entrusted her father, William T. Smedley, a wealthy and successful businessman, with the financial side of the club, including the establishment and maintenance of the clubhouse.

Frau Geheimrat Broicher.   Frau Fia Wille.   Frau Hedwig Heyl.   Miss Smedley,   Frau von Siemens.   Frl. Else Schulhoff.   *Spezialaufnahme fürs „Berliner Leben"*
                                               (Gründerin des Londoner Lyceum-Klubs), geb. Helmholtz.   Frau Paczka-Wagner.   *von Zander & Labisch*
                                                       Frl. Helene Lange.   Frl. Marie von Bunsen.   Frau von Bülow.

FIGURE 2.10. Constance Smedley (seated, middle) posing with local Lyceum Club board members in the entrance hall of the clubhouse on Potsdamer Strasse, 1905. From *Berliner Leben* 8, no. 11 (1905): 13.

He founded the club on a proprietary basis rather than requiring the members to own and manage it themselves, which, although common practice in St. James's, would have been difficult for women with limited financial resources and expertise.[62] As the club's financial director, Mr. Smedley also took charge of setting up and managing the clubhouse in Berlin, which existed as a separate entity from the club itself. Publicly, Heyl expressed her gratitude for "the marvelous gift of this fully furnished club."[63] Privately, she harbored doubts: Perhaps this was a Trojan horse after all.[64]

Speaking at the club's opening, Constance Smedley emphasized the native character of the new institution: "The club is German in all its contents, from the silver spoons to the wallpaper."[65] Although she wished to bring attention to the German contribution, the dominance of an English model was undeniable. As Luise Marelle, the club's longtime secretary, later admitted, the clubhouse had been "set up completely in the English style."[66] Heyl's memoirs recount her growing anxiety as she watched the clubhouse take alien form. "The many luxurious purchases" and the extravagant services, such as hiring "two very expensive chefs" for lavish and costly formal dinners, seemed not only fiscally reckless but also ill-suited to German tastes and customs. When she attempted to intervene, she was told that

FIGURE 2.11. Garden façade of the Lyceum clubhouse on Potsdamer Strasse, 1905. From "Der Lyzeumklub," 753.

her expertise did not extend to managing a club, a rebuke that still stung twenty years later. Unlike Smedley (who was barely out of her teens when she conceived the idea for the club), Heyl knew a thing or two about running a business. Widowed in 1889 with five children, Heyl, defying social convention, assumed the directorship of her late husband's factory. She employed her wealth and organizational skills to become one of Berlin's leading female philanthropists.[67] In other respects, she and her colleagues had more success in battling the English management. With much effort, they secured contracts for the club's own designers to furnish the rooms (Figures 2.12–2.14). Even so, the broader clubhouse environment remained outside the members' control, as revealed in a letter Smedley wrote to her father:

> Poor Countess Groeben! [Groeben chaired the club's influential social committee.] I found her in *despair* at the *awful* pictures yesterday morning. They are awful and do make the Club "ridiculous"—she implored me to ask you to forbid *all pictures* downstairs. I said I was sure you sympathised with her. The Club must be more dignified.

Although the letter does not identify who is responsible for hanging the "awful pictures" in the first place, Mr. Smedley's authority over building matters is clear. In the same letter, Constance presses her father to make a decision about electric light and to finish rooms that have been left incomplete.[68] "I had absolutely no restraining influence on the manager," Heyl wrote of Mr. Smedley, "who appeared like a meteor from London, slipped around like an eel, and disappeared again without results. One can imagine how unhappy this relationship made us, despite the fact that the internal work of the club developed splendidly."[69]

In a highly dramatic confrontation involving lawyers, moving trucks, and an eleventh-hour departure from the clubhouse, the Berlin club severed its financial ties with the English management in 1908. Tensions had been escalating for some time. In an effort to assume control over the club's financial management, Berlin members had legally founded the German Lyceum Club on December 31, 1906. They continued to occupy the Potsdamer Strasse clubhouse, paying rent to Mr. Smedley (who still managed the club's restaurant). Relations remained strained, however, and worsening financial disagreements led Heyl and the club's all-female board of directors to decide to abandon the clubhouse altogether in the spring of 1908. As a result, the club was expelled from the International Association of Lyceum Clubs, and Berlin members were barred from the London and Paris clubhouses.[70] Although Heyl's grievances suggest multiple causes for the rupture, I would like to focus on the issue of luxury, which occupies a dominant role in her narrative of the events as well as in subsequent club histories. The mistranslation of the aesthetics of luxury from

London to Berlin, I argue, underscores the necessity of attending to the specificity of place—in terms of national discourses as well as local geography and politics—in analyzing women's strategies for appropriating space in the modern Western city. For what worked marvelously in Piccadilly failed abysmally on Potsdamer Strasse.

Conspicuous displays and consumption of luxury in London clubhouses signaled exclusivity, privilege, and power.[71] As Smedley emphasized in her autobiography, having access to this symbolic capital, and the status it conferred, translated into real material advantages. In this context, mimicking the opulence of male clubland made strategic sense; certainly, the Lyceum Club did nothing to tone down the luxurious setting of the Imperial Service Club it inherited. Indeed, its likeness to the other clubhouses on Piccadilly was part of its special appeal, communicating to outsiders that its members stood on the same playing field as elite men.

When the Lyceum Club's management sought to re-create the success of the London clubhouse in Berlin, they fell into the trap of imperialist thinking, failing to see that the aesthetic culture of clubland was not universal but uniquely English. They were also unlucky in their timing, for the Potsdamer Strasse clubhouse made its debut in the midst of a widespread debate in Germany on luxury. As historian Warren Breckman points out, this discourse ignored the aristocracy, focusing instead on the corrupting effects of luxury consumption on middle-class identity. Bourgeois authors, writing for a middle-class audience, contrasted the parvenu's bombastic show of wealth to the bedrock ideals of Germany's educated middle class: self-restraint and *Bildung*, or personal cultivation.[72] As Wilhelm Bode, the powerful director of Berlin's royal museums, wrote in 1906, "The splendid king *Luxus* has a philistine face."[73] Bode might well have substituted the term *Queen Luxus*, for women were often blamed for the descent of the respectable middle class into luxury. Their subservience to foreign tastemakers, particularly to French couture, was especially decried. One can understand why members of the Lyceum Club in Berlin, forging an institution for bourgeois women modeled on elite English clubs, would have been sensitive to conspicuous displays of luxury. Extravagant purchases and glamorous dinners courtesy of an English master sent exactly the wrong kind of public message about these educated women: It suggested, as Bode argued, that those who lacked *Bildung*, the true cultivation of the spirit and mind, hid their deficiencies behind the spectacle of their riches.[74] Whereas in London, the appearance of luxury, as Smedley noted, concealed the taint of women's economic poverty, in Berlin it exposed the shaming spiritual poverty of the nouveau-riche mind.

Under the right circumstances, however, these same clubwomen were quite willing to be associated with luxury. As we will see in chapter 4, luxury dominated the design and displays of the national women's exhibition hosted by the German Lyceum Club in 1912. In that setting, luxury was marked by its artistic creators as specifically German—dignified, not ostentatious. This accommodation supports Breckman's argument that middle-class Germans were concerned less with eliminating luxury than with learning how to manage it.[75] In this light, the "problem" of the clubhouse on Potsdamer Strasse was not luxury per se but luxury that was foreign and beyond the control of those with the redeeming power of *Bildung*.

After the break with London, the Berlin club advertised the "exclusively German character" of the organization, even as, somewhat paradoxically, it continued to welcome members of all nationalities.[76] In the following years and culminating in the construction of their own clubhouse in 1914, members reclaimed control over their public identity, putting forth an image that spoke to their national and class ideals. Seeking new premises, the club's board of directors, led by Heyl, chose a stately neoclassical residence that Berlin architect Martin Gropius had designed for his family and offices in 1868–69.[77] The location at Am Karlsbad 12–13, only a block away from the old clubhouse, offered a quieter, more residential environment. Rather than turning away from the bustle of the metropole, however, this choice

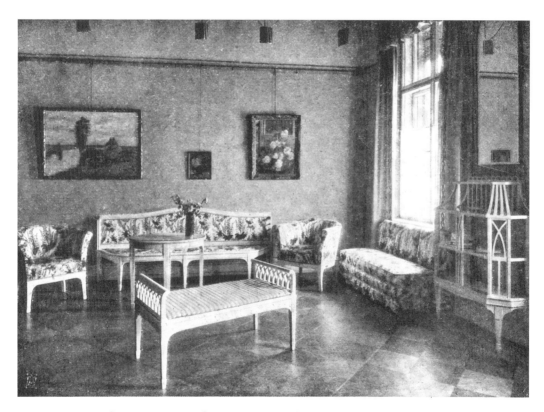

FIGURE 2.12. Conversation room by Maria von Brocken, Lyceum clubhouse on Potsdamer Strasse, c. 1907. From Jarno Jessen, ed., *Angewandte Kunst: Deutscher Lyceum Club Berlin* (Berlin: Lipperheide, c. 1908).

signified the embrace of an urban heritage that spoke directly to the club's identity struggles. A follower of Karl Friedrich Schinkel, Gropius made his mark with projects that combined restrained classicism with local brick traditions in the search for ideal Prussian form. He found receptive patrons among the city's well-to-do bourgeoisie, for whom his domestic architecture struck the right chord of enduring cultivation in the face of increasing prosperity.[78] By taking up residence in Gropius's former home, the club donned the mantle of an architect whose nativist principles represented a kind of antithesis to grandiose, Piccadilly-style clubhouses.

Inside the club, English services and amenities underwent naturalization. The restaurant, sans the two expensive chefs, served only cold dishes in the evening and sandwiches during the day. Three rooms were set aside for guests, as opposed to the thirty Mr. Smedley had envisioned.[79] Interestingly, the club advertised its bathing facilities, which members could use from ten in the morning until nine o'clock at night. Given the inadequate housing of many single women and the rarity of private baths in Berlin, this was a "luxury" members willingly condoned.[80] More broadly, the club's communal spaces displayed elegant comfort and an intimate disposition (Figure 2.15). Furniture, reclaimed from the old clubhouse, was arranged for conversations and in cozy settings. In describing the new location, Heyl evoked a particular notion of Germanic domesticity, associated with Nordic simplicity, vitality, and *Gemütlichkeit*.[81] Such rhetoric as well as the images published by the club signaled a turning away from the black-tie formality and luxury associated with the earlier clubhouse, a tone that had been set from the moment one entered its regal foyer.

Significantly, the model for the clubhouse had always been domestic. As noted earlier, gentlemen's clubs in London drew on domestic architecture to suggest privacy and a retreat from the city's social heterogeneity. The earliest and most prestigious clubs, such as Brooks's and Boodle's, adopted the eighteenth-century aristocratic country mansion as the model for their clubhouses.[82] Along with this house type came associated formalities (such as evening dress for dinner), decoration reflective of aristocratic tastes ("hippophilic," according to a club historian), and a large staff of servants in black knee-breeches.[83] At the Lyceum Club in Berlin, a good deal of that legacy had been retained, down to the butler.[84] Yet in those spaces controlled by the club's German designers, another, more meaningful model of domesticity prevailed. In late eighteenth-century Berlin, a new institution of the Enlightenment public sphere arose in the homes of the educated middle class: the salon. Hosted by a woman, these weekly gatherings united people from different class, gender, and religious backgrounds for free intellectual and cultural exchange in a relaxed, informal environment.[85] What better model for the Lyceum Club, which sought to create a similarly mixed arena for the mutual cultivation of women? The informal sociability of the club interiors designed by German members recalled the settings of these older salons, down to the requisite divan or sofa of the *salonnière* (Figure 2.12).[86] Against this forced marriage of English country squire and *salonnière*, the new premises initiated a more holistic approach to domestic models in the club's staging of a new community of modern women.

Far more than a backdrop for that community, the clubhouse enabled bonds of fellowship to emerge. A club brochure from 1911 recognized the interdependence of social and spatial innovation:

A new development creates new needs. Today's women, insofar as they have turned away from playful dilettantism, are no longer served by either purely social get-togethers among women or female trade organizations. What they want from one

FIGURE 2.13. Reading corner by Grete Hart, Lyceum clubhouse on Potsdamer Strasse, c. 1907. From Jessen, ed., *Angewandte Kunst.*

another is understanding, stimulation, exchange, mutual support. For this they need common ground, a meeting place.[87]

By providing such a venue, the clubhouse made possible a new form of interaction among women oriented toward the growth of the whole person—her *Bildung*. In their writings on women's clubs, present and future Lyceum Club leaders presented the modern woman's *Bildung* as a process of self-cultivation dependent on female community and an engagement with the difficult yet rewarding modernity of the metropolis. The fruits of this labor did not fall to women alone but contributed to the progress of society as a whole.[88]

Through her club, the modern woman became cognizant of belonging to a collective. "Women's esprit de corps is strengthened in the clubs," Eliza Ichenhaeuser wrote, "and realized in philanthropic and social work." Ichenhaeuser spoke from her personal experience in steering a Lyceum Club committee devoted to building Berlin's first women's hospital.[89] The club's integrative role, she believed, was

FIGURE 2.14. Japanese tearoom by Marie Tscheuschner-Cucuel, Lyceum clubhouse on Potsdamer Strasse, c. 1907. From Jessen, ed., *Angewandte Kunst.*

especially important for single women living on their own. Having fallen through the cracks as the patriarchal foundations of modern society gave way, these women looked to their club as a replacement home.[90] This view was reiterated by others within the Lyceum Club, including Emma Stropp, a feminist and journalist who cochaired the club's press committee. In an essay on women's clubs published in *What a Woman Must Know about Berlin,* Stropp portrayed them as a sanctuary for the single woman, both from her family, who little understood her desires and abilities, and from an alienating city that also refused to embrace her. In the club, amid her peers, she experienced "the feeling of definitely belonging together." The clubhouse, Stropp contended, physically expressed this empowering sense of a united female community.[91]

This collective body was, furthermore, a civic one. Ichenhaeuser maintained that women's clubs were not like those of men: a place to go smoke a cigar and forget the world.[92] Rather, they were a place to engage with the city and, in the process,

FIGURE 2.15. Library, Lyceum clubhouse, Am Karlsbad 12–13, Berlin. Through the open doors, one glimpses the new Japanese tearoom. From *Frauen-Rundschau* 11, no. 3 (1910): 67.

forge an identity as a female citizen. Contrary to Ichenhaeuser's claim, men's clubs in Berlin—their emphasis on leisure and recreation notwithstanding—were also venues for consolidating influence in the public sphere. Women's clubs, however, had to construct the idea of citizenship *and* a realm of influence for their members in the absence of a legitimate political voice. Drawing consciously on the experience of American women's clubs, German feminists such as Ichenhaeuser sought to recast clubwomen as socially and politically aware citizens "enfranchised" by their commitment to and performance of a feminine civic duty.[93] The making of this virtual citizen involved a personal and collective transformation, and clubs were seen as the training grounds for the values and skills needed for public service. Alice Salomon and Josephine Levy-Rathenau, leading voices of the bourgeois women's movement and Lyceum Club members, described the clubs as small women's states, where women learned to think democratically and acquired the language of diplomacy and statesmanship.[94] The Lyceum Club, for example, staged mock debates to teach its members parliamentary form.[95] Because of professional and social differences among members, Salomon thought the clubs combated sectarianism and fostered women's public spirit by allowing the idea of a common good to develop in free discourse.[96]

An incident in 1909, recorded in the club's newsletter, reveals some of the issues at stake in training women for the public sphere. Seeking no doubt to provoke a stimulating intellectual discussion, the club's literary commission invited the German psychoanalyst and antifeminist Georg Groddeck to speak on his new book, *Hin zu Gottnatur* (Toward Divine Nature). In the theory of personality he developed therein, he argued that women's proximity to nature and God meant they lacked the self-consciousness that drove men: They were symbols rather than actors in the world. Biology rendered them needy, obedient, and simple-minded, yet also glorious as a force of nature—in motherhood. Groddeck opposed the women's movement because it perpetuated the dangerous lie of women's progress while robbing men of their sense of self. This loss, he warned, would extinguish all of mankind's greatest achievements, indeed, would bring an end to the future itself.[97] Such essentialist, doomsday claims met with little patience from the gathered audience of 120 clubwomen, who openly insulted the guest. Their rude behavior embarrassed the hosts, and Margarete Danneel, an executive member of the club's social committee, responded with a strong reprimand in the club's newsletter. Urging greater restraint in such male–female interactions, Danneel carefully laid out a discursive model based on logical refutation rather than derision. This was not simply an exercise in rhetoric. The ability to debate Groddeck effectively promised a greater empowerment: credibility in the struggle against the reigning ideology of the German state, which maintained that women had no right to a public voice because they lacked the rationality to use it. As this event makes clear, the ideal expressed in writings on women's clubs sometimes fell short in reality. But mistakes, Danneel noted, also represented an opportunity to learn and grow stronger.[98]

Construction of a new clubhouse in 1914 gave visual expression to the mature identity of this group of women, who, a decade after stepping out collectively into the public sphere, confidently proclaimed their leadership in municipal and national reform campaigns. Already in 1912, this can-do spirit filled the air inside the exhibition halls of the Zoological Garden. The club's monumental show on women's work made tangible its members' myriad social and economic contributions to city and state and sought to position the organization at the center of the German women's movement. Berliners who lined up to admire (or belittle) the extravaganza filled the club's coffers and thus helped realize a lasting architectural symbol to a new community of women.

Success compelled the search for larger quarters: By 1912, the club's nearly eleven hundred members tested the capacity of the Gropius house. Activities and publicity surrounding the exhibition had increased membership significantly, and further growth was anticipated.[99] In her memoirs, Heyl admitted she had long coveted "a well-built patrician house" on Lützowplatz, a square with stately homes close

FIGURE 2.16. Aerial view of Lützowplatz in Berlin, showing the Lyceum clubhouse in the upper left-hand corner of the square, c. 1930. Postcard, author's collection.

to the zoo and Tiergarten and amply served by trams (Figures 2.16 and 2.17).[100]
The residences of many of Berlin's leading feminists (and Lyceum Club members)
were located in the adjacent streets.[101] The townhouse did not come cheaply, being
situated not only in one of Berlin's most prestigious neighborhoods but also on a
particularly advantageous corner lot. Since costs exceeded the club's accumulated
capital, members helped finance its purchase and renovation, begun on the drawing
board in December 1913 and executed the following summer and fall. Clubwomen
also directly shaped the new premises: Emilie Winkelmann thoroughly redesigned
the existing structure and supervised construction, and the interior decoration was
undertaken by a committee of architects and designers, including Winkelmann,
Elisabeth von Knobelsdorff, Fia Wille, and Marie Kirschner.[102] Their transformation of a "patrician" nineteenth-century home into a public space for bourgeois
women boldly asserted a new female agency in the city.

The renovated building (Figure 2.18) rose four stories above a partly submerged
basement floor, one story higher than the original structure. Municipal records indicate that the architect juggled demands driven by the functional need for diverse
spaces (social, commercial, and residential) with aesthetic and budgetary concerns, as
well as restrictive zoning codes in a wealthy residential neighborhood. Winkelmann's

VERLAG U. LICHTDRUCK VON KNACKSTEDT & NÄTHER HAMBURG 222

FIGURE 2.17. Lützowplatz around the turn of the twentieth century. Postcard, author's
collection.

creative solutions underscore the economic and symbolic potential of adaptive re-
use of domestic architecture, a strategy common to women's institution building
efforts of this era, both in Germany and abroad.[103] Rather than restore the crumbling
decorative stucco on the exterior, for example, Winkelmann seized on the possibilities of less is more. She stripped the street façades of neoclassical ornament,
leaving strikingly bare surfaces that were highly unusual for the time. Elaborate
window casings, floral railings, pilasters, and rusticated plaster were removed, and
plain frames, simple railings, and flat plaster took their place. What little ornament
remained focused on the club entrance. Framed by Doric pilasters, the doorway
was located on the short end of the building; the name of the club was engraved on
the entablature, above which an oval medallion bore its symbol, a tree. On the long
side of the building, a loggia and bay windows formed an asymmetrical protruding
block. Painted a lighter color, this block provided an element of dramatic contrast.

FIGURE 2.18. Lyceum clubhouse at Lützowplatz 8, as redesigned by Emilie Winkelmann.
From Jarno Jessen, "Der Deutsche Lyzeumklub und seine bildenden Künstlerinnen,"
Westermanns Monatshefte 120, no. 716 (1916): 165.

A comparison of the renovated exterior to that of its neighbors reveals how "modern" the building would have appeared in this context, even as its size and forms echoed the surrounding domestic architecture.

In its height and simple, bold masses, the clubhouse achieved a dynamic monumentality. Various elements visually unified the two façades of the building: a continuous cornice, the row of flower boxes spanning the top story, a band course above the basement and first floors, as well as the repetition of identical window frames. This horizontal movement was counterbalanced by the ascending rhythm of the stepped rectangles formed by the entrance (large), loggia (larger), and bay windows (largest). As the viewer's eye mounted this "staircase" of rectangles, it ascended from the tallest feature, the bay windows, to the flagpole at the center of the roof. Beyond accentuating the visual drama of the façade, the fluttering German flag marked the building as a public and national institution. By eliminating an existing loggia to the right of the bay windows, Winkelmann broke up the symmetry of the original façade, creating a diagonal thrust that emphasized the height of the building and sharpened the tension between horizontal and vertical elements. The only nonrectilinear shape on the building was the oval medallion above the entrance, which brought the viewer's attention to the club's emblem.

Jessen, championing a rather different set of design values from those lauded in her review of the first clubhouse, praised Winkelmann for harmoniously fusing past and present. Employing concepts from the design reform discourse, Jessen noted how "the simple exterior continues the dignified tradition of old Berlin, and yet freely admits the *sachlich* (objective) spirit of the new age." For reformers, the redemption of modern architecture, corrupted by capitalism, necessitated shedding historical ornament in order to excavate and resuscitate the organic spirit that presided over an older *Wohnkultur*, or culture of dwelling. Winkelmann's creation of a "modern functional building" that kept alive "the elegant and comfortable character" of "an old patrician house" exemplified aesthetic progress in its ability to unite *Sachlichkeit* and functionalism with cultural traditions.[104] Although the original structure dated only from 1874, the reference to an old patrician house stirred up— or, rather, invented—memories of a noble past, a German Rome. This romantic image served to recuperate what was, in fact, problematic about the house: Overlooking its complicity with nineteenth-century historicism, Jessen recast it as a symbol of the republic's founding years.

Even more emphatically than the Gropius residence, the sobriety of the new clubhouse declared the group's loyalty to bourgeois ideals of practicality and reticence. Design reformer and Werkbund cofounder Hermann Muthesius identified the *sachlich* spirit applauded by Jessen with the aesthetic tastes of Germany's middle classes. With the ascendancy of bourgeois culture, he believed *Sachlichkeit* would eradicate the use of luxury (whether simulated or real) as a means of asserting class difference.[105] By transforming the home of a wealthy gentleman into a model for *sachlich* taste, Winkelmann put into practice Muthesius's goals of visually constructed social unity. At the same time, her reconceptualization of the façade went beyond design reform concerns to embrace the feminist agenda articulated by the Lyceum Club. Winkelmann's design materialized the club's intention to create modern women engaged with the metropolis. By stripping away rusticated plaster and other ornament, the surface of the walls appeared naked and the windows more pronounced, an effect that suggested a more permeable boundary and greater interaction with the outside world than traditionally associated with the hidden, fortified spaces of the home. With almost no decoration to obfuscate its form and with its large apertures, the clubhouse presented an "open" face to the city.

Inside, the club's new spaces reiterated the promise of exchange. Unlike men's clubs in London, which adamantly refused entrance to nonmembers, the German Lyceum Club cast itself as a public venue for women's events. To this end, the most celebrated feature of the new clubhouse was an auditorium for 190 people that doubled as an exhibition hall. A restaurant and a tearoom, connected by sliding doors, could be merged to form a generous space for receptions. Having mended its relations with the International Association of Lyceum Clubs, which it rejoined in 1909, the German Lyceum Club encouraged foreign visitors, for whom it created additional guests rooms. Even in the midst of war, the club maintained the hope that it would become a meeting place for women of all countries.[106]

At the same time, the club respected its members' need for privacy by articulating a hierarchy of public and intimate spaces. Inside the building, commercial and domestic and public and private spaces were vertically arranged. The most open was the first floor, which was accessible to the invited public, both male and female. It contained spaces for events and refreshment as well as for commercial activity, including a shop selling members' products (which had its own display window on the street, to the right of the entrance). The second story held common rooms intended for the "comfortable lingering" of members: a salon, a music room, a library with terrace, and a smoking and billiards room. This represented an inner public space, more intimate than the fully public rooms below. The third floor carried this transition further with one semipublic but exclusive space, a board room, and a number of guest rooms. The top floor, reserved entirely for guest rooms, was the most private and shielded area in the clubhouse.[107] Flowerboxes on the exterior marked it as a domestic realm.

With funds for new purchases scarce, club designers reused existing furniture, arranging it to reflect recent trends in interior design toward airy, uncluttered spaces (Figures 2.19 and 2.20). Tall, lightly draped windows "flooded [rooms] with light and sun."[108] Contemporary photographs reveal that even with more space, the tone remained one of elegant but understated comfort rather than luxury. The lightness and practicality of the interior, Jessen wrote, mirrored the aesthetic qualities of the exterior.[109] As in the club's previous locations, designers were given their own spaces to decorate, which served as a showcase for their work. Thus, in addition to external commercial venues developed by the German Lyceum Club, as well as its own shop and exhibits, the clubhouse itself served as an ongoing showroom for its members' work.[110]

As an architecture of engaged and productive women, the clubhouse articulated a new dynamic between feminine identity and the urban environment. By 1914, the German Lyceum Club had come a long way from Mr. Smedley's suffocating tutelage. Through the process of rejecting his vision and reformulating its public image, the club arrived at a stark modernism that spoke not only to the changing identity of women but also to that of Berlin as a center of industrial and artistic reform. Moreover, this modernism offered an alternative to the modernism of certain members of the artistic avant-garde, who viewed the metropolis through the lens of a depraved female sexuality. A comparison of *Frauen am Potsdamer Platz* (Figure 2.8) with the clubhouse, both created in the same year, reveals how differently progressive Germans understood the role of the feminine in constructing the modern

FIGURE 2.19. Music room by Fia Wille, Lyceum clubhouse on Lützowplatz. From Else von Boetticher, "Das neue Heim des Deutschen Lyzeumklubs," *Die Welt der Frau*, no. 1 (1915): 16.

city: Whereas Kirchner objectified women and suggested danger and instability in his aesthetic choices, Winkelmann represented female mastery of a bright, rational world. In this juxtaposition, we see how pessimistic and misogynistic strains in the "crisis" of modernity articulated by German artists and intellectuals, who often focused their attention on issues of gender and sexuality in the metropolis, met with resistance from women producing counternarratives that cast female agency and urban life in a far more positive light.

Beyond the statement made through its own physical presence, the club became a forum for discussions of architectural issues affecting women. In March 1910, for example, the theme of the club's weekly debate was the kitchenless dwelling (*Einküchenhaus*).[111] A wide range of speakers, from a woman architect to a nationally renowned suffragette, delivered lectures on housing.[112] Advocacy groups concerned with women's needs and the built environment met at the clubhouse, among them the Association for Modern Women's Apartments and Alice Salomon's Association

FIGURE 2.20. Reception room by Fia Wille, Lyceum clubhouse on Lützowplatz. From Boetticher, "Das neue Heim," 15.

for Female Workers' Homes.[113] The club also became an architectural patron, leading the effort to build Berlin's first women's hospital. The clubhouse thus stood as a symbol and locus of a broad movement of new women who, in exploring the limits and potential of their modernity, understood its intimate connection to the physical structures of their city. For that reason, too, an idea begun in London required a process of naturalization to take root in Berlin, for the struggle to take space that united women internationally could be won only at street level.

3 A Home of Our Own

Single Women and the New Domestic Architecture

THE PAGES GLOW WITH DOMESTIC BLISS. A serene young mother, sun-filled interiors, feast-laden tables, verdant house plants, and—everywhere—robust, beautiful children as full of life as the garden outside, its boughs laden with blossom and fruit. The idyllic images of home life that Swedish painter Carl Larsson presented in *Das Haus in der Sonne* (The House in the Sun) enchanted German readers, and the book became a best seller when it was published in 1909. During the First World War, it was reputedly a popular gift to departing soldiers, bestowed perhaps as a sustaining fantasy of the good life they were meant to protect (and hopefully return to) or as a talisman to ward off the undomestic horrors of the trenches.[1] By this time, the book had also given its name to a most unusual type of home: a retirement villa for single professional women. Built in Potsdam and designed by Emilie Winkelmann, the Haus in der Sonne welcomed its first elderly residents in 1914. Mainly teachers, they had supported themselves with life-long careers, for which they had sacrificed (or been denied) marriage and children. How did these women come to claim the light and happiness of Larsson's domestic bliss, and why did they choose a name that, for many Germans, defined the very antithesis of their spinster lives?

Their story begins with a kind of expulsion from Larsson's Eden. By the end of the nineteenth century, a new homeless population had been identified in Berlin: single middle-class women who, by choice or necessity, made their own way in the urban world. In a culture that expected girls to exchange parental abode for marital hearth, the unorthodox lifestyles of these women created a serious architectural problem: they fit neither of the two domestic models available to them. Unwilling or unable to remain with parents or take a husband, these so-called new women discovered there was nowhere in the city where they could be at home.

It was writers for the women's press, themselves often struggling with the problem, who raised awareness of the plight of these domestic outcasts. In a chapter on housing for the women's guidebook *What a Woman Must Know about Berlin,* journalist Margarete Pochhammer surveyed the limited options available to single women and recommended a *Pensionat,* a boardinghouse. These were usually run by women, often widows from "the better classes" who needed to support themselves; in addition to furnished rooms, residents enjoyed maid service and meals, as well as the opportunity to socialize with others in a respectable environment. For those who could not afford a *Pensionat* or wanted long-term accommodations, there were few good alternatives. "Living as a lodger," Pochhammer asserted, "without a connection to a *Pensionat* or family is awkward for single ladies in the big city and leads easily to embarrassing situations and false judgments." Conversely, setting up a "proper household" of one's own was too expensive or time-consuming for some, and others felt uneasy living in "just any apartment."[2]

Nor were single rooms or apartments easy to find, for the majority of landlords rented only to men. In the press, women complained of doors shut in their faces when they inquired about vacancies. Gertraut von Beaulieu, a social satirist, captured the all-too-common humiliating experiences of the prospective female lodger in her 1892 book, *Das weibliche Berlin* (The Feminine Side of Berlin). Seeking to let a room, she records the following exchange between herself and a landlady:

> "To women?" she shouted at me, looking me up and down with a policeman's gaze. . . . "The owner does not allow us to rent to women; it is stipulated in the contract."
>
> "But why not? Tell me, where should these poor women go?"
>
> "Doesn't concern me. And why? Because it involves so much that is unwholesome. Wantons—you understand—that's out of the question, and reputable ladies always want to cook. I would never accept even a respectable lady, even if the owner did allow it."[3]

This scene was hardly atypical: The clause "not rented to women" was included in many Berlin rental contracts. The reasons for this exclusion varied, as was discussed in a 1912 article by Ella Mensch, editor of the journal *Frauen-Rundschau* and one of the first German women to earn a doctorate. Some landlords feared for the reputation of their building, since women living on their own were suspected of being prostitutes (hence the policing gaze reported by Beaulieu). Single women were also considered difficult tenants, paying the smallest rents but demanding extra services, such as the use of ironing boards and cooking facilities. Because so few landlords would rent to women, competition for the small number of rooms and apartments available increased their price.[4] To make matters worse, these were often the least desirable accommodations; one disappointed seeker described the dark, cramped spaces she was shown at the back of buildings, guaranteed to induce "suicidal thoughts," instead of the bright and airy front rooms that had been advertised. These, she learned, were reserved for bachelors.[5]

Neither a *Pensionat* nor a furnished room offered much of a home.[6] Even if it served a semipermanent clientele, the *Pensionat* was essentially a hotel, and it was difficult to control one's privacy or create meaningful social bonds.[7] Furnished rooms, conversely, often necessitated an uncomfortable proximity to the landlord's family and offered little freedom to create a space of one's own. Annie Ohlert, a Hamburg social worker, described the dispiriting experiences of single teachers living in rented rooms for Mensch's *Frauen-Rundschau.* She quoted a teacher who warned her fellow female lodgers not to come home an hour earlier than usual lest they discover that their "private" room was being used by the landlord in their absence. Anything not locked away, this source further claimed, became the object of scrutiny. Along with such intrusions, women bore the fear of eviction for a better-paying tenant; for some, the fortnightly expiration of leases meant constant anxiety.[8] "Cold" and "uncanny," in the words of journalist Käthe Schrey, these forms of living bore "only too clearly the stamp of modern nomadic existence."[9]

Because the problem was chronic, beginning with the single woman's first steps toward economic independence as a college student, extending through her career years, and continuing into retirement and old age, new domestic types developed for different stages of her life. By looking at the architecture of this life cycle, we can trace how such housing experiments involved a redefinition of the notion of family, one that centered the female self in a web of intimate relationships formed within community. This effort to refit hearth and home for the single woman, which forms the focus of this chapter, took place within a larger context of domestic transformations. Profound economic and social shifts in Europe and the United States in the nineteenth century, foremost industrialization and the struggle for women's emancipation, spawned widespread debates about how to design and run a household as traditional domestic structures and family roles yielded to modern pressures.[10] In Germany, the women's movement immersed itself in a broad range of design and lifestyle issues, including centralized housekeeping, institutional residences, housing inspection, the garden city movement, and land reform.[11] While discussions about housing single women drew on these broader debates, they also addressed concerns about morality, individual freedom, communal life, and public integration specific to the New Woman. In this chapter, I introduce three new residential types in Berlin created for the young, mature, and aging single woman as realized in the Victoria Studienhaus, the Lehrerinnenheim, and the Haus in der Sonne. All three buildings still stand, although none continues its original function.

In the absence of historical markers, the casual passerby has no reason to suspect their once radical role in the quest for modern living.

A HOME FOR DAUGHTERS OF THE ALMA MATER: THE VICTORIA STUDIENHAUS

At the instigation of Georgina Archer, a Scottish tutor of the future Wilhelm II, Crown Princess Victoria founded the first institution of higher learning in Germany for women, the Victoria Lyceum in Berlin. Opened in 1869, it served to improve the education of female teachers and governesses through lectures given by professors from the Friedrich Wilhelm University, which did not admit women. Courses ranged from art history to physics, and prominent names on the teaching roster attracted a large student body, reaching over nine hundred within a decade. By the spring of 1888, the newly crowned empress seems to have been working toward creating a centralized campus for women's higher education in Berlin. As historian James Albisetti notes, this project, "the one serious opportunity for a women's college or university in Imperial Germany," was undermined by the emperor's sudden death in June.[12]

By the turn of the century, women's struggle for advanced study focused on integrating male universities. In 1907, Ottilie von Hansemann, widow of the powerful Berlin banker Adolph von Hansemann, offered the Friedrich Wilhelm University a generous scholarship endowment of two hundred thousand Marks if women were permitted to matriculate under the same conditions as men. In 1908, after the Prussian government opened universities to women, the Berlin rector declared that the conditions of her gift had been satisfied and requested a transfer of the money. The law admitting women stipulated, however, that for "special reasons" a professor could petition the education minister to bar them from his courses. Since the Ministry of Education refused to remove this clause, Hansemann withheld the scholarship. Instead, she channeled the money into building a residence for female college students.[13] Opened in 1915, it was called the Victoria Studienhaus as well as Haus Ottilie von Hansemann in honor, respectively, of its royal patron and its largest donor (Figure 3.1).

The desperate housing situation of female students had long been recognized. Unlike English residential colleges and many American campuses, German universities did not provide dormitories. The types of accommodation available to male students were either inaccessible or considered inappropriate for women. A few male students had rooms in their *Burschenschaften*, the student dueling societies that formed an elite fraternity within the universities and left their members proudly scarred by the end of their studies. Women, needless to say, were excluded from these societies, as were other "undesirable" minorities, such as Jews. More common was a room let in a private residence, a form popularly known as the student *Bude*.

The *Bude* symbolized the liberties associated with university study, including drinking and sexual experimentation (with prostitutes, waitresses, maids, and other morally dubious women). In the years before the First World War, the *Bude* increasingly came under attack as an immoral and unhygienic form of living. Reformers such as Theodor Temming and Carl Sonnenschein portrayed the *Bude* as a dangerously sexualized space. Innocent young men, they warned, were corrupted by landladies who justified astronomical rents by offering their daughters in the bargain, and bright futures were lost when they were forced to marry low-class women they had made pregnant in their *Buden*.[14] With this kind of reputation, even the most liberal supporters of women's higher education found it "unimaginable" to associate a young German woman with a student *Bude*.[15]

The class status of female university students aggravated the housing dilemma. In the Wilhelmine period, the majority of women attending university came from privileged socioeconomic backgrounds.[16] To maintain their social standing, as well as that of their families, daughters had to appear respectable in their behavior and circumstances. A woman attending university in her hometown avoided damaging gossip (and heavy expenses) by continuing to reside with her parents. For

FIGURE 3.1. View from Berliner Strasse of the Victoria Studienhaus, 1916. Postcard collection of the Zentrum für Berlin-Studien, Zentral- und Landesbibliothek Berlin.

nonresidents without relatives or family friends to whom they could turn, housing
represented an enormous hurdle. Since even wealthier families begrudged daughters
the financial support for study that they offered sons, and scholarships for women
were rare, a woman's choices were limited.[17] Religious hospices offered inexpensive
shelter, but their strict house rules stifled youthful freedom. Private rentals, in turn,
posed their own set of difficulties. In Berlin, women did not dare rent lodgings
in the immediate vicinity of the university because of its many nightclubs and their
association with prostitutes.[18] As a result, female students often bore a long com-
mute, in some cases up to an hour. Landlords, moreover, viewed them as a nuisance,
preferring to rent to someone who would leave early in the morning and return late
at night.[19] If reformers depicted landladies as a moral threat to naïve young men,
student journals and the women's press more often portrayed them as mean and
neglectful—a poor substitute for a mother—to the female student.

The Victoria Studienhaus defined itself against such housing perils and practices. When it opened, an article in the feminist journal *Die Frau* stated, "One can
hardly imagine a greater contrast to the usual student *Bude.*"[20] Indeed, if unbounded
liberty and the pursuit of pleasure constituted the tenets of the *Bude*, radically different ideals of university life guided the conception of the Victoria Studienhaus.
In the absence in Germany of women's colleges, which then existed in the United
States and England, the Victoria Studienhaus played an important role in defining
the collegiate experience for German women.

According to Helene Lange, a relentless campaigner for women's educational
rights, the project arose like a phoenix from the "death" of another institution.
After forty years of schooling women, the Victoria Lyceum closed its doors in 1910
after its courses were made redundant by the advent of coeducation at Prussian
universities. Still committed to helping women study, the board of trustees shifted
their attention to the creation of a residence for women attending Berlin's institutions of higher learning.[21] The city had a single precedent: a boardinghouse for
female university students, the first of its kind in Germany, in the Tiergarten district.[22] It was far too small, however, to meet the pressing demand, and, in any case,
the Victoria Lyceum trustees envisaged something quite different in nature, larger
not only in the number of women who could be accommodated but also in the
scope of its mission. On an extensive research trip, Ottilie Fleer, the first director
of the Victoria Studienhaus, visited over forty colleges and universities in Europe
to gather information on the academic and housing conditions of female students.
Hansemann's keen interest in what women at German universities had to say on their
housing needs prompted Fleer to attend female student conferences in Wernigerode
and Weimar in 1912 and 1913, respectively.[23] From this period of intense deliberation,
a vision emerged of a residential center for female student life. With Hansemann's

financial sponsorship and capital from the Victoria Lyceum, the dream assumed built form.[24]

For their architect, the trustees chose Emilie Winkelmann, who must have seemed the ideal candidate for the job. She was a seasoned builder with a thriving architectural practice in Berlin. Her residential projects, among them an apartment building and boardinghouses, garnered press attention and positive reviews.[25] Her portfolio boasted an impressive and growing list of design work for women, including the municipal girls' school in her hometown of Aken an der Elbe.[26] As a woman architect, Winkelmann was expected to possess a natural affinity for domestic design and greater sensitivity to the needs of female inhabitants.[27] Finally, she had personally experienced the difficulties of academic life, having struggled to obtain an architectural education at Hanover's Technical College in the decade before women were permitted to study.[28]

The residence stood on Berliner Strasse in Charlottenburg, a site distinguished by its easy access to the university as well as to other schools and cultural resources (Figure 3.2).[29] Construction began in April 1914, and, despite war shortages, the

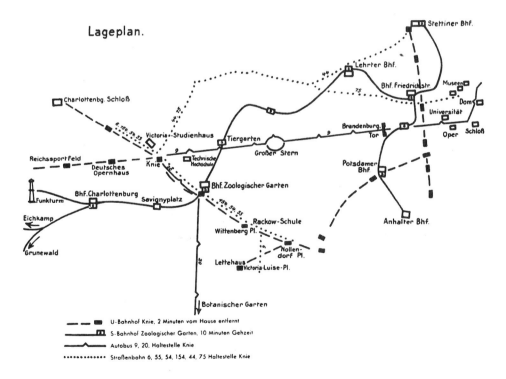

FIGURE 3.2. Map illustrating the location of the Victoria Studienhaus (upper left) in relation to other cultural and educational resources in Berlin, c. 1930. From an undated brochure in the collection of the Heimatmuseum Charlottenburg-Wilmersdorf.

residence opened on October 25, 1915.[30] It introduced a novel form of architecture to Berlin, the closest thing the city had to an American-style college campus. This was achieved on the limited space of a (slightly irregular) city plot by creating a hook-shaped building that presented an impressive, uniform façade, accommodated a range of functions internally, and maintained a sense of open landscape at the rear (Figures 3.3 and 3.4). Two unequal wings projected back from the street: tall and narrow to the west with six floors (including the attic), broad and truncated to the east with just two floors. The east wing housed facilities for the Victoria Lyceum, which reinstituted a limited educational program: a two-hundred-seat lecture auditorium with projection facilities on the ground floor and classrooms above. In the rest of the building, the ground floor contained service areas (isolated in the west wing) and the residence's main communal spaces: a well-appointed foyer, living and reading rooms, and a dining hall (Figures 3.5 and 3.6). Ninety-six single rooms for students, shared baths, maids' rooms, and the director's apartment were located on the upper floors. The attic story held a library, darkroom, art studios with natural light, and a gym. When weather permitted, gym and dance classes—with the students dressed in colorful, Grecian robes they had made themselves—took place in the large garden to the rear of the building, which also encompassed a terrace (for dining) and a sports area with tennis courts (Figure 3.7).[31] Abundant modern conveniences included elevators, central heating, baths with hot and cold running water, and hall telephones.[32]

Although it boasted luxurious facilities, the residence did not cater to a rich clientele. To the contrary, its founders intended to "benefit educated but not wealthy circles," that is, Germany's *Bildungsbürgerinnen,* women of the educated bourgeoisie. Winkelmann explained her decision to put some of the communal facilities in the attic as a cost-saving measure that avoided diminishing the number of rooms, which also would have necessitated raising rents (since this income was expected to finance maintenance of the residence).[33] Yet, as Lange pointed out, "first-rate board and lodging" came at a corresponding price. Rents varied depending on the size and location of the room, ranging from forty to eighty Marks per month. Meals, if taken, added another sixty-five Marks monthly. These costs compared favorably to what female students paid for full board at private pensiones in Berlin, with far fewer resources.[34] Lange observed that although one received good value, the expense over an academic year was considerable for "a meager parental purse." She pleaded with readers for donations to make possible the renting of rooms at half or no cost to students from economically constrained backgrounds.[35] In 1914, Winkelmann had stated that the Victoria Lyceum intended to offer a few rooms free of charge to needier students, but Lange's comments reveal this did not happen when the residence opened.[36]

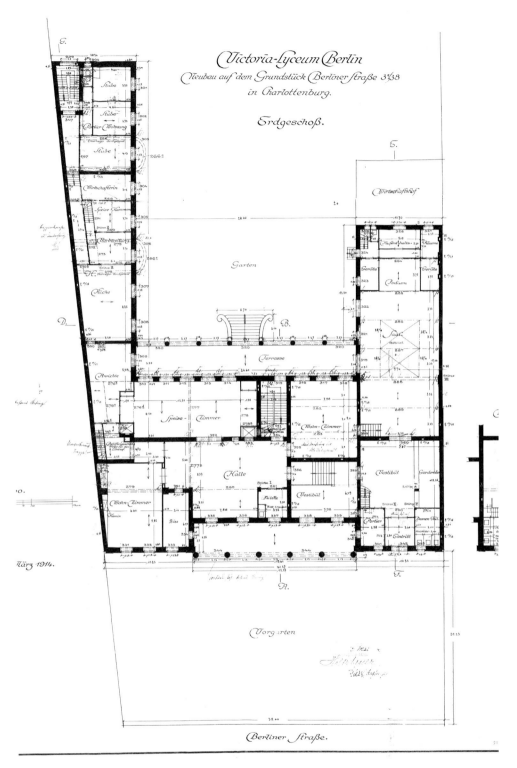

FIGURE 3.3. Victoria Studienhaus ground-floor plan by Emilie Winkelmann, 1914. Archiv, Bau- und Wohnungsaufsichtsamt, Bezirksamt Charlottenburg-Wilmersdorf.

In 1915 and 1916, numerous articles praising the residence appeared in Berlin's newspapers and in the national women's press. Commentators lauded the Victoria Studienhaus for offering a "real" home to women students, a physically healthier and spiritually loftier alternative to the student *Bude.* This impression was reinforced by the representational strategy of the building, which, despite its complexity, was exceptionally successful in communicating the ideals of the project. Instead of producing a uniform *Gesamtkunstwerk* (a visual environment all of one piece), the architect employed two architectural styles, neoclassical and Biedermeier, to evoke different layers of meaning and to create a dialogue within the building itself.

Describing her design, Winkelmann wrote that the building's exterior evoked the architecture of the second half of the eighteenth century, the period in which neoclassicism was ascendant in Berlin and other European cities (Figure 3.8).[37] To cloak a women's residence in neoclassical forms was a significant and unusual choice. Since its advent in the mid-eighteenth century, neoclassicism had been represented by architects and critics as a masculine style, a return to "disciplined," strong forms after the feminine "capriciousness of rococo."[38] This was especially true of the heavy, unadorned Doric columns Winkelmann used for the front entrance, considered the most muscular and robust of all the classical orders.[39] Yet, despite being defined

FIGURE 3.4. View of the garden and rear façade of the Victoria Studienhaus, c. 1930. From an undated brochure in the collection of the Heimatmuseum Charlottenburg-Wilmersdorf.

against imagined "feminine" qualities, neoclassical forms had cultural associations deeply meaningful to this new community of women.

At the most basic level, the style alluded to the Enlightenment and its emphasis on reason and secular learning, a heritage claimed by the young women of the Victoria Studienhaus. Numerous architectural examples in Berlin linked classicism (from various periods) to higher intellectual pursuits. These included the university (Georg Wenzeslaus von Knobelsdorff and Johann Boumann, 1748–53), Karl Friedrich Schinkel's Altes Museum (1823–30), and Friedrich August Stüler's Neues Museum (1841–59) and Nationalgalerie (1862–76). After the turn of the century, the association was reinforced by projects such as the new Royal Library (1903–14) by Ernst von Ihne, which also housed the Academy of Sciences, and the Pergamon Museum by Alfred Messel (1906–30). By drawing parallels through a shared classical language, the Victoria Studienhaus partnered itself visually with state institutions of public education.

FIGURE 3.5. One of the Victoria Studienhaus's communal living rooms, designed by Winkelmann, c. 1916. Landesarchiv Berlin.

The stateliness of these royal projects undoubtedly resonated with the founders of the residence, which bore the name of its royal patron. Contemporary descriptions of the building as "imposing," "giant," "monumental," "proud," and "powerful" suggest an authoritative presence.[40] By evoking the classicism of Berlin's grand royal projects, the Victoria Studienhaus appealed to the legitimacy of the state and tradition to sanction what was, after all, a radically new institution. Moreover, as Barry Bergdoll argues, Enlightenment philosophers looked to monumental public buildings such as schools and museums to reawaken civic life and forge an engaged citizenry. Imagining the vibrant public life of the antique polis, symbolized by the "architectural grandeur of the Athenian agora or Roman forum," reformers drew on ancient paradigms to shape a new civic urbanism.[41] The monumental classicism of the Victoria Studienhaus can be read as a continuation of this Enlightenment project, specifically as an attempt by the patrons and architect to signal to Berliners an expanded public realm that encompassed the New Woman.

In the austerity of its classicism, the Victoria Studienhaus also referred to contemporary uses of the style to express modern, German functionalism. Responding

FIGURE 3.6. The Victoria Studienhaus's dining hall, c. 1930. Small tables promoted a sense of intimacy and domesticity, countering the depersonalizing aspects of institutional living. From an undated brochure in the collection of the Heimatmuseum Charlottenburg-Wilmersdorf.

to a growing discourse on how to design for the modern age, architects such as Paul Bonatz and Peter Behrens mixed pared-down classicism with industrialism. Behrens's Allgemeine Elektrizitäts-Gesellschaft turbine factory in Berlin became iconic of a "modern and timeless" functionalism, even if its classicizing design elements were not, strictly speaking, functional.[42] Perhaps Winkelmann, too, wished to indicate something eternal and new in this residence for young scholars. Yet if the home, or women, possessed some (imagined) immutable trait to be cherished, such as coziness or femininity, that was not to say that domesticity or women remained unchanged. The suggestion of functionalism that adhered to Winkelmann's spare classicism communicated the message that the residence was a new functional type addressing the needs of modern women. In other words, what the AEG factory was to twentieth-century industry, the Victoria Studienhaus was to urban domestic life: a symbol of continuity and progress.

The aesthetic redefinition of women and domesticity continued in the interior spaces, which Winkelmann designed along with all of the furniture.[43] The monumental classicism of the residence's public face gave way to the intimacies of

FIGURE 3.7. Dining on the terrace, c. 1930. By the time this photograph was taken, vegetation had softened the severity of the Victoria Studienhaus's neoclassical architecture. From an undated brochure in the collection of the Heimatmuseum Charlottenburg-Wilmersdorf.

FIGURE 3.8. Partial view of the Victoria Studienhaus façade. The name Haus Ottilie von Hansemann is inscribed on the architrave. From "Das Heim unsrer Studentinnen: Haus Ottilie von Hansemann, Berlin," *Daheim* 52, no. 47 (1916): 23.

Biedermeier. Flourishing in Austria and Germany from the early to mid-nineteenth century, Biedermeier represented a style of living centered on the bourgeoisie and the home. Its influence, which touched all the arts, was most profound in the areas of furniture and interior design. Admired for its simple, unpretentious comfort, Biedermeier enjoyed a revival among early twentieth-century architectural reformers searching for more utilitarian forms. Against Schinkel's contemporary and very public classicism, Biedermeier stood for the architecture of private life, and books such as Paul Mebes's *Um 1800* popularized the association of domesticity with this period.

Interestingly, both public and private dimensions of the Victoria Studienhaus interiors served to reinforce a sense of the intimate and personal. In her designs, the architect labored to avoid any sense of the loss of self associated with large institutions. The communal rooms on the ground floor were not particularly large, and the arrangement of furniture broke up the space into intimate clusters. The dining hall was set with small tables and was divided into indoor and outdoor sections. Most important, no two of the ninety-six student rooms were alike. Variations in the design of the rooms, such as in the wall coverings and furnishings, created a sense of individuality that students further enhanced with their own decorative touches.[44] Because Biedermeier was understood as a style embodying personal taste, the Biedermeier-style decoration of the rooms signaled personal domestic space, helping to avert institutional overtones.

Finally, Biedermeier evoked the grand era of the Berlin *salonnière*. In the homes of salon hostesses such as Rahel Varnhagen, whose guests included Heinrich Heine and Alexander von Humboldt, men and women of different classes, nationalities, and religious faiths mingled to discuss art, music, literature, and politics. The salon, a distinctly feminine and domestic form, helped shape a new realm of heterogeneous social discourse that philosopher Jürgen Habermas identifies as the bourgeois public sphere.[45] It also represented an institution of self-cultivation for women, who welcomed the public worlds of learning, culture, and politics into their homes.[46] One can easily imagine the symbolic appeal of the *salonnière* for a project such as the Victoria Studienhaus. Biedermeier's urban and progressive associations were reinforced by architectural reformers such as Joseph August Lux, an influential Austrian theorist. To him, the style emblematized the rich hybrid of local and cosmopolitan cultures in Vienna and prefigured the rise of "great-city urbanism" and "the new, modern individual."[47] All of these meanings—simple functionalism, bourgeois domesticity, private life, salon culture, urbanism, and modernity—recommended Biedermeier to the Victoria Studienhaus, which was to be a practical home for a new type of educated and emancipated urban woman.

The serious mission that the Victoria Studienhaus set itself was inscribed in the architect's careful use of neoclassicism and Biedermeier. Nothing about the place struck visitors as frivolous. To the contrary, the lofty ideals of the Enlightenment seemed to permeate the building: "The highest classical ideals of the spirit-filled bliss of youth appear to come alive in the delightful new home for female students." The "spiritual and noble" façade greeted the public, and "no clumsy ornament or pretense" marred "the simple truth and health of the whole powerful building."[48]

Similarly, the functional simplicity of the student rooms bespoke the honest work that took place therein (Figure 3.9). One journalist noted how the "practical" design of the room gave it a feeling more of workspace than bedroom: "The bed is placed in a niche behind a curtain, washstand and closet are built in, so that the large sunny room utterly gives the impression of a pleasant workroom."[49] Smaller rooms contained a sofa that converted into a bed, preserving the appearance of a

FIGURE 3.9. A student's room in the Victoria Studienhaus, 1916. Of the ninety-six student rooms Winkelmann designed, no two were alike in their decoration, emphasizing the unique character of each resident. Landesarchiv Berlin.

workroom by day. As the journalist mentioned in passing, each room possessed a small vestibule with a built-in closet and washstand for tidier living. (The double set of doors also created a sound barrier, eliminating noise from the hallway.)[50] Winkelmann thus resolved a design problem addressed repeatedly in the discourse about housing the single middle-class woman on a budget: namely, how to merge the function of rooms so that both private and public needs could be accommodated with dignity.

In discussing the students' rooms, commentators paid particular attention to their big desks.[51] Although the desks appear small by today's standards, they were large compared with the traditional secretary's desk used by women.[52] The secretary desk had been designed for correspondence, whereas the desk in the Victoria Studienhaus served for study. For one observer, the setting evoked a modernized genre scene: "In my mind's eye I see . . . a youthful face at the desk eagerly bent over thick books—a subject for a painter of interiors that would be a right healthy counterpart to the dainty little fashion ladies of certain Frenchies!"[53] This xenophobic gibe, typical of the war rhetoric of the period, promoted a robust model of Teutonic femininity and domesticity in German painting against the "effeteness" of eighteenth-century French masters, such as Fragonard. More than nationalistic tensions, however, the comment underscores changes in women's occupations and the need for new kinds of design in the early twentieth century. Interestingly, in a 1913 survey asking female university students what furnishings would be most useful to them, respondents singled out a big desk.[54]

The large windows and abundance of light also drew notice (Figure 3.10).[55] Sanitation reformers, campaigning for hygienic urban buildings, promoted such features in the fight against disease.[56] In the context of a women's residence, the airy windows suggested not only health but also Biedermeier interiors, the hallmark of which was their light. Art historian Ellen Spickernagel has discussed the gendered representations of light in Biedermeier interiors and the tendency to attribute a spiritual or noble quality to women's rooms through their luminosity.[57] Here, again, is an instance of how Winkelmann's design could evoke a sense of modernity and timelessness, using light to appeal to both the "healthiness" of (reformed) modern life and the "spirituality" of the past.

In devising a representational strategy for this novel type of building, the architect thus mined many levels of cultural meaning. Instead of a singular story, she offered a cluster of narratives about identity and destiny. One could be domestic and stately, individual and communal, modern and timeless. Meanings reflected and altered one another, especially in the relationship between exterior and interior. In an 1812 painting by Georg Friedrich Kersting, a woman embroiders at a small table bathed in the sunlight of a nearby window (Figure 3.11). As Spickernagel explains,

FIGURE 3.10. Published descriptions and images (such as this one from 1916) of the students' rooms infused with light evoked a Romantic tradition associating women and the domestic realm with spirituality and enlightenment. Original photograph from the Landesarchiv Berlin. This image was published in "Das Heim unsrer Studentinnen," 23.

FIGURE 3.11. Georg Friedrich Kersting, *The Embroideress*, 1812. Klassik Stiftung Weimar, Herzogin Anna Amalia Bibliothek.

to a contemporary audience, such images signified the uplifting aspects of a woman's isolation from the world.[58] By contrast, the neoclassical façade of the Victoria Studienhaus inflected the Biedermeier interior: The light streaming in through the windows brought with it Enlightenment ideals, transforming a bedroom into a scholar's study. The building's Biedermeier "heart" similarly spoke to the façade of the necessary infusion of a "spiritual," domestic femininity into the public worlds of government, commerce, and culture—the central argument of the bourgeois women's movement. Although it is true that strangers passing by on the street encountered only one of those dimensions, it is important to remember that residents experienced a dynamic. The visual signs of domestic life and citizenship were placed into dialogue, reminding the young students that neither could exist in isolation, as in the idealized image of the woman at her sewing table. Moreover, as indicated above, the character of Biedermeier domesticity was highly complex, and it introduced, through its association with the salon, a notion of porousness to the public realm. Winkelmann manipulated domestic codes to undermine a simple polar opposition between home and the world beyond, unlike the designers of earlier women's colleges in England, who employed domestic idioms precisely in order to signal this sort of separation as well as to reassure parents that their daughters had not truly left home.[59]

The unprecedented nature of the Victoria Studienhaus encouraged commentators to explore the relationship of form to function and, in particular, the influence of design on the moral and physical formation of the young residents. A law student writing in *Die Studentin,* a journal for Germany's female university students, argued that because of women's greater sensitivity to their surroundings, unfavorable living conditions weighed more heavily on women than on men. A decrepit and ugly dwelling caused the young female student physical and moral damage, as well as aesthetic distress.[60] The carefully planned interiors of the Victoria Studienhaus struck visitors as an antidote to the environmental horrors of the traditional student *Bude.*[61] Measuring it against the worst stereotypes of the *Bude*—dirty, noisy, smelly, and outfitted with "brown plush chairs," an "artificial palm tree," and a "painted green head of Apollo"—the women's residence seemed a haven of health and good taste.[62]

For these writers, good design was a moral and physical imperative, not an indulgence. Nonetheless, assertions that women were frivolous spendthrifts, voiced in the discourse on luxury in Wilhelmine Germany, produced a certain defensiveness:

These charming rooms! How each one looks like an outrageous spoiling. But are comfortable, functional simplicity; solidity of materials; beautiful, quiet form and color not the most permissible spoiling? Indeed, the only one that we should all allow ourselves? Here, in any case, one that is bestowed with full and cheerful awareness on the young female bearers of German culture. There is nothing junky, nothing half done, nothing unclear in the entire building; stillness, light, pure atmosphere—all conditions of self-absorption, a concentration of powers that any person who suffers from the external clamor of public life could envy these heaven-blessed young women in their lovely home, which, while communal, nonetheless enables the strictest isolation.[63]

Appealing to the guiding tenets of the design reform movement (functionality, solidity, clarity, light), which endowed aesthetic form with culturally redemptive powers, the author recast "spoiling" by design as the protection and nurturing of Germany's most valuable asset, its young female bearers of culture.

As much as it might have provided a contemplative setting, the Victoria Studien-haus was not perceived as a passive vessel. Rather, the building was depicted as a formative agent, interacting with and shaping its residents. Together with Fleer, the resident director, the house enacted the role of moral parent: "Student mother Ottilie Fleer, one feels your good, refined spirit after spending only a few hours in the building, and one says to oneself with blunt emotion that here, for once, people have it really good—unrestricted and simply *committed to noble thought and action through the stamp of the house*, secure in confidence and trust, in carefree safety."[64] Through a diffuse maternal spirit and virtuous architecture, the residence left its mark like the imprint of a good upbringing. In keeping with the whole project, Fleer's parenting style was depicted as modern: She allowed her girls the liberty required by youth—"the students are on the whole their own mistresses"—but was there with "advice and help" if needed.[65] Still, this was not a total, *Bude* freedom; if not Fleer, then the building itself was expected to impose limits on the women's behavior by compelling them to be good.

The presence of the Victoria Lyceum in the east wing accentuated the formative element of the Victoria Studienhaus. In its large auditorium, the Lyceum's popular lecture series, which had ceased in 1910, was reinstituted.[66] The classrooms were used for a variety of courses, which were closely coordinated with the university.[67] During the war, for example, Turkish was added to the language curriculum to compensate for overenrollment in the university's Oriental Department.[68] Although the Lyceum occupied its own wing, there was direct access to the residence (a side door from the auditorium foyer opened onto the residence's entry hall), and the two shared a common living room. As one reviewer noted, "The Studienhaus does not want to offer just a home; the scholarly development and academic studies of its inhabitants should also be fostered—specifically, through courses and lectures."[69]

The residents' minds and bodies were further cultivated through nonacademic offerings, such as musical evenings and dance classes.[70] By combining living quarters,

instruction, cultural activities, and athletics, the Victoria Studienhaus attempted
to re-create the vibrant campus life of women's colleges in the United States and
England. If, as noted above, the idea of same-sex colleges had fallen out of favor
among German champions of women's higher education long before the Victoria
Studienhaus was built, the advantages of American- and English-style campus life
continued to be recognized. Women's colleges, it was argued,

> allowed the students to fill their minds with knowledge and yet, at the same time,
> happily enjoy their youth and train and toughen their bodies with all kinds of
> sports. These things could be united because the lecture halls and departments were
> affiliated with a residence for female students with its own living rooms, dining hall,
> work and common spaces, park, and sports fields. And so, with no time lost, one
> activity could flow into the next.[71]

Despite working within considerable financial and spatial restraints, Winkelmann
fulfilled the desire for a centralization of resources as then existed at women's
colleges.

Equally appealing was the idea of community that women's colleges represented.[72] An aggressively masculine student culture at German universities excluded
women from important bonding rituals and practices, such as heavy drinking.[73]
Concerned about this isolation, the founders of the Victoria Studienhaus sought
to provide young female scholars with an alternative experience of academic community. Like the clubs discussed in the previous chapter, the Victoria Studienhaus
was shaped by the notion of *Frauengeselligkeit*, the empowering development of the
female self within a community of peers. This shared ideology reflects, in part,
the influence of clubwomen on the project: Hansemann, Winkelmann, and Fleer,
three key figures, were all members of the German Lyceum Club. *Frauengeselligkeit* at
the residence, as at the club, was defined in "international" terms, even if the war
narrowed its scope: "Here the woman from Vienna comes to know the one from
north Germany, the woman from Westphalia the one from East Prussia, and with
a pretty similar educational background, the exchange of experiences is doubly
important and instructional."[74] Weekly meetings between Fleer and her "student–
daughters" ritualized this exchange. At these gatherings—a kind of minisalon—
house rules were worked out, talks might be given, and a stream of ideas, conversations, and suggestions flowed among women from various academic disciplines.[75]
Like the women's clubs, the residence fostered dialogue across differences, creating
a new public sphere of social exchange.

While nurturing the bonds of a peer community, the Victoria Studienhaus
rejected insularity. This distinguished it from the emphasis on spatial segregation

at early women's colleges in England and the United States.[76] Although national differences in academic culture played a role (male students were also isolated to some degree on English and American campuses), this attitude did not result simply from adopting the German university model, which, as noted above, was seen by many as inappropriate for women. Founders of the Victoria Studienhaus attempted to construct a positive image of the urban integration of female students without raising the libertine values associated with male student life (typified by the nightclubs and prostitutes surrounding the university). In a 1916 speech to the German Lyceum Club, Fleer emphasized physical and intellectual proximity to Berlin's academic institutions: Easy access to schools had determined the site of the Victoria Studienhaus, and its educational program (operated through the Victoria Lyceum) maintained contact with the university.[77] The map from a 1930s brochure (Figure 3.2) locates the residence within a network of schools and cultural resources, such as opera houses and museums, underscoring the desire for connectedness. Thus, while the Victoria Studienhaus sought to shelter young women's bodies and minds, it also promoted engagement with broader civic and academic communities. It did so, however, from a position of strength and security. Agnes Harder, a writer and German Lyceum Club member, described the students as bees leaving the hive to gather the pollen of science, bringing it back to their cells, manufacturing it into knowledge for themselves, and then using it to better society.[78] Like the women's clubs, the residence was conceived as a gateway to the city as well as a place apart, where one could prepare for and process this encounter. This experience was expected to benefit not only the individual but also the greater progress of humankind.

The residence's creation for the most part by an older generation of women (Ottilie von Hansemann died in 1919, at age eighty) raises questions about whose ideals it reflected. Unfortunately, memoirs and descriptions of the home by its earliest inhabitants are rare.[79] Fleer, in her club speech, noted that the *Studienhaus* had been fully booked since its opening and that demand was so great, applications were submitted semesters in advance, proving, in her eyes, the institution's necessity.[80] One wonders, however, what young women would have chosen had there been more alternatives at their disposal. A survey of female university students questioned about their housing preferences and published in *Die Studentin* in 1913 reveals that many preferred apartments to student dormitories. This suggests that young women as well as men valued the freedom and independence of the *Bude* so decried by reformers. At the same time, student residences held their own appeal:

One would be among one's own there, among female comrades pursuing the same goal. Opportunities for making friends would exist, without the need for seclusion being taken amiss. Of course, this presupposes a director who understands student life and her residents' legitimate needs for freedom. If one managed to create such homes, which offer young women suitable lodging and social contact without impeding their freedom of movement, it would eliminate restrictions on the capacity to work for many a female student as well as great worries for many parents.

The ease of living among one's peers, moreover, contrasted sharply with the uncomfortable feeling induced by being an object of curiosity as the *Emanzipierte*, the liberated woman, at a pensione. [81] In their responses to the questionnaire, students identified features they desired in a student residence. These included good reading and common spaces, basic cooking facilities in their rooms in addition to a central dining hall, and modern comforts such as electric lighting, baths, and central heating. The Victoria Studienhaus offered almost everything these students demanded and probably owed its success to good design and the balance between community and independence.

The residence remained popular for many decades. By its tenth anniversary, in 1925, over one thousand women had lived there.[82] Time brought some alterations: In 1919, the auditorium was converted into an experimental expressionist theater. During the Second World War, the building was appropriated for a makeshift hospital.[83] In 1956, it resumed its original function and continued as a women's residence until the early 1970s. At that point, the building's outdated facilities as well as its increasing operating expenses, no longer covered by the rents, led to the decision to close the residence.[84] Changing social mores also played a role. As a former trustee put it, "When the students began to sneak men into their rooms, we knew it was time to quit."[85] Once again, a transformed social landscape compelled the Victoria Lyceum to rethink its purpose. In 1972, the trustees sold the Victoria Studienhaus and used the proceeds, together with public funds, to build student housing for women and couples with children. The new Haus Ottilie von Hansemann, on neighboring Fraunhoferstrasse, opened in April 1977. The Victoria Lyceum then disbanded, and its remaining capital was absorbed by the Land Berlin on condition that it uphold the mission of the new residence. A private institution founded and sustained by women thus passed into state hands.

Redefining Hearth and Home for the Career Woman: The New Building Cooperatives

Residents of the Victoria Studienhaus enjoyed the backing of committed patrons, who assumed responsibility for housing female students. After graduation, however, those who pursued a career over marriage were on their own, along with thousands of other single middle-class women supporting themselves in the metropolis. Without an Ottilie von Hansemann to lend a hand, they were forced to rely on their own meager resources. Few earned an income beyond subsistence level. Teaching, the most popular profession among women, paid its female practitioners two-thirds of male salaries. Justifications for this disparity ranged from the assertion that women were simply earning pocket money before marriage to the presumption that they could get by on less than male colleagues, who were expected to support families.[86] Alone, single women could do little to alleviate their desire for more than the furnished rooms they habitually occupied. After the turn of the century, however, the growth of women's housing and building cooperatives encouraged pooling resources. Thus began a striking transformation that witnessed new women acting collectively to become their own landlords and building patrons.

In 1911, a novel organization appeared in Berlin exemplifying the convergence of new domestic ideals and innovative financial strategies among women. The Association for Modern Women's Apartments (Vereinigung für moderne Frauenwohnungen) believed it had a solution to the problem of housing single women: the "hearth collective" (*Herdgenossenschaft*). The concept implied small groups of women, drawn together by bonds of friendship and mutual interest, forming communal households. The arrangement was economical: By sharing service areas, such as kitchen and bath, residents could afford to rent a large and comfortable apartment. Moreover, housework performed among friends transformed drudgery into a "convivial, healthy activity" and reduced the need for servants. Alongside these pragmatic advantages, the hearth collective offered "a real home" to women who shied away from single rooms, pensiones, and institutional residences.[87] It represented intimacy, a supportive environment, individual freedom, and affordable rent—all rolled into one. Not surprisingly, the concept was deeply appealing: At a public meeting held by the association in October 1911, the hall was crowded with prospective clients.[88]

The association functioned as a managerial and mediating agency. It began by acquiring leases for a number of properties that it sublet to women.[89] Although landlords, as noted above, were reluctant to rent to single women, they were amenable to dealing with an organization that assumed responsibility for finding and replacing tenants. The association also acted as a matchmaker: "Ladies" registered their wishes (about area, price, and housemates) at the office, which coordinated groups.[90] Bringing together housemates with similar life experiences, attitudes, and education levels was considered essential.[91] Potential residents had the opportunity to meet one another at the office or at association meetings in order to measure their compatibility and build their hearth collective around shared interests and expectations.[92] Although this may strike us as self-evident or even routine, it is important to keep in mind that the association was pioneering a new concept, the cooperative flat.[93] The intended balance between the individual and the social unit in the hearth collective attempted to redress the solitude experienced by many single women by creating new "families" that nurtured their desire for independence. In the attention to social station, a Prussian sensibility for boundaries remained—here, however, not dividing the hearth collective internally (by reinstating familial hierarchies), but rather distinguishing it from the mixed society beyond its doors.

As demand increased, the association expected that builders would step forth to design apartments specifically for hearth collectives.[94] In anticipation of this new architecture, the association became a forum for discussing women's design needs. Members were invited to tour a new building in Berlin being considered as a possible model for women's dwellings. Monthly evening lectures provided further food for thought. Guest speakers included Mathilde Kirschner, the Berlin mayor's daughter, who had founded a home for female workers in Berlin in 1908, and a Frau Philip, the inventor of the "Philaküche."[95] This appliance, which Frau Philip named after herself, was designed primarily for single women living in cramped quarters. Described as a "kitchen in a cabinet," it consisted of a compact box on wheels that, once unfolded, revealed compartments for cooking, cleaning, and storing kitchen utensils.

By 1914, the association had shifted from relying on the private market to its own initiative. In order to heighten public interest in a planned residence, it issued two series of colored promotional stamps. The first series pictured six women in different professions. The second series illustrated the proposed building, including views of the exterior, an interior common space, and different sides of a furnished room.[96] The themes of the two series interwove the modernity of the New Woman with that of architecture—a juxtaposition that would become widespread in the Weimar era, which twinned the *Neue Frau* with the *Neues Bauen*. Yet the Wilhelmine example was far more radical in its conception of the occupant: Her unconventional (to some, heretical) way of living became the foundation on which to build. Although architects of the 1920s accommodated the needs of the New Woman, through, for example, communal laundries and efficient kitchens, they ultimately intended to create better and happier housewives.[97]

The Association for Modern Women's Apartments spawned a limited liability cooperative, the Women's Apartment Cooperative Limited (Genossenschaft "Die Frauenwohnung" eGmbH), to oversee construction of the new buildings.[98] Such cooperatives were a recent phenomenon in Berlin, appearing around the turn of the century in response to the chronic inability of the private market to produce good, affordable housing.[99] Share certificates in the women's cooperative cost two hundred Marks and could be paid for in monthly installments as low as three Marks, so that even those with little money could join. Representatives on the cooperative's board of directors suggest the peculiar confluence of interests sparked by this housing experiment. Among them were Hedwig Rüdiger, the president of the powerful Association of Female Postal and Telegraph Employees, noted ethnologist Caecilie Seler-Sachs, and Elisabeth von Knobelsdorff, the first woman to earn an architectural degree in Germany.[100] Knobelsdorff may have been the architect responsible for creating the building prototype.

An article from 1916 described the design of the proposed buildings, which were to be located in various districts of Berlin. The upper floors incorporated studios for women artists, as well as one-room apartments that carefully maximized the comfort and utility of their small spaces. These units featured a cooking pantry with cold and hot running water and a gas stove; a balcony, loggia, or bay window; and built-in closets. Bathrooms were situated in the corridor. Larger, self-contained apartments were planned for the lower stories. These consisted of two to four rooms and were intended as apartments shared by several women. The larger units could also be rented by single women who wanted more space without forfeiting community. Visiting, music, and reading rooms for common use were located on the ground floor, as was a larger apartment for two women who operated a canteen for residents not wishing to cook.[101] This urban project—mixing domestic, work, and public spaces; designed for female professionals, possibly by a woman architect; and funded by a women's building cooperative—was unique not only within Berlin but also internationally. Similar projects, established on a for-profit basis and designed by male architects, had begun to appear in London in the late 1880s, the most famous of which was Sloane Gardens House.[102] As with other ventures, Berlin women pushed both the social and economic implications of such precedents further by seeking all-female (or nearly all-female) productions. The advent of war, or perhaps the collapse of the Women's Bank in 1916, which had provided support to the Women's Apartment Cooperative, undermined the project's realization.[103] Nevertheless, this collaborative undertaking, which united an ethnologist and an architect, among others, opened up new ways to imagine the single woman's home life.

As the brief description above makes clear, the Women's Apartment Cooperative sought a compromise, accommodating both women who wished to live alone and those who preferred to live with others, while providing all residents with the possibility of social interaction in the ground-floor common rooms. It is notable that shared dining space was limited to a canteen, revealing a desire to avoid the unwanted institutional domesticity of group homes. Nonetheless, it is equally important that this project, as well as the others discussed in this chapter, included some form of dining facilities for women too tired or unable to cook. In a period when women felt neither welcomed nor comfortable dining alone in public restaurants, the option of prepared meals remained too valuable to discard altogether.[104]

Despite the absence of centralized housekeeping arrangements, the communal element of the Women's Apartment Cooperative raised, for some critics, the issue of the *Einküchenhaus* (the kitchenless dwelling) and its lack of success in Germany. Journals such as *Hohe Warte* introduced German audiences to English experiments with residential living that centralized housekeeping with the intention of reducing the labor and cost of private housework. In 1909 Hermann Muthesius and Albert Gessner designed five apartment buildings in Berlin for married couples and families, which contained kitchenless dwellings served by a central kitchen (but without a communal dining room). While cooperative developments met with success in other European cities, *Einküchenhäuser* faced financial difficulties and public skepticism in Berlin. Among women, the idea was advocated with enthusiasm by some members of the socialist movement but found less currency among centrists. Historian Günther Uhlig has argued that the German bourgeoisie failed to perceive the advantages offered by the *Einküchenhaus* for its increasingly embattled way of life. Rather, it was seen as threatening the bourgeoisie's very foundation, the privacy of the family. Moreover, the role of conspicuous consumption in determining the social status of a family, including the visibility of superfluous servants, militated against household strategies that, although more economical, did away with such displays of abundance.[105]

Writing in 1914 on the Women's Apartment Cooperative, Elisabeth Eichler claimed that an "extremely developed Germanic sense of individuality" had contributed to the rejection of the *Einküchenhaus* model. She continued,

> Now I read in a commentary on the women's apartment project about a five-room apartment set up for four ladies with a common veranda, hallway, kitchen and servant's room. A communal kitchen for four ladies! Well, what does one imagine? What remains here of the lovely saying: One's own hearth is golden? Peace would never reign in this kitchen. And the servant girl? Should she obey four ladies at once? Which of them would be her boss? Utterly unthinkable!

Eichler thus mocked the feasibility of cooperative living among women. She maintained that if the proposed dwellings were to avoid an institutional character, which "holds no appeal for the wage-earning, independent woman of the twentieth century," then autonomy must be prioritized, allowing the resident to cook her own meals "without a stranger's eyes peering into her pot." To this end, Eichler favored separate, individual apartments (with thick dividing walls) over shared living space. Yet despite disagreeing with the cooperative's architectural vision, she strongly supported its broader goals.[106]

Eichler's assumption that cooperative living was institutional in nature is illuminating. Traditionally, homes for genteel spinsters were associated with *Damenstifte,*

residences run by religious organizations. Educated bourgeois women, who struggled to assert their social and economic independence, felt no affinity for such
homes. Indeed, the recurring emphasis on autonomy in the discourse about housing single career women suggests an aversion to any institution perceived as limiting
individual freedom. For some, the *Einküchenhaus* fell into this category and was thus
rejected, even though socialist feminists such as Lily Braun argued that it was an
instrument of liberation for womankind. Nonetheless, the idea of community was
of central importance to single women. Rejecting the *Einküchenhaus* did not necessarily mean rejecting communal living. The smaller cooperative structure of the
hearth collectives found an eager audience, because it allowed for group living while
avoiding the regimentation of a larger-scale institution.

Despite such objections, bourgeois women appear to have been more supportive
of centralized housekeeping than has been previously recognized. Writing in the
women's guidebook to Berlin, Pochhammer claimed that *Einküchenhäuser* were "much
in demand" among single women. While admitting that Berliners, on the whole,
did "not yet seem to be quite ready for this 'modern' form of domestic life," she laid
the blame more on men than women.[107] In an article weighing different housing
options for single career women, Schrey advocated centralized housekeeping as the
best solution.[108] Writer Anna Behnisch-Kappstein hoped that the issue of women's
dwellings would bring about a reconsideration of the maligned *Einküchenhaus*.[109]
Other commentators praised the centralized housekeeping system developed by the
Damenheime (Ladies' Homes), a cooperative-based organization founded around
the turn of the century. By 1906, it had eight buildings in Berlin and Potsdam, with
over two hundred female residents. This population included single women of all
ages, from students to widows, stemming predominantly from the educated middle class.[110] Apartments ranged in size from one to four rooms, all of which were
advertised as fully self-sufficient.[111] Centralized facilities and services, including a
staffed dining hall (Figure 3.12), professional kitchen, and by-the-hour maid service, were available to residents on a voluntary basis.[112] In addition to convenience
and economic saving, the Damenheime offered a balance between social community
and individual freedom. Advertisements promised "social contact without personal
limitation."[113] By emphasizing the autonomy they permitted their residents, the
homes distinguished themselves from similar but more restrictive institutions. In
1905, journalist Margarete Zepler noted that a women's residence in Lichterfeld,
intended for working daughters of the educated classes, imposed rules that were
inconvenient and uncomfortable for its residents, such as a compulsory midday
meal at fixed hours, an obligation to undertake heavy housework, and no male visitors, including relatives.[114] Despite the Damenheime's initial success, however, only
three buildings remained by 1911.[115] Perhaps the homes experienced financial or

managerial difficulties similar to those that befell the *Einküchenhäuser* designed by Muthesius and Gessner. Such enterprises were, notably, far more expensive than the humble hearth collectives.[116]

Heterogeneity may have further contributed to the Damenheime's decline. The mixture of widows and students, who shared little beyond their status as single women, may have felt too random to those seeking "a real home." In April 1911, a residence opened in Pankow that articulated a more exclusive vision of domestic community. The Berlin Association of Female Elementary Teachers, under the auspices of its own housing cooperative, commissioned Paul Mebes to design a fifty-unit apartment building for its members and other female teachers (Figure 3.13).[117] The housing crisis for female teachers was particularly acute, because, by law, they could not retain their positions if they married.[118] The Lehrerinnenheim (Female Teachers' Home) was hailed as an important advance in the housing question for single professional women. It addressed both general needs associated with working women and concerns specific to teachers, namely, the space to do the at-home work

FIGURE 3.12. Advertisement for the Damenheime (Ladies' Homes) cooperative, illustrating the communal dining room of one of its residences. From "Damen-Wohnungen," advertisement, *Centralblatt des Bundes Deutscher Frauenvereine* 5, no. 7 (1903): 56.

(such as grading) required by their profession. Neither the general housing stock, it was argued, nor institutional residences for women met these special needs.[119] The Lehrerinnenheim thus acknowledged that marital status and gender were not the only determinants in the women's housing question.

The teachers' home offered self-contained apartments of one to three rooms, all of which boasted an entry hall, kitchen, bathroom, balcony, and built-in closets, as well as central heating and hot water (Figure 3.14).[120] The largest apartments also included a servant's room, and maid service could be arranged for the others. Communal reading and writing rooms were located on the first floor, as were guest rooms. Those who wished to dine in company could do so in the common dining room (Figure 3.15), while those who sought privacy could have meals delivered to their apartments at a slightly higher cost. This combination of centralized housekeeping features and fully autonomous households allowed residents to make choices on the

FIGURE 3.13. Wisbyer Strasse façade of the Lehrerinnenheim in Pankow, designed by Paul Mebes. From M. Heeren, "Lehrerinnenheim in Berlin," *Deutsche Bauhütte* 16, no. 40 (1912): 330.

basis of personal preference or shifting needs. Beyond these amenities, teachers who fell ill could rely on the assistance of the house manager, as well as proximity to helpful friends. Faced with job insecurity, heavy workloads, ceaseless financial difficulties, and the loneliness of legally enforced celibacy, female teachers experienced a relatively high incidence of illness.[121] Living in isolated quarters, they struggled to recuperate on their own. In this and other respects, founders viewed the new home as a "blessing" for the single teacher.[122]

The conception of community at the Lehrerinnenheim encapsulated more than professional, marital, and gendered identities. Most female teachers came from educated middle-class backgrounds, and their sense of belonging drew on shared class sensibilities. An early advertisement for the home promoted the possibility of forming connections with social peers.[123] Ohlert's article on the housing crisis of female

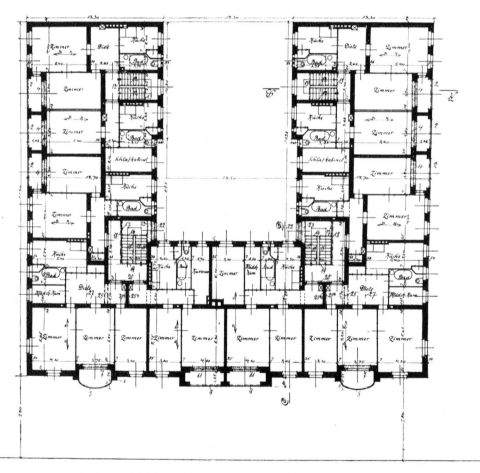

FIGURE 3.14. Plan by Paul Mebes of the upper residential floors of the Lehrerinnenheim. From Heeren, "Lehrerinnenheim in Berlin," 330.

teachers noted that an important stimulus to creating their own residence in Hamburg had been the discomfort teachers experienced while living in rented rooms with families who were "uneducated." "Living together with people who share the same level of education, pleasures, and sorrows as oneself," Ohlert wrote, "offers its own particular contentment."[124]

Mebes's design responded to the importance of class identity in the teachers' new home. Restrained terracotta ornamentation, including medallions of female heads that announced the building's occupants, decorated the façades (Figure 3.16). A contemporary observer remarked that the exterior avoided "all grandeur," yet achieved a "dignified" appearance. Similar characteristics defined the interior, executed in "solid, genuine materials without unnecessary extravagance or magnificent display."[125] Such modest elegance, shaped by Mebes's interest in Biedermeier (as explored in his book *Um 1800*), was expected to appeal to teachers' equally modest but refined tastes.[126] The simplicity of the home, according to its director, had been

FIGURE 3.15. The Lehrerinnenheim's communal dining room. From Heeren, "Lehrerinnenheim in Berlin," 330.

FIGURE 3.16. Detail of the Max-Koska-Strasse façade with its large terracotta medallions of female heads (alternating with floral motifs). From Heeren, "Lehrerinnenheim in Berlin," 330.

intended from the start, and she praised the architect for understanding his clients' needs and desires.[127] His previous work for the Civil Servants' Housing Association of Berlin (Beamten-Wohnungs-Verein zu Berlin) gave him ample experience in planning small apartments for bourgeois patrons. These projects demonstrated the "tasteful simplicity" sought by the founders of the Lehrerinnenheim, who "borrowed" Mebes from the Civil Servants' Housing Association, which also sold them the plot of land for their residence.[128] Highly critical of the shoddiness of most housing constructed for the lower and middle classes, Mebes strove to establish a new standard through small, thoughtfully planned dwellings that rejected the expense of superfluous decoration for healthier, more comfortable living spaces. Instead of the typical structure of Berlin's tenements—a long row of increasingly dark and airless buildings connected by courtyards—he devised more open forms in accordance with the ideals of sanitary reformers. The U-shaped layout of the Lehrerinnenheim delivered cross-ventilation and sunlight to all units on its five floors, features doubly important to inhabitants already concerned about their health.[129] The home was hailed as a functional and formal success, meeting the needs of its residents while also crafting a stylistically representational image in keeping with the modest but dignified public persona of the female teacher.

Despite its somewhat remote location, the teachers' home soon filled to capacity. Its founders hoped to construct additional residences in other parts of Berlin but failed to attract sufficient members or financial capital for the planned expansion. Such hurdles were typical of women's building cooperatives, whose members generally had far fewer resources at their disposal than those of comparable organizations. The Civil Servants' Housing Association, for example, boasted over ten thousand members in 1905 as well as strong government support.[130] The female teachers' housing cooperative, by comparison, numbered only a few hundred members. Published pleas to Berlin's female teachers to support the creation of a second home suggest they were hesitant to invest their money in new ventures, despite the guarantee of a solid return.[131] Women's cooperatives were also unfortunate in their timing. Emerging in the years before the First World War, they suffered from a worsening economy and the turmoil of the war itself. Nonetheless, these organizations did succeed in establishing a new model for building, which encouraged women to actively revision hearth and home.

The search for new forms of domestic living among single career women represented a process of both unification and division. Although gender was a common denominator, it alone did not define a woman's identity. Class, education, employment status, professional affiliation, marital status, and age also played a role. Consequently, in the search for a community of peers, the notion of peership shifted according to these many variables. Community itself was a fluid concept, and the debate over what a women's home should be was a contentious issue. With-out exception, however, the idea of community was valued in all its varying formu-lations. The experience of social isolation, so common to career women, fueled the desire for meaningful social bonds. Although a concern for independence shaped each of the projects discussed above, all provided opportunities for social intercourse through communal spaces, whether dining halls, reading rooms, or shared kitchens. While economic necessity influenced some aspects of design, this communal element was both desirable and intentional, and it distinguished these projects from conventional notions of the urban residence, whether a private home or an apartment building. Whereas the traditional family abode sheltered a group united by ties of matrimony and blood, the new domestic forms pioneered by single career women envisioned peership, friendship, and community as their foundation.

THE NEW WOMAN GROWS OLD: THE HAUS IN DER SONNE

At the dedication ceremony in early June 1914, a residence for single women retired from professional careers was officially christened the Haus in der Sonne after a German best seller.[132] As Cecilia Lengefeld has shown, the popularity of *Das Haus in der Sonne* was sudden and unprecedented, and for a very long time, it remained one of the nation's favorite books.[133] No one in the audience that day, then, could have missed the intended connection between Carl Larsson's domestic idyll and the new home for elderly spinsters. If the analogy raised eyebrows, no trace remains in the glowing accounts of the residence published in the women's press. And yet, was it not an odd name? As noted at the start of this chapter, the book cele-brated the blessings of home, focusing on Larsson's eight children. Like a family album, anecdotal texts and images captured merrymaking in a house teeming with boys and girls, whose antics included finger painting on Larsson's still-wet canvases. Their rambunctiousness, born of vitality and good health, tried the patience of their loving painter–papa, although nothing seemed to disturb the equanimity of their beautiful mother. Contemporary stereotypes of the barren, forsaken spinster could not have been further from this vision of fulsome domestic joy.

To dare to claim this dream says a great deal about the determination of single women to challenge such stereotypes and rethink the perimeters of domesticity. The appropriation of Larsson's title conveyed the belief that the pleasures of home life could be enjoyed even by a group of elderly spinsters. Their house might not be filled with the patter of little feet, but it would be inhabited by happiness all the same—symbolized, as we will see, by Larssonian light and sunshine. Geography suggested a further parallel to Larsson's book: *Das Haus in der Sonne* depicted the artist's summer home in Sundborn, a rural village two hundred kilometers northwest of Stockholm.

Larsson idealized the simplicity of country life as a balancing counterweight to the unhealthy strains of urban living; the home he pictured was specifically a place of refuge for the city dweller. The idea of returning to nature appealed deeply to the founders of the retirement home, even if they were not yet ready to forfeit the city.

With the Haus in der Sonne, we come to the final stage of the New Woman's life cycle. Once again, a demographic shift prompted architectural experimentation. In the years preceding the First World War, a German generation of bourgeois women who had begun careers in the last quarter of the nineteenth century was reaching retirement age. A comfortable retirement threatened to elude them in their common dependence on modest pensions to support themselves. Journalists sympathetic to their plight represented these women as deserving orphans: Having suffered homelessness their entire working lives, leading a nomadic existence in the furnished rooms of others, these aging women now sought and had earned the peace and stability of "a real home."[134] But Berlin offered few such options: "Urban apartments are either expensive or located in bad, noisy neighborhoods or unhomely buildings, and lack all the coziness and comfort that an older woman living on her own especially needs."[135]

The traditional recourse, retirement in a charitable institution, was wholly unacceptable. Like ill-fitting clothes, such modes of living rubbed against the very grain of the career woman's self-conception:

> Today's woman, who has gained independence through her work and by right highly values this self-sufficiency, especially wants to retain the greatest possible freedom in old age. She does not want to receive the charitable favors that religious foundations and old people's homes bestow to a greater or lesser degree. She also does not want to have to fit into a larger community, but would rather shape her domestic life according to her own strengths and means.[136]

And yet, in preserving this independence, women did not wish "to be damned thereby to total isolation."[137] They sought fellowship based on shared interests and life experiences.[138] How might one live independently in a meaningful community and maintain self-reliance as it became increasingly difficult to depend solely on one's own resources?

Beginning in 1910, Clara Richter organized a series of meetings in Berlin to search for an architectural solution.[139] From her vantage point as director of the Pestalozzi-Fröbel-Haus, a school that had been training women for professional careers since the 1870s, she perceived the housing crisis looming for her older alumnae and their peers.[140] So, too, did leaders of women's professional organizations who accepted Richter's invitation to participate in the discussions. At the meetings, the representative of the Berlin Association of Female Elementary Teachers spoke of her organization's experiences with their own residence, then under construction. What she related must have been persuasive, for the talks ended with a consensus to establish a building cooperative modeled on the "indisputable success" of the Lehrerinnenheim in Pankow.[141] This decision constituted a rejection of a more directly relevant precedent: retirement homes for female teachers that had begun to appear in German towns and cities, including Berlin, by the 1870s.[142] These were deemed insufficiently modern in their conception, being modeled on charitable institutions that failed to accommodate changing conceptions of the single life. Richter's meetings clearly evinced a new approach to housing needs that drew on the idea of "social politics" rather than charity.[143]

Thus, the Cooperative for Women's Homesteads, dedicated to creating healthy and inexpensive dwellings for educated women retired from careers and living on low incomes, was launched in the fall of 1912.[144] The cooperative's goals were at once more limited and grander than those of the Lehrerinnenheim. The limitation pertained to the cooperative's desire to build on a more intimate scale than that of the teachers' residence, which occupied nearly a city block. The country house, rather than the urban apartment building, was its domestic model. But the group's aims were also larger in two important ways. First, and as its name suggests, the cooperative envisioned a settlement rather than a single structure: a villa colony consisting of multiple houses subdivided into self-sufficient apartments, as well as a main building for administration, dining, and lodging vacationers.[145] Like the garden cities then developing outside Dresden and London, the retirement colonies would be located in rural or forested areas. This setting promised not only health benefits but also inexpensive land. The cooperative's bylaws stipulated the purchase of large plots in order to accommodate future growth. Second, the colony model was meant to be replicable. Although the prototype would be built in Berlin, where the cooperative's headquarters would also be based, a network of settlements would eventually span the country.[146] By 1914, preparations for sister colonies had begun in Cologne, Hamburg, and Hannover.[147]

From the start, the cooperative struggled to finance its ambitious program. Membership, acquired through the purchase of share certificates, grew more slowly than anticipated. In December 1912, when the cooperative was legally registered, it had only ninety members, a number insufficient to carry out its plans.[148] Moreover, most of these shareholders were retired women, a group with limited capital. Desperate appeals went out in the women's press to increase membership beyond this circle so that funds could accumulate and construction begin. Women still active in their careers were told that duty, as well as their own self-interest, compelled them to help their aging colleagues.[149] Ella Mensch played on different sympathies, based perhaps on her own experiences as a teacher. She entreated wealthy women who depended on female teachers to educate their children, whether as private tutors, schoolteachers, or music instructors, to repay this debt by supporting the cooperative.[150] Ultimately, however, it was professional associations that came to the rescue. They possessed not only the requisite capital reserves but also members anxious to see the residences completed. A Berlin association that trained female home economics teachers donated five thousand Marks, and the national pension institute for male and female teachers provided a mortgage to construct the first house.[151]

Compared with this slow financial start, attracting tenants was no problem; indeed, most apartments were rented before construction was completed.[152] Eligible residents were members of the cooperative, retired from professional service, and solvent. Although rents were low relative to the private market, a minimum income requirement made clear that the cooperative would not and could not function as a charity.[153] In return for fulfilling their contractual obligations, tenants were guaranteed never to be issued an eviction notice. Such security was dear to women who, as noted above, lived with the constant fear of being turned out for a better paying tenant.

By 1913, the cooperative had located an ideal site for its prototype retirement colony: two acres of forested land in Neubabelsberg, an elegant residential development on the south bank of Griebnitzsee, adjacent to the summer palace of Germany's first emperor.[154] The natural setting and large vacation houses, designed in divergent styles by architects such as Mies van der Rohe and Hermann Muthesius, attracted Berlin's wealthy bankers and industrialists as well as intellectuals and artists. In devising a site plan, the cooperative sought to maintain the wilderness aspect of the terrain. Residences would be nestled among the pine trees, and only trees that obstructed breezes or light would be removed.[155]

The architect steering the physical creation of the settlement was Emilie Winkelmann. She had been involved from the earliest stages, participating in the working committee that devised the initial plans for the cooperative and, in February 1912, exhibiting a model of the future home that was seen by thousands of Berliners.[156] Her qualifications for the job were indisputable: Beyond apartment design, she had extensive experience constructing villas for wealthy patrons in Berlin and renovating manor houses in the agrarian northern provinces.[157] She was also familiar with the Neubabelsberg district, having built a cottage and studio there for two female artists, Margot and Adele Grupe, in 1909. In addition to her professional acumen, Winkelmann may have brought a personal interest to the project. As a single career woman, then in her late thirties, she was in the unusual position of creating what eventually might have been her own retirement home. This experiment in living was directly relevant to her own life choices.

Construction of the first of four planned residences began in the fall of 1913 and was completed the following spring.[158] Viewed from the street, the Haus in der Sonne resembled a single-family villa, articulating in visual terms the cooperative's primary goal: to create a genuine home, not an institution (Figure 3.17). Stylistically, Winkelmann combined different sources to suggest multiple meanings, as she did for the contemporary Victoria Studienhaus. The imposing effect of the building, noted by one reviewer, owed much to the use of a pared-down classicism.[159] Almost completely unadorned, the simple forms and masses produced a certain monumentality. Abstracted Doric pilasters, framing the loggia windows, heightened the impression of dignified sobriety. The severity of the whole was tempered, however, by the façade's modulating planes and varying roof lines. As in the case of the Victoria Studienhaus, the use of functional classicism may have been inspired by the modernity of the residence and its inhabitants. Advocates of the new retirement lifestyle equated the Haus in der Sonne with the spirit of the age: "The idea of establishing such homes for educated women . . . corresponds perfectly to the attitudes of our time. We have outgrown the old retirement homes."[160] By contrast, incorporation of vernacular elements appealed to notions of domesticity and tradition. These

FIGURE 3.17. Street façade of the Haus in der Sonne in Potsdam, designed by Emilie Winkelmann. From Else von Boetticher, "Heimstätten für Frauen," *Berliner Frauenclub von 1900* 3, no. 10 (1915): 6.

included the red-tiled, steeply pitched roof (typical of the neighboring villas), painted green accents, flower boxes, and window shutters. Whereas the architect sought to update the image of domesticity in the Victoria Studienhaus, here the appeal to home evoked a deeply rooted ideal, as celebrated in *Das Haus in der Sonne*. Winkelmann's design can thus be seen as a cross, or a compromise, between a modernizing classicism and a comforting vernacular.

The interior of the Haus in der Sonne was divided into self-contained dwellings. Residents could choose from fourteen apartments, on three floors, ranging in size from one to three rooms. Each had its own entrance hall, kitchenette (Figure 3.18), loggia, and toilet. The largest units were equipped with baths, while the others shared a bathroom located on each floor. Befitting its "modern" inhabitants, the house boasted the latest conveniences, including central heating, hot water, and electric lighting.[161] Such domestic luxuries were still a rarity for most Berliners.

It was less technological sophistication, however, than pastoral charm that captured the imagination of the home's first occupants. Marie Schulze, a teacher who vacationed there in the summer of 1914, recorded her impressions for a professional journal:

FIGURE 3.18. Haus in der Sonne kitchenette, 1926. From Dora Martin, "Heim der Genossenschaft für Frauenheimstätten," *Frau und Gegenwart*, no. 40 (1926): 9.

> A pretty white house with a red roof and green window shutters. . . . Red geraniums
> adorn its windows, flowerbeds surround it, the pine forest at the back sends its won-
> derful hot scent toward us. Curving above, the radiant blue sky sends us its warmest
> sunshine. . . . Berlin, with its life and bustle, lay behind me, and in this I rejoiced, for
> here is peace and quiet.

Emphasizing the connection to land and sky, Schulze portrayed the residence as
a sanctuary for all professional women who "wish to conclude the autumn of their
life in tranquility and comfort."[162]

And yet, proximity to the city, as Schulze herself noted, was equally important.
Nature exerted a deep appeal, but so did landscapes in art museums.[163] As urban
women, the residents of the Haus in der Sonne were not about to relinquish the
advantages of the city, even as they sought a more restful environment for their retirement years. Promotional articles touted not only the home's natural surroundings but also its convenience to Berlin, which was reached by a short train ride.[164]
From the initial planning stages, the founders understood that the residence must
be so situated that "the occupants, who have hardly given up on life, can easily reach
the city."[165] Even in retirement, and despite their faith in pastoral renewal, these
women's identities were tightly interwoven with the urban fabric.

The house's most lauded characteristic, however, was its focus on independence.
Mensch, writing in *Frauenkapital*, Germany's only financial journal for women, imagined the residents as contented rulers of their own small empires. In her view, the
absence of "the communal dining room of most retirement homes" spoke volumes.
Later in the article, she mentioned that those not wishing to prepare a midday meal
had the option of eating at the "Zentrale."[166] This was, in fact, the communal dining room, which was located on the ground floor of the Haus in der Sonne until
it was moved to a nearby building in 1915. Although Mensch appears to contradict
herself, she was making a distinction between the forced communalization of larger
institutions and the freedom to choose offered by the Haus in der Sonne. A strong
selling point was precisely this balance between independence and community. A
resident could prepare her own meals or "spare herself the trouble of cooking and
take her meal in company, thereby passing a pleasant hour in conversation."[167] With
regard to housework, she could undertake this herself or arrange to have her rooms
cleaned. Mensch pointed out that these arrangements were flexible and, in the case
of meals, required little advance notice. The caretakers, a couple who lived in an
apartment on the ground floor, were also available to help with housekeeping needs.

Significantly, choice was incorporated into the very design of the dwellings in
the form of the loggia—a colonnaded, porchlike room reached from the interior.
As several commentators noted, this structure possessed a unique feature: retractable

windows that disappeared into the ledge, allowing each woman to transform the space as desired from a completely open balcony to a sheltered sun room, with a range of variations in between.[168] Equipped with heating, it could be used in winter or bad weather, giving each resident her own "piece of nature" year round.[169] The loggia integrated those natural elements—light, greenery, and air—central to Larsson's idealized vision of domestic health and happiness.[170]

Every inhabitant, furthermore, was free to select her own décor (Figure 3.19). A cacophony of styles resulted: "Modern artistic taste or old-fashioned comfort rule in the different rooms, each according to the character of its resident."[171] The liberty to decorate according to one's own taste represented a much valued freedom to women who, having spent years in rented furnished rooms, had hitherto been constrained in this form of personal expression. In this context, being able to hang a picture one had chosen or decorate as one wished was deeply meaningful, indeed, even politically significant. What would have been anathema to many architects of this period—stylistic anarchy—was celebrated here as the measure of true independence.

The overwhelming success of the Haus in der Sonne, evidenced not least by its full occupancy, immediately prompted calls to build the second on-site residence.[172]

FIGURE 3.19. Interior of a two-room apartment in the Haus in der Sonne, 1926. Photograph by W. Herrmann. From Martin, "Heim der Genossenschaft für Frauenheimstätten," 9.

The outbreak of the First World War halted those plans, although the cooperative managed to complete the renovation of an existing house on the property, which created, as originally intended, separate facilities for a dining hall, office, and vacation home.[173] Even without this disruption, it is uncertain that the next residence would have been constructed as scheduled. The cooperative's finances continued to provoke concern. By 1917, there were 150 members, a substantial number for this sort of organization. Nonetheless, membership was too low to embark on additional buildings or expand into other cities.[174] In 1918, urgent appeals went out once again to wealthy women.[175] Much of this potential base of support disappeared, however, in the catastrophic hyperinflation of the early 1920s. Political upheavals after 1918 further undermined the social and financial networks that had supported women's projects.[176] Thus, despite the unabated need for such housing in the Weimar Republic, the second residence was constructed only in 1927.[177] For the next fifteen years, until its sale in 1942, the pioneering homestead in Neubabelsberg continued to serve women who, in retirement as in youth, strove to remain true to their modern ideals.[178]

4 Exhibiting the New Woman
The Phenomenal Success of Die Frau in Haus und Beruf

O N A LATE FEBRUARY EVENING IN 1912, the fog blanketing the city was pierced by two towers of light that beckoned to Berliners to leave the gloom of the streets and enter a dazzling world unlike any they had seen before.[1] Inside the exhibition building at the Zoological Garden, amid blooming flowers, silk architecture, and brilliant chandeliers, visitors encountered a vast and intricately ordered cosmos devoted to women, from which "mere man is conspicuously and universally absent." Women designers had arranged the halls filled with displays of women's labor, an all-female orchestra serenaded the crowd with music by female composers, and female writers stocked a library with books authored and bound by women. "The greatest exhibition ever devoted to the work of women," according to the *New York Times*, encompassed "every sphere of activity, domestic, industrial, and professional, which women have so far invaded."[2] Marveled at by some, abhorred by others, this show of female self-sufficiency exerted an enormous attraction. In the four weeks the exhibition remained open, half a million people passed through its portals.[3]

Ironically, the origins of this groundbreaking event had more to do with keeping women cooking over hot gas stoves than with female emancipation. Concerned about the growing appeal of electricity, the director of a national lobby group for gas interests asked Hedwig Heyl to organize a show for his industry.[4] Known as the "Hindenburg of the kitchen" for her authority in the field of German domestic science and the military-like efficiency of her reform campaigns, Heyl possessed formidable influence over female consumers: Her classic cookbook, *The ABC of the Kitchen*, was "to be found in every German household."[5] Although the project to emerge from this collaboration turned out rather differently from that initially proposed, the gas industry's sponsorship of the women's exhibition proved felicitous.

With Heyl at the helm and the combined labor force of the German Lyceum Club behind her, a grand vision began to take shape. Announcements in the club's newsletter described an ambitious program that would shed light on the work of some ten million employed women in Germany.[6] The title chosen, Die Frau in Haus und Beruf (Women in the Home and at Work), reflected the desire to honor equally the paid and unpaid contributions made by women to the nation. Hoping to strengthen its ties to other women's organizations while also promoting itself as a center of the women's movement, the Lyceum Club invited women's groups across the nation and in the colonies to participate, and thousands of women responded to the call. When the exhibition opened, the scope of their combined labor astounded visitors: From the *Architektin* (female architect) to the *Zeichnenlehrerin* (female drawing teacher), from town planning in Silesia to housework in German Southwest Africa, every profession and sphere of activity seemed occupied by women. Within the confines of the halls emerged a network of productive German women radiating from Berlin to Togo, China, and Samoa.

The effect of totality was both calculated to impress and determined by the adoption of a prevailing cultural type: the universal exhibition. Beginning with the Great Exhibition of 1851, in London, and honed by subsequent world's fairs in continental Europe and the United States, a new form of mass education emerged in the nineteenth century, aiming for "a total view of any given subject."[7] In this context, what was excluded was often as important as the object of display. Leaders of the Lyceum Club understood the power of exhibitions to reveal and obscure as well as to influence public opinion. In an article published on opening day, Alice Salomon explained the women's show to readers of *Der Tag* precisely in these terms. She began with comments made by a "well-known" German politician on a visit to an industrial fair. Noting the absence of female representation, he deduced that men were solely responsible for the nation's major economic achievements and concluded that what he had (not) seen discouraged him from supporting the women's movement. Salomon presented Die Frau in Haus und Beruf as a corrective to such attitudes as well as a tool of propaganda.[8]

For education, important as it was, did not stand alone: The encyclopedic display of women's labor was driven by the same inspirational motives that filled the world's fairs to the bursting point. The spectacular massing of objects at the world's fairs was meant to signify the irresistible forces of progress (whether imperial, technological, or social) and to convince onlookers of "the certain glory of the future."[9] The feminist progressivism on view in Berlin was framed in terms of not suffrage but rather a bourgeois faith in self-improvement. In her inaugural address, given before an illustrious audience that included Empress Augusta Victoria and carried widely in the German press, Heyl boasted of having materialized a new female spirit within the walls of the exhibition. This essence—manifest in women's thoughts and actions, desires, and in their "toughened" bodies—was still in the process of becoming, and therefore the exhibition could claim to be, she said, only a snapshot of an ongoing metamorphosis. Although traditional and unconventional realms of female work were included, "house" and "profession" were to be considered not opposing halves of the exhibition but rather intertwined elements of this larger evolution in womanhood.[10] Organizers thus represented all German women as modern. They hoped the visual surfeit of female progress would persuade visitors, both male and female, to do what the German politician had resisted: aid women's causes.[11] Heyl believed that monumentality was needed to attract men, who avoided small, artsy presentations.[12] But a young Theodor Heuss, then political editor of the liberal journal *Die Hilfe* and later president of the Federal Republic of Germany, predicted the effect would be greatest on women: The "massive impression of female accomplishments," he argued, would instill pride and self-confidence, providing a needed boost to the women's movement.[13]

Even older advocates of change, such as Helene Lange, the author of the famous 1887 "Yellow Brochure" on women's education, recognized that words were no longer enough to reach people in an increasingly visually oriented culture.[14] Images and objects, not speeches and texts, were necessary to educate, persuade, and rally the public. This imperative for visibility strongly influenced the exhibition's physical realization, from the site chosen to the interior arrangements of the halls. Here, crucial support came from the gas industry, which sought maximum publicity for its products. As the show's main sponsor, it provided a large financial guarantee that enabled Heyl and her colleagues to secure the Zoological Garden Exhibition Building. This stately structure, located in the city's well-to-do Tiergarten quarter, sat adjacent to the Zoological Garden Station, a transportation hub connecting local and regional trains, subways, trams, and buses and serving tens of thousands of commuters and tourists daily (Figures 4.1 and 4.2). It was a highly visible site in Berlin, not only because of its function as a traffic thoroughfare, but also because of the presence of the Emperor William Memorial Church (1891–95), one of the city's tallest structures and the hub of its newly developing western center.[15]

As Berliners rushed to and from the station, they must have been struck by the transformation of its somber, gray-stoned neighbor, its façade now adorned with orange drapery and spruce garlands.[16] Designed in 1905 by Carl Gause (the architect of the contemporary Adlon Hotel), the exhibition building was part of a neo-Romanesque complex on Auguste-Victoria-Platz (now Breitscheidplatz) that included the memorial church.[17] The plaza's architectural specifications, down to the style of the street lamps, were ordained by Wilhelm II, who identified his reign with the first German rulers of the Holy Roman Empire.[18] Although Heyl loathed the emperor's infamous solution to the woman question, which called on German women to limit themselves to the three K's of *Kinder, Küche,* and *Kirche* (children, kitchen, and church), her elevated social station and connections to the court undoubtedly contributed to her appreciation of the authority and majesty of the site, which she and the other organizers strove to harness for women.[19] The significance was not lost on one reporter who saw the exhibition as a direct response to the kaiser's antifeminism.[20] Above the main portal and below the imperial eagle perched atop the pediment hung a large semicircular banner with the Lyceum Club's emblem, a verdant tree, announcing the women's show (Figure 4.3). On either side, monumental torches, courtesy of the gas industry, spewed flames at their summit. Visitors interpreted the symbolism of the torches according to their own sympathies, seeing therein everything from "the holy zeal" igniting the feminist movement to "Bengali flames," a double-edged insult evoking the great harems of the Moghul emperors.[21]

On opening day, after the inaugural ceremonies ended and the empress departed, the doors opened to the public, and ten thousand visitors streamed into the exhibition.[22] They were greeted by the scents of lilac, primrose, orchids, and other flowers,

FIGURE 4.1. The Zoological Garden Exhibition Building on Hardenbergerstrasse in Berlin, designed by Carl Gause, as it appeared in 1907. Landesarchiv Berlin.

which, for organizers and audience alike, marked the space as feminine.[23] High above, brilliant gas chandeliers burned with the intensity of 120,000 candles (Figure 4.4). The gas industry donated the fuel for this cascade of light, as well as for the myriad gas lamps illuminating the displays.[24] Beyond its advertising value, the spectacular luminosity, which bedazzled reporters, reinforced the exhibition's symbolic message.[25] In the poetic lyrics sung by the character of "the productive woman" in a cantata with Wagnerian overtones performed by an all-female choir at the opening festivities, "the world blossoms with light and color" for the New Woman striving toward the sun.[26] With the assistance of their main sponsor, organizers made manifest the show's promise of emancipation and enlightenment.

The use of light for dramatic effect and its association with progress had important precedents at industrial fairs and in department stores. By 1912, however, it was incandescent electrical lights, not flickering gas flames, that symbolized modernity at these venues.[27] Displays of advanced technology at the Berlin Trade Exhibition

FIGURE 4.2. Aerial view of the Zoological Garden Exhibition Building (the long rectangular complex of buildings in the center, part of which was converted into a movie theater in the Weimar period) and the busy train station to the left, 1926. Landesarchiv Berlin.

of 1896, dedicated to the city's industrial and economic achievements, included a promenade festooned with electric lights.[28] Over the next ten years, Alfred Messel introduced Berliners to the luxury emporium with his designs for the Wertheim store on Leipziger Strasse (1896–1905). As part of the imagery of contemporary commerce, he incorporated strings of electrical lights in the store's atriums.[29] By flowing against the current, so to speak, the "resurrection" of gas lighting at the women's exhibition attracted attention.[30] In this publicity gamble, gas lobbyists sought to defeat their electrical competitors at their own promotional game by associating gas power with the dynamism of modern women.

If the desire to sell gas influenced some aspects of the physical realization of the exhibition, particularly the bold illumination, commercial concerns of another sort inspired the creation of the interior space, which demonstrated a similar attention to visibility. In Berlin, a public space of such size and splendor dedicated to women was unprecedented. The nearest prototype was the department store, which was closely associated with the female consumer. Organizers of the show were well acquainted with this modern institution: The Lyceum Club had a long and successful relationship with the Wertheim store, which also employed several of the exhibition's designers. It is not surprising, then, that in searching for a model for a grand female space, Wertheim came to mind.

FIGURE 4.3. Street façade of Die Frau in Haus und Beruf exhibition at night. Two gas pylons placed on either side of the main entrance frame the exhibition banner depicting a tree, the symbol of the German Lyceum Club. From *Berliner Lokal Anzeiger*, March 14, 1912.

Indeed, the similarities already existing between the exhibition hall and the
department store may have pushed the designers in that direction. As historians
have demonstrated, the two types developed interdependently as architectures of
display.[31] A comparison of Wertheim's atrium (Figure 4.5) with the original structure of the exhibition hall (Figure 4.6) reveals matching open, elongated spaces,
vaulted ceilings, and multiple vantage points (floor, balcony, staircase) from which
one could see and be seen. Designers for the women's exhibition increased the viewing possibilities within the main hall by extending the space of the stage and making
it accessible to the public via a double staircase, as well as by creating an elevated
reception pavilion with portico, from which the empress had watched the opening
festivities while being herself on display. The prominence of the row of shop windows, mounted on the stage, further emphasized the act of looking (Figure 4.4).

The reliance on department store aesthetics is examined at length later in this
chapter; here I am concerned with the implications of the scopic regime of shopping

FIGURE 4.4. Main hall of Die Frau in Haus und Beruf exhibition. At the lower right-hand
side we glimpse the porticoed pavilion, from which the empress enjoyed the opening
ceremony. From Emma Stropp, "Die Ausstellung 'Die Frau in Haus und Beruf,'" *Illustrirte
Zeitung* 138, no. 3584 (1912): 448.

FIGURE 4.5. Atrium of the Wertheim department store in Berlin, designed by Alfred Messel, 1896–97 (photograph c. 1905). The female allegory *Work*, created by the sculptor Ludwig Manzel, presides over the ladies' handglove department. From *A. Wertheim GmbH, Berlin* (Berlin: A. Wertheim, c. 1905), the Wolfsonian–Florida International University, Miami Beach, Florida, the Mitchell Wolfson, Jr. Collection.

for the creation of a female public space. By tapping into an already established architectural type and its visual practices, the designers, I believe, eased the transition to a novel form of gendered space. The show's predominantly female and middle-class visitors, who were also the department store's main clientele, came equipped with a ready-made set of visual tools with which to absorb and process the encyclopedic display. As in the department store, their discerning, comprehensive gaze took it all in, scanning objects, spaces, and, also important, other people.[32] Prompted by the show's design, they saw throngs of women and became conscious of being part of the multitude. On the opening day of the exhibition, the majority of the ten thousand visitors in attendance were women—a pattern that would be repeated over the next four weeks. The effect, according to a reporter, was among the most astonishing of the show.[33]

Admittedly, department store architecture had already materialized crowds of female shoppers, which critics in turn-of-the-century Germany (and elsewhere) portrayed as dangerously unruly, a kind of shopping cyclone that ruined husbands and national economies with its mindless and voracious consumption (Figure 4.7).[34] The women's exhibition attempted a profound reorientation of this gendered mass away from consumption toward production: Women were exhorted to reach for the "sun" of emancipating labor, not the glittery bijoux. In this new context, the consuming female public of the department store was transformed into a civic body—self-conscious, enlightened, and empowered. Salomon affirmed that organizers strove to make visible a new feeling of unity among women, a sense of shared responsibility and agency spanning all fields of productive work.[35] With her empowered gaze, as described by Anne Friedberg, the department store *flâneuse* was addressed not as a consumer but rather as a citizen.[36] The political implications of making women aware of their collective potential did not escape the attention

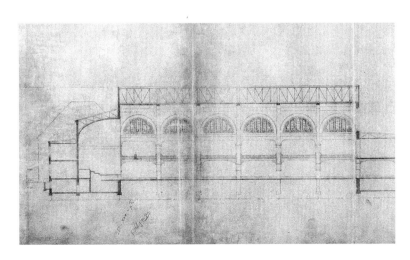

FIGURE 4.6. Cross-section drawing (detail) by Gause of the main exhibition hall, 1905. Landesarchiv Berlin, A Rep. 3502/2.

of state officials. A report by the Royal Police Authority in Berlin concluded that the exhibition must be deemed political for stirring "the consciousness of unity."[37]

If this awakening posed a threat, it emanated not from the chaotic female mass envisioned in discourses on shopping but rather from an orderly one. The show's organizers, had they known of the police report, would have been pleased with the reference to unity, for they took pride in their careful construction of an ordered whole that was seen to challenge prevailing cultural conceptions of women as selfish, irrational creatures incapable of cooperation or organizational thinking.[38] Developing a coherent scheme had not been easy: As Salomon recounted, the novelty of the exhibition meant inventing new frameworks for display.[39] Although pavilions and sections devoted to women's work had been included in national and world's fairs since the nineteenth century, they were widely disparate affairs and not always considered a success.[40] Perhaps for this reason, creators of the 1912 show did not acknowledge such precedents, even when borrowing—as in the broad definition of women's work—is evident.[41] In a narrower sense, however, they navigated uncharted

FIGURE 4.7. Crowds of female shoppers in a Berlin department store. Wood engraving after a drawing by Edward Cucuel, 1901. Bildarchiv Preussischer Kulturbesitz/Art Resource, New York.

waters: In Germany, no one had attempted, or even come close to, a women's show on the scale of Die Frau in Haus und Beruf. Four broad themes structured the exhibition: home, professions, club life, and public and private interests. They were further subdivided into dozens of smaller groupings, such as "Woman in Architecture" (included under the professions category). Numerous reviewers praised the clarity of the structure. The emphasis on order, however, also had its detractors: An anonymous reviewer in *Die Welt der Frau* disparaged the "embarrassingly exact, clean divisions" as indicative of the female mind.[42] Thus, where some saw a complex world unfold before their eyes, others perceived the unimaginative "tidiness" of the housewife.

In fact, the architectural structure of the exhibition rendered these categories more dynamic than they appeared on paper. Fia Wille, Else Oppler-Legband, and Lilly Reich were charged with the aesthetic conception of the show, from the layout of rooms to the broader physical environment.[43] Wille and Oppler-Legband, the show's principal designers, were well established and respected artists. Wille, together with her husband, Rudolf, owned a successful design firm in Berlin, and their work was regularly featured in architectural journals. Oppler-Legband, a longtime member of Wertheim's board of artistic advisers, was director of the German Werkbund's Professional College for Display Art in Berlin (the Höhere Fachschule für Dekorationskunst), an influential position within the design reform movement. The younger Reich, who worked in clothing display for Wertheim and also taught at the Werkbund school, was on her way to becoming one of the most important exhibition designers in Germany, later forming a partnership with Ludwig Mies van der Rohe.[44] With ninety-two hundred square meters of exhibits (a new record for the building) distributed between two vast halls, each with two floors, the designers faced an enormous challenge in bringing harmony and legibility to the whole.

Judging from floor plans, photographs, and contemporary descriptions, their strategy involved breaking up and rearranging the four themes according to two aesthetic criteria: luxury and mechanization. The first hall, arranged by Wille, represented the former; the second, codesigned by Oppler-Legband and Reich, the latter. The exhibition thus united the two dominant codes of display in the early twentieth century, derived from the department store and the industrial world's fair, respectively. The division between luxury and mechanization, combined with the juxtaposition and overlap of the four categories, produced new layers of meaning. Within the two main halls, ninety-two smaller rooms or spaces framed individual groupings and at the same time often served more than a single purpose. For example, displays and activities associated with the model apartment for a working-class family, designed by Reich and discussed below, bridged three categories: home (the working-class housewife and mother), professions (the middle-class woman as designer), and club life (social welfare associations). Through overflowing bound-aries and multiple-use spaces, the designers helped emphasize the complexity of women's labor and activities.[45]

The initial effect on the public, however, as they entered the main hall from the street, was of a monumental *Gesamtkunstwerk*, a total work of art. Wille wanted the visitor to experience "a unified overall impression at first, giving the effect of the exhibition as a complete whole, from which the sequence of the individual groups then develops."[46] She minimized the obstruction of sightlines to create a sweep-ing panorama that allowed the viewer to take in at one glance the exhibition's vast scale (Figure 4.4). Smaller pavilions and displays broke up the space of the main hall and suggested paths to follow without obstructing the viewer's gaze. A repeat-ing color scheme dominated by royal blue and golden yellow reinforced the sense of visual harmony.[47]

Directly across from the entrance, a semicircular structure greeted entering visi-tors (number 1 on the floor plan, Figure 4.8; bottom right-hand corner of Figure 4.4). Also designed by Wille, it created a dramatic focal point in the main hall with its sweeping baldachin of golden silk. Visible behind the pavilion's square posts and decorating its curved exterior wall, Ida Stroever's life-size, twenty-two-meter-long frieze, titled *Woman's Path,* depicted women's progress from crepuscular bondage to sun-filled freedom.[48] On entering, the visitor encountered a bust of Empress Augusta Victoria, the "protector" of German women's work, surrounded by glass cases housing collections assembled by aristocratic and bourgeois women, including a thimble collection owned by a baroness. While some perhaps scoffed at the inclu-sion of such activity under the rubric of labor (the catalog defended collecting as culturally productive), these displays promoted the exhibition's class-bridging aspi-rations.[49] They also contributed to the domestic ambience of the pavilion, which served primarily as the Lyceum Club's reception area, an intimate space within the vastness of the main hall. Symbolically and physically, it represented the gathering, sheltering function of the Lyceum Club as an institution, which the subsequent construction of the clubhouse reenacted in the urban landscape. Afternoon teas hosted daily in this space, made elegant with flower arrangements, lace tablecloths, and wicker furniture by Wille, reinforced those meanings. At the same time, the pavilion's design avoided isolating or separating women from one another. The partly open baldachin as well as the connection to adjacent rooms created visual continuities with other spaces in the exhibition, so that the reception area remained integrated into the larger whole.[50] Moreover, the exhibition floor plan (Figure 4.8) suggests that the curve of the pavilion acted like the prow of a ship around which currents of circulation flowed, uniting the two halves of the main hall in a broad arc of movement.

From the reception pavilion, the visitor's eyes gravitated toward the large semi-circular space at the northern end of the hall that contained a stage for performances and a brightly lit shopping promenade, the form of which reiterated the curve of the apse (number 15 on the floor plan, Figure 4.8; see also Figure 4.4). The "shops" were designed by Elisabeth von Hahn, Wertheim's trend-setting artistic director of window displays, and their glowing interiors and domes strongly enhanced the exhibition's theatrical luminosity.[51] Directly above them rose Stroever's monumental painting of a green tree surrounded by three-meter-tall clothed and naked women, some of whom were drinking at the stream of productive life. The combination of the Lyceum Club's emblem with the nude figures in a churchlike apse raised unwanted associations, and a special exhibition edition of the club's newsletter emphasized that this was not the biblical tree of Eden that bore the fruit of knowledge that tempted Eve and destroyed humanity's bliss. Rather, this tree's flowers (there was no fruit) blessed and sheltered the work of all women.[52] The visually dominant placement of the tree in the hall, towering over the fragrant flowers on the floor below, reinforced the idea of the women's exhibition as a real, spatial extension of this mythical garden of female empowerment.

As the visitor moved through the main hall, the display of luxury goods magnified the initial impression of splendor. From pearl pendants to a marble-clad bathroom, women's design work dominated the ground-floor exhibits. Some items were for sale and bore price tags; the back of the catalog also advertised the exhibitors'

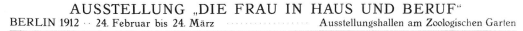

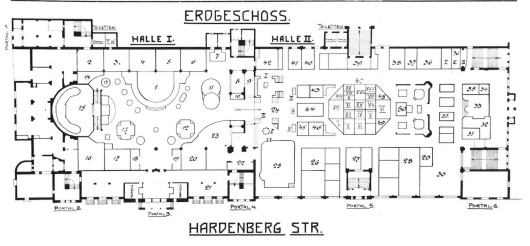

FIGURE 4.8. Ground-floor exhibition plan of halls I and II, Die Frau in Haus und Beruf. From *Die Frau in Haus und Beruf* (Berlin: Mosse, 1912).

offsite showrooms.[53] The combination of luxury goods, commerce, and architectural grandeur reminded some visitors of Wertheim. And indeed, there were striking similarities. As noted above, both had large, atrium-like spaces with dramatic lighting and multiple vantage points from which women could view displayed goods and one another. In addition, the visitor to Wertheim, like one to the women's exhibition, entered through a flower garden, marking the passage from the street into the pleasurable world of the store with a burst of sensual delight. Cascading silks, long a feature of department stores, formed a baldachin that spanned the exhibition's two floors. And the external sign of the department store, the shop window, was brought directly into the exhibition space (by Wertheim's own master of window display), creating a commercial–theatrical backdrop against which women performed daily. At a more metaphorical level, the exhibition transformed *Work,* Ludwig Manzel's female allegory, who presided over Wertheim's main atrium, into the real products of women's labor (Figure 4.5).

Similarities between the exhibition and the department store disappointed some visitors. Writing in the Berlin culture magazine *Der Türmer,* Agnes Harder, a Lyceum Club board member, defended the exhibition from middle-class visitors' repeated criticism that there was nothing here that they had not already seen at Wertheim. While acknowledging some justification for this observation, she argued that it was precisely the organizers' intention to make the public aware, through an encyclopedic display, of the vast and manifold contributions that women were already making to home and industry. Familiarity, not novelty, was the point. At the same time, Harder dismissed the apparent similarity to Wertheim, which she ascribed to the eye of the superficial observer who flounced through the halls looking at pretty things but did not take the time to study the all-important statistical and textual materials. Harder's defense suggests the problematic aspect of adopting the scopic regime of the department store: The shopping gaze, with its fleeting appraisal, did not promote sustained analysis and reflection. In a speech to an audience of young women, Gertrud Bäumer, the conservative president of the Federation of German Women's Associations (Bund Deutscher Frauenvereine, or BDF), recommended a different visual strategy. At the entrance to the main hall, organizers had placed two large columns graphically depicting the millions of women working in different trades and professions in Germany. Bäumer advised "young ladies" not to rush past the columns to see the beautiful objects on display but to study the sobering statistics and, having pictured themselves in those figures, proceed through the exhibition with an eye toward planning their future careers.[54] Organizers thus acknowledged the necessity to work against the pleasures of the exhibition in order to educate oneself. If the New Woman was represented as striving toward the sun of productivity, she could, it seems, still be waylaid by the sparkling bijoux.

After this show of opulence, the second hall, designed by Oppler-Legband and Reich, came as something of a surprise. "From the ballroom to the pigsty," as one Berlin bard put it, and not without some truth.[55] The main hall's final exhibit, devoted to haute couture, featured a gold-brocade ball gown.[56] "From this glittering finish" the visitor passed into "a totally different realm of female work. Cheerful green, alluring fruit garlands, fragrant fruit, and delicate vegetable shoots announce the woman gardener." The visitor had entered an exhibit on the horticultural school for women. "Not far away from this high palms sway; they shelter 'Woman in the Colonies.'"[57] By placing the work of horticulturists and colonists at the entrance to the second hall, Oppler-Legband and Reich signaled a transition with a sudden burst of earthy fragrances and the "shock" of the exotic. Sound enhanced the spatial dislocation: Unlike the harmonious voices of the women's choir singing in the first hall, the second hall was filled with loud clanging noises from the gallery, which housed industrial exhibits. Aristocratic elegance thus gave way to themes of labor centering on the middle and working classes. Ground-floor exhibits displayed the activities of housewives, farmers (hence the pigpen, with a live sow and piglets), colonial settlers, teachers, and social welfare workers, among others. Much of the upper gallery was devoted to working-class women in industry (primarily garment and textile), skilled trades, clerical occupations, and domestic service. Sponsored by particular firms, such as the Berlin fashion house Herrmann Gerson, "live" exhibits presented women operating looms and Singer sewing machines or cutting hair in a women's hair salon.[58]

The shift from luxury to labor was accompanied by a change in aesthetic strategies. Avoiding ornament, Oppler-Legband and Reich emphasized functionality (Figure 4.9). In contrast to Wille's rich hues, white dominated the color scheme.[59] Gone were the curvilinear forms of the main hall, visible in the structures as well as in the elegant arcs embedded in the floor plan that swept the visitor from one exhibit to the next. A new angularity replaced the curves, both in the rectilinear shapes of the pavilions and in the ordered regimentation of the floor plan. A comparison of the floor plans reveals how differently bodies moved through the two spaces, with the flowing grace of the first hall transformed into the right-angle discipline of the second (Figure 4.8). That these distinctions were predicated largely on class suggests how conceptions of the aristocratic female body differed from those of the middle or working classes, even when all groups were gathered under the rubric of the productive woman. Although the aesthetic differences between the two halls were partly suggested by preexisting structures—the architecturally more elaborate first hall retained traces of Jugendstil, whereas the plainer second hall favored industrial idioms—the choices made by the exhibition designers heightened and sharpened the existing contrast and harnessed it to convey specific meanings in the context of the exhibition.

Aesthetically and conceptually, the second hall owed a large debt to industrial fairs and their grand galleries of machines. Beginning with the Great Exhibition of 1851 and reaching a high point with the World's Fair of 1889, in Paris, displays of gargantuan turbines and engines mesmerized crowds flocking to the palaces of metal and glass. Modern industry was represented as innovative technology from which the laborer's body had all but disappeared. Such aestheticized views dominated the Machine Hall of the Main Industry Building at the pivotal 1896 Berlin Trade Exhibition, the memory of which must have lingered in the minds of many visitors to Die Frau in Haus und Beruf (Figure 4.10). In a reversal of the ascendancy of the machine, the latter exhibition maintained the idea of the machine hall but made women's bodies the engine driving the nation's productivity.[60]

FIGURE 4.9. A partial view of exhibits in hall II, designed by Oppler-Legband and Reich, Die Frau in Haus und Beruf. The large octagonal *Jugendheim* pavilion appears behind the horticultural displays. Above, we glimpse exposed skylights that contributed to the hall's more industrial look, a tone further accentuated by the designers' functional, angular forms. From Jarno Jessen, "Das Reich der Frau: XIII: Die Frau in Haus und Beruf und Deutscher Frauenkongress," *Westermanns Monatshefte* 56, no. 9 (1912): 417.

Visually speaking, the road from ballroom to factory floor might seem difficult to have navigated. But in the eyes of Max Osborn, an architectural critic and Werkbund member, the journey proved seamless. Wille, Oppler-Legband, and Reich had achieved a magnificent totality, smoothly guiding the visitor through the rich diversity. None of their male predecessors, he claimed, had similarly overcome the pernicious vastness and ungainliness of the halls.[61] Other reviewers agreed that the place had never looked better, and they sought the key to the designers' success in entrenched cultural notions of a "feminine" aesthetic. Heuss admired the "genial grace of the ornament" as well as the "vibrant, colorful decorations" that mitigated the building's architectural failings.[62] Others focused on the designers' "good taste" and their ability to harmonize the various parts into a balanced whole.[63] All of these aspects of design—a flair for ornament and color, tastefulness, and a coordinating talent—were considered inherently feminine.[64] Indeed, according to writer Anna

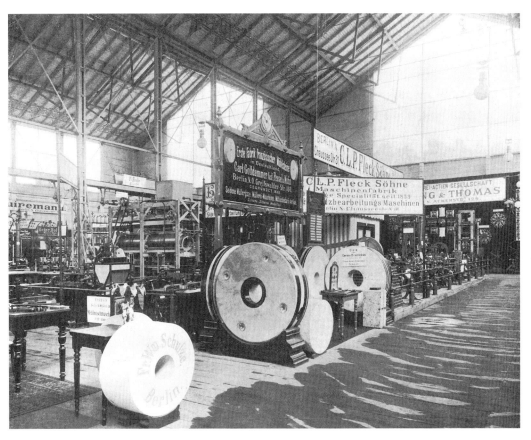

FIGURE 4.10. The Machine Hall in the Main Industry Building, Berlin Trade Exhibition, 1896. From Paul Lindenberg, *Pracht-Album photographischer Aufnahmen der Berliner Gewerbe-Ausstellung 1896* (Berlin: Werner, 1896).

Plothow, a Lyceum Club member and organizer of the show, these qualities made visible the show's female difference. "One has asked whether this exhibition differs from men's work. Yes, it distinguishes itself through its grace and tasteful presentation, through the womanly joy in flowers and colors that shines throughout."[65]

Paul Westheim, an influential design critic and Werkbund member, generally concurred with these positive assessments, although not with their logic. The work of his colleagues clearly interested him a great deal, for he wrote three reviews of the women's exhibition. He called the halls' presentation "a declaration for the modern" and credited Wille and Oppler-Legband's familiarity with contemporary trends in exhibition design for the "decency" of their production.[66] But he disliked Wille's "completely unspatial reception hall with the clumsily dangling yellow baldachin," as well as the "ridiculously decorative frieze" by Stroever.[67] Flabby silk architecture and excessive ornament were symptoms of what Westheim identified as women's innate tectonic lack, a "problem" addressed in all three reviews.

Like many of his male colleagues in the design reform movement, Westheim aggressively resisted integration of the "feminine" into modern design, considering them mutually exclusive in nature.[68] His appreciation of Wille and Oppler-Legband's aesthetic achievements rested on their perceived adoption of a masculine-style modernity. Whereas other reviewers proclaimed the merits of pursuing supposedly feminine drives, Westheim encouraged their rejection, and he was quick to point out where the designers faltered. Still, whatever influence his views had in progressive artistic circles, they were in the minority. For most journalists speaking to non-specialist audiences, the Zoological Garden halls had been transformed into a recognizably and appropriately feminine public space by the very decorative qualities that Westheim abhorred. Notably, at the 1914 Werkbund exhibition in Cologne, when these same designers shaped public space for women explicitly through architecture (creating the severely unornamented Woman's Building), the response from critics and the public alike was far more negative.[69]

By looking feminine, imitating the Wertheim department store, and distantly echoing the Berlin Trade Exhibition, this novel cultural experiment fostered a sense of the familiar. Yet the comfort (or boredom) aroused by these apparently familiar spaces made their potential all the more radical. In appropriating known models, the designers also subverted them. The female garden, with its bright colors and floral scents, was revealed to be a political meeting place. The department store became a venue where women produced rather than consumed. And the "machine hall" made visible the laboring female bodies that German politicians failed to see. Aesthetic strategies thus helped launch the women's exhibition directly into the chief political, economic, and social debates of the time, which concerned Germany's commercial and industrial strength vis-à-vis other European nations, particularly

England. The spaces of these discourses, as they were shaped by male politicians, economists, and sociologists, tended to exclude women as subjects. When women were noticed, it was often in negative terms: as an absence, a problem, or a destructive force, the last view being especially prevalent in debates about consumerism.[70] By creating physical spaces that engaged these discourses as women and in the midst of the nation's capital, the show's designers made tangible a powerful, submerged female agency that had for too long been denied.

On a smaller scale, individual exhibits revealed women designers' engagement with a broad range of social and economic concerns, including urban issues such as housing reform and education of the poor. Individual objects, too, embodied design solutions to problems faced by women in traditional and novel domains of their lives, from folding baby's beds for poor mothers to multiuse furniture for female teachers living in cramped quarters. The preeminence of design work (Westheim estimated that it constituted half of the show) mirrored the commanding position of designers at the Lyceum Club itself.[71] Dynamics within the club thus ensured that the representation of women and the shaping of the visual environment would be closely allied at the exhibition.

Three fully furnished apartments, created for different social classes in an urban setting, were among the most discussed features of the show. These model homes represented an important public statement about a new, professional relationship between women and domestic space. In keeping with the underlying class divisions of the exhibition layout, the residence for the well-to-do was nestled among the splendors of the main hall, while the bourgeoisie and working poor were housed in the more industrial environments of the adjacent hall.

The "Grand Apartment" was a luxurious, multiroom exhibit conceived as a dwelling for a wealthy family (rooms 1 to 8, Figure 4.8). It boasted a salon, an office, a library, a music room, a dining room, a bedroom, a bathroom, and a children's playroom (Figures 4.11 and 4.12). The rooms' stylistic diversity reflected the range of idioms favored by the design movement, from sturdy Arts and Crafts to simplified neoclassicism and graceful Biedermeier. Despite the conventionality of the room types and predictability of the styles, however, this was a most unusual space, created by seven prominent designers for activities and inhabitants hardly common to most Berlin homes. The office (by Bremen-based Elisabeth von Baczko) was not the bastion of a cigar-smoking paterfamilias: It was created for a female editor and housed a display on female journalists. Portraits of these newspaper ladies, rather than the usual stuffy oils of noble ancestors, hung on its walls. Similarly, the library (by Oppler-Legband) contained nearly two thousand works by female authors, and the music room (by the Berliner Marie Tscheuschner-Cucuel) was devoted to exhibits on and performances by female composers, the latter on a Steinway piano,

FIGURE 4.11. Library by Else Oppler-Legband in the "Grand Apartment" exhibit, Die Frau in Haus und Beruf. From H. von Hagen, "Zimmereinrichtungen von der Ausstellung 'Die Frau in Haus und Beruf,'" *Die Welt der Frau*, no. 45 (1912): 718.

also designed by a woman. Although the catalog suggests that organizers believed these displays would not interfere with a traditional reading of the dwelling, the professional presence in these spaces—manifest by the designers, the exhibits, and the rooms' usages—complicated the accepted meanings of domesticity. In this context, a woman did not realize herself within the home as housewife, but rather the home was realized through the woman's professional identity and needs.

This reversal of the conventional Haus–Frau dynamic provoked a scurrilous review in *Die Fackel*, a satirical Viennese journal founded (and, after 1911, wholly written) by Karl Kraus. Kraus used the journal as a forum to propagate fin-de-siècle views of the sexual woman and the intellectual man. Not surprisingly, his response to the professional feminine spirit inhabiting the grand apartment was one of disgust

FIGURE 4.12. Luxury bathroom by Ilse Dernburg in the "Grand Apartment" exhibit, Die Frau in Haus und Beruf. From Hagen, "Zimmereinrichtungen von der Ausstellung 'Die Frau in Haus und Beruf,'" 717.

("Ugh! Away!"). It was only in the bedroom, "where no women journalists hang on the walls," that he found some respite. "In the name of God," he summoned women "made hot by progress" to this room.[72]

On the whole, however, the grand apartment garnered far more acclaim than venom. Reviewers praised the intelligence and execution of the rooms, even while some acknowledged their unaffordable luxury for most Berliners. With a mixture of sarcasm and admiration, the writer Marie Heller noted that the playroom "brings home the whole lot of splendors with which one can surround one's spoiled darlings if the means permit" while nonetheless demonstrating women's ingenuity for domestic design.[73] Similarly, in a city where only a small fraction of homes had baths, Ilse Dernburg's stately bathroom remained a pleasurable fantasy in green faux marble, where one could imagine soaking in the recessed tub and stretching out on the floral divan, warmed by the fireplace and other gas appliances (Figure 4.12).[74] Somewhere in this reverie, a lasting impression was hopefully made on the viewer by the catalog's long and prominent list of companies that produced Dernburg's design, evidence of the growing cooperation Heyl and others wished to foster between women and industry.[75]

Despite the costly beauty and comfort of the rooms, designers avoided ostentation. Photographs reveal interiors that were elegantly but not profusely furnished, with a controlled use of ornament. The absence of prodigality and pomp gratified observers, whose opinions reflected debates in the Wilhelmine period on the "problem" of luxury and its potentially destructive impact on the nation's cultural and economic development as well as on its social stability.[76] Politicians, intellectuals, artists, and the popular press grappled with how to curb tendencies among the working and middle classes to emulate the lifestyles of those higher in social standing. Leaders of the design reform movement believed in a radical aesthetic solution. Hermann Muthesius proposed a national style based on *Sachlichkeit* (objectivity), a sober, "scientific" approach to design that rejected nostalgia for past styles and excessive ornament in favor of a simple "inner truthfulness."[77] These values, as Werkbund scholar Frederic Schwarz has argued, were both "classed and classless": By cultivating a universal aesthetic true to the modesty of the bourgeois citizen, Muthesius sought to eliminate "both the upper classes' visual assertion of difference and the lower classes' imitation of these forms."[78]

With several Werkbund members among the participating designers, the idea for the three dwellings possibly developed as an attempt to put Muthesius's idea of a "classless" style into practice.[79] At the top of the scale, the grand apartment set an example of subdued luxury for those who could afford its costs while also communicating the superiority of simple taste over conspicuous consumption to the vast majority of viewers who could not. As such, its designers walked a fine line between stimulating admiration for its beauty without arousing envy (or worse, class hatred). Moreover, because the problem of luxury was identified strongly with women, it was especially important that the female designers of the grand apartment demonstrate their own self-discipline.[80]

Judging from the critical response, they mostly succeeded. An article in the mass circulation *Die Welt der Frau* hailed the dwelling as quintessentially "*sachlich,* a word that one has only recently been wont to associate with women." Instead of the flamboyant "extravagance" that had become commonplace, decorative restraint and harmony reigned.[81] Reporting for design journals, Westheim gave a more mixed assessment. He approved of the "*sachlich,* decent spaces" created by Baczko (office), Dernburg (bathroom), Oppler-Legband (library), and Wille (dining room). But he found some of the other rooms distasteful, with "a shade too much coquetry and theatrical direction" in the bedroom by Elisabeth von Hahn and a disturbing fragility and moodiness in the music room by Tscheuschner-Cuceul.[82] In contradistinction, these two rooms were singled out by the *Welt der Frau* reviewer as evidence of the apartment's *sachlich* character, a disagreement that reveals the inherent subjectivity of the values Muthesius portrayed as scientific. Moreover, Westheim's terms of criticism (e.g., "too much coquetry") suggest that *Sachlichkeit* was understood in deeply gendered terms, reflecting on the gender of the maker as much as on the objects themselves.[83]

Whereas the grand apartment showcased the talents of the Lyceum Club's senior designers, two young artists, Lotte Klopsch and Lilly Reich, earned a share of the limelight with their solo creations of the middle- and working-class dwellings, respectively. Like the wealthier model, both of these domestic spaces hosted affiliated exhibits: The bourgeois home served as a functioning classroom for housekeeping schools, and charitable organizations illustrated their care of postpartum mothers and invalids in the working-class home.[84] The varying nature of the displays and activities associated with the upper-, middle-, and working-class apartments suggests fundamental differences in how organizers identified with those places. In the case of the upper- and middle-class dwellings, the creators envisioned living quarters for themselves that also housed their professional identities, whereas for the lower-class home, a professional identification with the space was applied from without.

The middle-class apartment encompassed seven rooms, as many as that for the upper classes (Figure 4.13). But this was no extravagance, for the apartment was conceived as a dwelling for three professional single women living together: a school director and two teachers. The director had three rooms to herself, the teachers two each. Klopsch focused her attention on formulating a rational plan for this nontraditional household while maintaining certain domestic comforts. Particular design

FIGURE 4.13. Bedroom by Lotte Klopsch in the "Middle-Class Apartment" exhibit, Die Frau in Haus und Beruf. From "Bürgerliche Innen-Räume," *Innen-Dekoration* 23 (1912): 223.

problems she faced included how to combine the functions of rooms (for example, bedroom and living room) and make furniture that could be easily moved, a reflection of the mobile lives of teachers.[85] Moreover, all of this had to be accomplished on a strict budget to accommodate female teachers' low salaries. Further complicating these demands was the expectation that Klopsch create the appearance of an integrated dwelling for a conventional middle-class family, allowing, as in the case of the wealthier dwelling, two different readings of the design.

Even greater financial restraints defined the project assigned to Lilly Reich: to design a dwelling for a working-class family (consisting of a man, his wife, and their infant) based on the principles of "simplicity, affordability, and functionalism."[86] As art historian Magdalena Droste has argued, this project placed Reich in the midst of an intense architectural debate on workers' housing and in direct competition with male colleagues such as Richard Reimerschmid, Peter Behrens, and Bruno Paul, who promoted their own solutions to the problem of tasteful-yet-affordable design for the working classes.[87] Reich limited herself to just two rooms, a bedroom and a combined kitchen and living area (with a scullery for washing and bathing), which is all that most working-class families in Berlin could afford (Figure 4.14). Like her colleagues, she adopted the multiple functions of rooms then common to workers' homes, rationalizing the plan and furnishings to create a comfortable and sanitary space.[88] The inexpensive pine furniture she designed for the dwelling was painted in the kitchen for easy cleaning and waxed in the bedroom and living area, with colors and types selected to maximize interchangeability within rooms. The catalog noted the "quality material, solid workmanship, [and] simple forms," as well as the elimination of "dust traps" and the free circulation of light and air.[89] The dual emphases on aesthetic and hygienic interventions typify reformers' medicalization of architects as doctors of homes. The total cost for Reich's "treatment," consisting of the complete interior furnishings, came to a modest 681.50 Marks. Despite proving thriftier than many of her male colleagues, she faced concerns that even this low price was beyond most working-class families.[90]

Reviews of the working- and middle-class dwellings tended to attribute the success of the designs to the special female talents of the artists. Evoking the ideal of the frugal housewife, a report in a medical journal applauded Reich for showing "how much can be achieved with humble means as soon as female taste and a practical gaze are brought to bear on the solution of such problems."[91] These same abilities could also rescue the gentility of the struggling middle classes: Klopsch was commended for achieving a graciously feminine atmosphere on a restricted budget.[92]

Yet the gendered stereotypes underlying these favorable reviews, which female designers manipulated to their own professional advantage, could just as easily be turned against them. A reviewer for *Bauwelt*, forced to concede the tremendous popularity of Klopsch's design, found in its "too tender softness" proof of women's inability to handle tectonic forms. With the discomfort of someone ingesting a cloyingly sweet pudding, the reviewer longed for a masculine counterweight— a dash of beefiness and a twist of acerbity.[93] Westheim similarly blamed the designers' gender for the failures of the working- and middle-class dwellings. Their work, he insisted, demonstrated "all the bad habits of the tectonically inept woman." Instead of a true, architectural solution to the problem of affordable housing, Reich offered a "bit of unconstructive prettiness," begat either by her inability to understand the task at hand or the desire to conceal her "weaknesses." Whatever the reason, the "crux of the problem has been sacrificed to a will for ornament" (*Schmuckwillen*).[94] As if she herself exuded decoration, Klopsch, too, was accused of "glazing" her materials with a "peculiar" self-indulgence.[95] Except for two pairs of small knobs in the middle-class dwelling, however, Westheim provided no examples to support or illustrate his objections. He seemed to expect his audience to know, without further clarification, what he meant by the "unconstructive prettiness" and *Schmuckwillen* of the female designer.

FIGURE 4.14. Bedroom by Lilly Reich in the "Working-Class Apartment" exhibit, Die Frau in Haus und Beruf. From "E. H.," "Die Frau in Haus und Beruf," *Die Welt*, no. 24 (1912): 477.

And it is quite possible that readers of the design journals in which Westheim's reviews appeared would have understood and sympathized with the critic's distress. For despite their specific focus on the 1912 exhibition, Westheim's texts engaged and contributed to a broader discussion on the role of gender in the professionalization of design. After the turn of the century, as men and women struggled to control a newly emerging field of professional activity—the design of everyday objects and spaces—gender norms became the axle around which their claims were made or refused.[96] Westheim did not need to point to specific examples, because he was re-hearsing stereotypes rather than proving an argument. Even so, a survey of reviews in other types of journals and newspapers reminds us that Westheim spoke for an elite minority. A reporter for the *Vossische Zeitung* noted that Reich's design elicited "great approval."[97] An article on Klopsch that appeared in 1913 credited the apart-ment's enormous public appeal for the young designer's sudden professional fame.[98] This response suggests that nonspecialists were more disposed to support the new professional design relationship touted between women and the home.

The working-class apartment extended the scope of that claim even further. In addition to being a model of professional domestic design, it represented the type of architectural intervention embraced by women as female social work. This double nature, design object and site of social work, was reinforced by the philanthropic activities associated with the dwelling. The erection of a *Jugendheim* (youth center) at the 1912 exhibition, also in the second hall, further bolstered the public claim to architectural social work. The *Jugendheim* consisted of a large octagonal pavilion (number 47 on the floor plan, Figure 4.8) with multiple rooms devoted to women's social work with disadvantaged urban children. Among them was a functioning reading room for children and adolescents, which the catalog described as a place where the disadvantaged had access to higher culture: "This reading room shall give the adolescent what his family has never given him, and can never give him, because a family, with few exceptions, can only transmit to its children its own level of cul-ture." Here their spirits would be nourished, they could participate "in the culture of their times," and they would learn "there is something more valuable than work and mere bread." The reading room was open to all children, and it was hoped that proximity would teach them to bridge class differences.[99] Charged with creating the physical space for these interactions, Ilse Dernburg emphasized *Sachlichkeit*. The room and furnishings (painted light gray) were simple, solid, and bright (Figure 4.15). Decoration, consisting of framed prints, a few rugs, and house plants, was muted. Here was the "classed and classless" aesthetic sought by Muthesius to dispel visual markers of difference, based on the hegemony of middle-class taste. Ostensibly neutral, this space, both in program and form, was, in fact, profoundly classist, inviting children to surmount the "inadequacies" of their working-class upbringing in order to assimilate bourgeois values. Jarno Jessen, a design journalist and Lyceum Club member, admired the project's totalizing "functionality," which extended from the aesthetic environment of the room to the content of the children's reading material.[100]

If the functionalism of the *Jugendheim* can be seen as an application of the Werkbund's design principles for social and aesthetic harmony, it was also a sign that marked this space (as it did those of the dwellings) as the object of professional attention. Bright, simple forms and a rationalized floor plan were the visual trademarks of the modern designer, and they proclaimed her difference from other, untrained practitioners. Wandering the halls of the 1912 exhibition, Westheim sensed the repudiation of traditional folk art, by which he meant the kind of work done "in olden times" by wives to decorate their homes or by nuns to glorify their churches.[101] Despite the heavy emphasis on the applied arts, folk art merited only a kiosk in the main hall. This paucity might be excused by the lavish folk art show

FIGURE 4.15. Reading room by Ilse Dernburg in the *Jugendheim* pavilion, Die Frau in Haus und Beruf. From "E. H.," "Die Frau in Haus und Beruf," 476.

the Lyceum Club had hosted just three years earlier as well as the ongoing display it maintained at the Wertheim department store. But Westheim offered another reason, which I believe was closer to the mark. The 1912 exhibition, he wrote, "attempted to size up the applied arts as a profession, [and] it presented woman as a designing artist."[102]

This astute observation captured both the tenuous position of design as a newly emerging profession and the struggle between men and women to claim it as their own. In this respect, design was not much different from other emerging middle-class professions represented at the exhibition, such as social work. Staking their claim to fields they had helped develop as amateurs, women now insisted on their professional transfiguration. In the popular weekly *Die Woche*, Heyl wrote that the exhibition sought to impress on the German public that women's dilettantism was a thing of the past.[103] The selection of displayed objects was carefully controlled, and education in all branches of women's work was made central to the exhibition. According to another organizer, the show displayed women's determination "to eliminate superficiality and dilettantism everywhere, to achieve a good education, to strive for a deep and fundamental knowledge, to foster efficiency, clarity, and truth."[104]

Westheim remained unconvinced. Making his rounds at the exhibition, his hawkish gaze detected the lingering presence of the *Dilettantin* (the woman dilettante). She was identified by her tendency toward kitsch, the signifier of aesthetic lack.[105] Almost as if describing the creators of the displayed ceramics, he called them "wretched little ornaments, little pictures, craftily coiffured, old-maid kitsch." The embroidered pictures of one artist prompted Westheim to note "how easily something like this can sink down to the level of old-maid arts."[106] Even favorable impressions stirred up bad memories of earlier, dilettantish efforts. (That is, progress was marked by a reminder of how bad things used to be.)[107]

This is not to say that Westheim's criticism was wholly unwarranted; as he himself acknowledged, with thousands of objects on display, a range of quality was inevitable.[108] Notable, however, is how readily the charge of dilettantism in particular was levied against the woman designer. To prove herself as a professional, the woman designer had to banish the ghost of Christmas fairs past. And it was precisely this shift from church bazaar to the department store, more than female aesthetic lack, that worried Westheim. In the past, he explained, a woman's handiwork had no influence beyond her home or a small circle of acquaintances. The new professional designers, however, needed to create a market. And what they initially brought to the marketplace, Westheim claimed, was uniformly bad.[109] Although he admitted some improvement had occurred, his reviews give the impression of someone coming to assess the damage after the floodgate has broken.

With its usual sarcasm, the avant-garde journal *Der Sturm* bluntly reiterated Westheim's objections in its review of the show: "A kitschification of the A. Wertheim department store. Everything for sale."[110] Both the quality of the designers' work and their crass commercialism were thus impugned. Although the reference to the Wertheim store was tailor-made for the women's exhibition—a response to the strong visual similarities and the types of objects on display (and for sale)— the criticism itself was hardly original. As Beth Irwin Lewis has shown, women artists faced accusations of dilettantism and economic motivation (over a genuine calling) in the 1890s, when their growing presence in the field prompted similar fears of overproduction.[111] By 1912, the dilettante card was still being played against women artists, as even positive reviews of the fine arts section (coordinated by the renowned painter Dora Hitz) attest.[112] Nonetheless, the "front" of this gendered battle had since shifted to the applied arts. The prominence, copiousness, and unprecedented scope of the design work at the women's exhibition represented both a thrown gauntlet and a unique opportunity to assess the challenger's strengths.

While Wille and her design colleagues captured the media's attention, the show's greatest novelty, according to Salomon, was the architects. Salomon expected visitors to be surprised not only by their existence but also by their success: "It is known only to a few that one of the German women architects maintains a large office, constantly has numerous buildings under construction, and has already won prizes in many competitions."[113] She was referring to Emilie Winkelmann, the organizer of the "Woman in Architecture" exhibit. Although two others, Elisabeth von Knobelsdorff and Therese Mogger, displayed their work, Winkelmann's presence dominated. She was the senior of the three, and by 1912 her practice was flourishing. This was the first time in Germany that women architects had exhibited as a group or category.[114] Writing in 1928, Gisela Urban, an Austrian feminist, looked back on the event as the turning point that finally "convinced the general public that women really are active in the field of architecture."[115]

The architecture display was located well away from distractions that could impede the quiet contemplation Heyl believed it required.[116] In a large room on the upper floor of the second hall, architecture nestled between areas devoted to the fine arts and to social work (room 79 on the floor plan, Figure 4.16). The latter category encompassed a broad spectrum of socially engaged labor, including the creation of female workers' clubs and women's retirement homes, as well as the newly minted career of female housing inspector.[117] This spatial contextualization is revealing. All three categories—fine arts, architecture, and social work—were included in the "Women in the Professions" section, directed by Salomon. For leaders of the women's movement such as she, architecture stood (literally) somewhere between art and social service.

Displaying the full range of her production, Winkelmann exhibited models and illustrations of her numerous residential projects (including hotels), factory buildings, agricultural structures, schools, and exhibition pavilions for an industrial fair in Köslin, as well as a bridge, a museum, and a popular Berlin theater. It was her houses, however, that entranced visitors. One reviewer noted the "envy-filled" apartment dwellers who lingered in front of photographs of the suburban villas built for the beloved Berlin writers Paul Oskar Höcker and Rudolf Presber.[118] The art historian Eduard Thoma, who generally opposed women artists, was thoroughly impressed with Winkelmann, whose handling of form and space reminded him of Messel.[119] Winkelmann's tour-de-force portfolio overshadowed the more modest contributions of her coexhibitors. Knobelsdorff, just graduated from Berlin's Royal Technical College, chose to include an apartment building from her diploma project, and Mogger, who had recently established an office in Düsseldorf, featured the pattern-book style drawings for single-family homes that would become the basis of her design periodical, *Unser Haus* (Our House), which began publication the following year.[120]

Of the many positive reviews of the architecture room, the most interesting, and ambiguous, appeared in the *Vossische Zeitung*, penned by the art critic Paul Fechter:

One encounters a series of tasteful, intelligent works, in which contemporary trends are skillfully elaborated. One feels oddly an atmosphere of self-renunciation, which

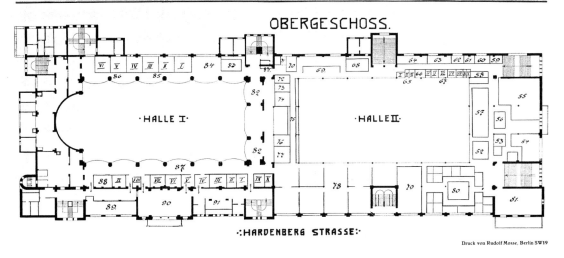

FIGURE 4.16. Second-story exhibition plan of halls I and II, Die Frau in Haus und Beruf. From *Die Frau in Haus und Beruf*.

this initially most unsensual form of human expressive activity produces in this environment.[121]

This intriguing statement, from a champion of expressionist art, suggests that in this feminine environment, the normally intellectual art of architecture produces feeling. But the feeling is of absence, a giving up of the self. The author, however, does not name the self being renounced. It might be the female self, which, with all of its emotive qualities, is inappropriate to a nonsensual art. Or it may be the architects, or even their works, that hold back from their feminine surroundings. Perhaps the work renounces itself as women's work. Or is it the producing woman architect who is made absent, so that the work creates itself? The above statement, while expressing admiration for the work, captures the sense of oddity that must have struck visitors contemplating the unusual, and to some unnatural, combination of women and architecture.

The architecture room, three dwellings, *Jugendheim,* and social work displays, as well as a host of other exhibits, made contemporary debates about women's architectural needs and their contributions to the urban built environment tangible to a popular audience. A lecture series, held onsite and free to exhibition visitors, further heightened awareness of these issues. Dora Martin, a champion of women's vocational training, gave a well-attended talk on homes for retired career women that employed an architectural model by Winkelmann (see chapter 3).[122] From a different standpoint, that of the artist shaping urban imagery, Elisabeth von Hahn spoke on the reform of window display and its professional opportunities for women.[123]

An even larger audience heard debates on kitchenless dwellings and female housing inspectors, among other topics, at the German Women's Congress planned by the BDF to coincide with the exhibition. The "women's parliament," as Berlin newspapers called it, convened during the first week of the exhibition in the zoo's majestic and newly constructed ballroom. Over five thousand women (and a small number of men) attended daily, and even though the speeches were repeated to accommodate the unexpected crowds, many were turned away for lack of space. The meeting was seen as an opportunity to theorize and debate the meaning of the objects on view in the adjacent halls.[124]

Closely watched by the press, the congress also contributed significantly to the visibility of the exhibition as a whole. Published photographs of the assembly gave Berliners a rare glimpse of a politicized mass of women (Figure 4.17). Such images were still newsworthy in a state that had only recently revoked the Law of Association, which from 1850 to 1908 barred women from public meetings on political affairs (including female suffrage). Beyond the size of the audience, its composition was strikingly unusual, with baronesses and "court ladies," previously resistant to the women's movement, openly showing their support and mixing with people from very different social and political backgrounds to do so.[125]

What was one to make of this newly constituted female mass? Through its editorial choices, *Der Tag* seemed to define it in relation to more radical "mobs" in London, suggesting a potential link between the two while also differentiating and domesticating the German feminists. The March 2 issue carried nearly contiguous stories about the shop window–smashing campaign of the London suffragettes and the final day of the women's conference in Berlin.[126] The contrast in journalistic styles could not have been greater. With dramatic theatricality, the London report began with vivid descriptions of the chaotic and fearful scene in Regent Street and went on to discuss the "manly" militancy of the "suffragette generals." The Berlin article, by contrast, first noted the absence, due to illness, of key speakers at the conference before continuing with a bland description of the day's speeches. Despite real differences in the nature of the two events, representational choices heightened, and perhaps exaggerated, those differences. Thus, the decision to foreground weak female bodies in the Berlin piece gave it a profoundly different tone from that which

FIGURE 4.17. Overflowing audiences filled the German Women's Congress held at the Zoological Garden in association with Die Frau in Haus und Beruf, February 27 to March 2, 1912. From *Gartenlaube*, special issue, *Frauen-Kongress: Illustrierter Bericht der "Gartenlaube" mit "Welt der Frau"* (1912): 14.

emphasized the physical strength of the "manly" English suffragettes. The striking contrast in the writing styles also contributed to this impression: While the London article deployed language to evoke the reader's fear, all passion was stripped from the Berlin account and, by extension, from the voices of the female speakers. This was reinforced by the use of indirect discourse (subjunctive) for the Berlin speeches, which was replaced by direct discourse (indicative) in the London narrative. Reports published that same day on the tea reception held for the congress delegates at the chancellor's residence, hosted by his wife, further softened the tone of the press coverage.[127] Nonetheless, the international events cast a threatening shadow over the women's congress, a shadow that could not be entirely ignored. At the exhibition itself, representatives of the suffrage movement, handing out flyers, were greeted repeatedly with sarcasm by Berliners who wanted to know when women in Germany would also begin breaking windows.[128]

For critics on the political left, an infusion of radicalism would have improved the women's events. Touring the newly opened exhibition, Minna Cauer, a leader of the left wing of the bourgeois women's movement and a Lyceum Club member, lamented the focus on "the grand and beautiful" to the detriment of more difficult and pressing social concerns. The resulting impression, she suggested, hardly encouraged support for the women's movement, for if a woman's life was all "glamour and cheer," why bother to protest? She looked to the upcoming congress, at which she would speak, as a potential corrective, a discursive space that might make room for the unpleasant realities banished from the exhibition.[129] Not all subjects, however, or all voices were included in that discussion. In a postscript to the congress, Helene Stöcker, president of the League for the Protection of Motherhood and Sexual Reform, complained that the presence of "court ladies" and the illusion of interclass unity had been achieved only by shutting out voices on the far left (namely, that of her own organization, which fought for the rights of unwed mothers). Although she agreed with much that had been said at the congress, she deplored the avoidance of entire topics of women's oppression, such as prostitution or enforced celibacy, deemed unsuitable for this genteel company.[130]

In far less diplomatic terms, Alfons Goldschmidt, an economist with socialist sympathies, excoriated the show's organizers for ignoring the daily struggle for existence faced by many German women. He called the exhibition arrogant and mocked the pretensions of "the lady on parade" with her tasteful "little things." In her train, "the triumph of the little crochet table" had banished human misery from the show. Nowhere could he find workers choking on the miasmic clouds of polluting factories or the victims of "manly slave owners." For Goldschmidt, the parading "Berlin lady" was a menace, the creator of "false ornament" and "pleasurable kitsch."[131] She was, in other words, an aristocratically decadent dilettante.

The feverishness of Goldschmidt's polemic, which threatened to subvert itself as caricature, suggests he struggled to revive a once-reliable stereotype of the lady as an absurd and destructive dabbler.

A cartoon in the satirical magazine *Simplicissimus* also drew on this stereotype to lampoon the exhibitors, but it depicted men, rather than poor women, as their victims. Two young and fashionable ladies are shown in conversation (Figure 4.18). The caption reads: "Me? I exhibited the death certificates of my first three husbands."[132] The German verb *ausstellen* plays on the meaning "to exhibit" the death certificates as well as "to issue" them. Thus, like Goldschmidt, the cartoon laughed at the exhibitors' conceit while also suggesting something sinister.

Whereas the *Simplicissimus* ladies were comically frightful because they produced only death, other male anxieties were aroused by the vast scale of female production made visible by the exhibition. A journalist for a popular illustrated weekly, confronted by the apparent self-sufficiency of this women's world, felt the need to reassure male readers that they were not obsolete and about to be "thrown onto the scrap heap." Prowling around the exhibition the day before it opened, the reporter was comforted by the presence of workmen. This secret knowledge, imparted to the reader, was meant to undermine the illusion of modern female independence: "Today, like the man, the woman designs a house, an apartment; but the construction will be carried out and the furniture made by a man. Woman cooks well with gas, man constructs the gas oven. Woman plans a garden and the man plants it."[133] Poking fun at such fears (while upholding the inviolability of the natural sexual order), a male writer confessed that he felt "elevated, enthused, and yet dejected" by the show. Returning home, he handed over his fountain pen and inkpot to his wife, asking her to replace him as the family breadwinner, since "you [women] can do it all so much better than we can." Luckily or unluckily for him, his wife scorned this gesture as a "lame excuse" to evade his husbandly duties.[134]

For the most part, organizers of the women's show did not respond publicly to their critics. The exhibition was in itself, after all, a confutation of a host of damaging cultural stereotypes, such as the femme fatale evoked by *Simplicissimus*. Nonetheless, some of the barbs stung, as revealed in a rare rebuttal by Henni Lehmann. Lehmann, an artist and Lyceum Club member, was not directly involved with the show but felt obligated to defend her colleagues against Goldschmidt's "spiteful attack." Her strategy was twofold. In certain instances, she acknowledged Goldschmidt's observations in order to dispute his interpretation. Thus, conceding the role of taste, she drew on the discourses of the design reform movement to argue for the national importance of such concerns. Moreover, Lehmann asserted that female taste impacted more than "little things," pointing to the architectural transformation of the halls to underscore the environmental scale of women's work

FIGURE 4.18. A cartoon and its caption mock the exhibitors as elegant but deadly: "Me? I exhibited the death certificates of my first three husbands." From "Die Frau in Haus und Beruf," *Simplicissimus* 16, no. 51 (1912): 891.

in contrast to Goldschmidt's evocation of the tiny and trivial. Even the smaller objects on display were not to be confused with "the embroidery grandmother made in her leisure hours." This was work of an entirely different order, professional and with market value—a defense that articulated Westheim's worst fears.

At the same time, Lehmann rejected what Goldschmidt claimed to have seen, suggesting his viewing was superficial, prejudiced, or simply hallucinatory. (There was no such thing, she pointed out, as a "little crochet table.") Whole rooms, she complained, had been reduced to some small detail ridiculed by Goldschmidt, which hardly did justice to the complexity of their contents. His selective vision, moreover, blinded him to displays that contradicted his criticism about the lack of attention to the lower classes. If there were not more on female workers, as Goldschmidt had demanded, Lehmann asserted that it was a problem of scale. Faced with "an enormous mass" (and it is not clear whether she meant of information or people), only a sampling was possible, which the organizers accepted "with resignation." Lehmann referred to the catalog entry on "Industry and Trades," which acknowledged the impossibility of an exhaustive review of women's contributions to these fields.[135]

While there is much in Goldschmidt's review that seems to have been inspired by his antipathy to "Berlin ladies" and that Lehmann convincingly refutes, her justification for the limited representation of female workers rings hollow, as does that of the organizers themselves. If the encyclopedic display of women's labor was the original premise of the show, it did not apply equally to all classes. Despite the substantial "Industry and Trades" section, the majority of displays addressed the work and concerns of bourgeois women.[136] Class issues at the exhibition were more complicated, however, than either Goldschmidt or Lehmann suggested. More than numbers or breadth shaped the representation of female workers. Equally important, but mentioned by no one, was their treatment as objects rather than subjects. Workers were represented not by their unions but as employees of exhibiting firms, such as the Gerson fashion house.[137] In the same vein, the working-class dwelling displayed what middle-class women, seeking new careers for themselves, could do for the poor, more than what the poor might do for themselves. Lehmann confirmed this viewpoint when, countering Goldschmidt's assertion that poverty had been excluded from the exhibition, claimed one could see it reflected in women's relief work.[138] This class-based subjectivity permeated the exhibition just as it shaped the vision of a gendered city that middle- and upper-class women sought to shape for themselves and for less fortunate others—but always on their own terms.

A lack of firsthand accounts by working-class women makes it difficult to assess how they responded to their marginalization within the exhibition. *Für die Frau Meisterin*, a journal for skilled tradeswomen, published an anonymous review asserting that working-class women had, on the whole, avoided "Fihub," and those who had attended had left disappointed. "No wonder," commented the reviewer, "the exhibition says nothing about the worries, work burden, or needs of a woman who truly depends solely on the labor of her own two hands." The writer went on to criticize the show's ostentatious displays, such as ladies' hats worth up to sixteen hundred Marks, a reality far removed from the lives of poor Berliners.[139] While these sentiments were undoubtedly shared by many working-class visitors, the show's astoundingly high attendance numbers suggest that its appeal, while primarily to the privileged, was not quite as narrow as the above reviewer claimed.

Beyond class biases, the "problem" of representing poverty at the 1912 exhibition raises important questions about the organizers' construction of urban narratives. Goldschmidt's discussion of women's poverty focused to a significant extent on sexual dangers. He conjured up for the reader abandoned pregnant women, dark corners of prostitution, harsh slave owners, and young girls traded on the international market.[140] His colorful prose evoked for Lehmann "monstrous images of scenes of horror," whose sensational effect she considered "undignified" for an exhibition.[141] Theodor Heuss, by contrast, wished the organizers had been less timid. The topic of prostitution was broached from such an oblique angle, he complained, that it threatened to disappear altogether.[142] Certainly, cultural notions of propriety made it difficult to represent sexual themes visually at a women's exhibition; as Lehmann argued, they were better left to the congress. At the same time, the figure of the desperate, impoverished prostitute hardly could have appealed to organizers trying to promote the educated, professional dimensions of women's labor.

But more than the dignity or professional focus of the exhibition was at stake, I believe, in the suppression of these most "public" of women. In creating female public space and putting women "on display" at the heart of the city, organizers of the 1912 exhibition sought new types of gendered urban narratives that did not foreground sexual danger.[143] The elimination of monstrous images from the exhibition went hand in hand with the construction of a modern female identity that responded to the urban environment as subject rather than object. The woman on view at the 1912 show traversed her city as a social worker, built homes, occupied university classrooms, decorated shop windows, and so forth; she produced and claimed urban space with an agency difficult to reconcile with contemporary discourses of "public women," either as sexual victims or as pariahs. A large map of Germany displayed by the BDF, pinpointing the locations of its member organizations with brightly colored flags, dramatically revealed the nation's cities to be hotbeds of female activism.[144] Goldschmidt's insistence on reintegrating sexual danger into the exhibition, whatever the economic or political justifications, must also be viewed as an attempt, whether conscious or unconscious, to undermine this new female subject and reassert male control in the creation of urban narratives and space.

Whatever the exhibition's real or imagined flaws, it was without doubt an overwhelming public relations success. A report by the Royal Police Authority noted the "unanimous praise bestowed on it by all the presses, daily and specialist."[145] And this was not much of an exaggeration: Hundreds of admiring reviews appeared in journals and newspapers from Königsberg to New York City. Goldschmidt, in frustration at the adulation, accused the press of robbing space from newsworthy stories, such as the coal strike in England or Italy's annexation of Tripoli, to give more coverage to the women.[146] It was probably because of such positive publicity that organizers felt little need to respond to criticism; for the most part, voices like those of Goldschmidt and Westheim were cold drops in an ocean of warm affirmation. And despite the occasional chivalrous tone of some of this coverage, the press treated the women's exhibition as a serious and important event, "a monumental milestone" in German women's history.[147] As a reporter for the *Norddeutsche Allgemeine Zeitung* observed, one left the premises with a new respect for the women's movement as a powerful force in the life of the nation.[148]

After four weeks of glorious visibility, at the center of Berlin and in the nation's press, the women's exhibition closed its doors. Its effects, however, did not immediately dissipate. Heuss seems to have been right about the radical potential of this gathering: The energy formed by the massing of women at the Zoological Garden soon flowed into the streets. As historian Ute Planert has argued, the spring of 1912 marked a high point in the politicization of German women.[149] Seven weeks after the exhibition closed, on 12 May, women took to the streets of Berlin to demand the vote—a dramatic shift in tactics for a movement that had shied away from the public unruliness of the London suffragettes. Except for a single, modest march in 1910, Berlin feminists had avoided street protests, partly because they lacked support for a compelling showing.[150] But on that spring day in 1912, the capital witnessed forty-eight well-attended demonstrations, with smaller events occurring in Frankfurt and Breslau.[151]

Heuss focused on the power of images to transform a woman's sense of political self-identity. Contemporary accounts also suggest that the exhibition and congress made the city itself feel different. So wrote a female reporter from Hamburg, who struggled to express the shared perception of a cosmological shift: "It is an extremely odd effect, compelling serious reflection, this impression that obtrudes on everyone who 'experiences' Berlin these days, that Berlin is under the sign of woman."[152] This feeling, which may have encouraged women to claim the streets as their own, was not necessarily fleeting. Subsequent physical interventions in the urban topography perpetuated the sign of woman. The half million people who visited, shopped, and ate at the exhibition produced a hefty profit for the German Lyceum Club, which it used to finance the construction of a permanent home. The silk architecture of the exhibition thereby morphed into the bricks-and-mortar clubhouse on Lützowplatz. Moreover, several of the building projects presented as drawings or models and discussed in lectures soon materialized, among them, the Victoria Studienhaus and the Haus in der Sonne. The visionary idea of a female topos that had so fascinated Berliners flocking to the Zoological Garden thus began (indeed, had already begun) to assume architectural flesh in the body of the city.

In her memoirs, Heyl looked back on the exhibition as a turning point for women, its consequences beyond measure.[153] An account published in 1920 claimed the show greatly increased trust in women's work and abilities, a feeling that had not diminished when the First World War began, and millions of women stepped into the shoes of departing soldiers.[154] Assessing the impact of the event some thirty years later, Salomon wrote: "The 'modern woman' became popular, almost fashionable, and in Germany that meant a lot."[155]

5 The Architecture of Social Work

Workers' Clubs, Social Welfare Institutions, and
the Debate over Female Housing Inspectors

REFASHIONING BERLIN THROUGH WORDS AND BRICKS, the bourgeois women discussed in previous chapters altered the urban built environment in order to realize a modern female identity that hinged on new kinds of spaces. In places such as the Lehrerinnenheim or the Lyceum Club, spinsters were reborn as independent women, and lone individuals became a visible collective. Such projects opened doors to new realms of activity and influence vis-à-vis the male public sphere; for example, the Victoria Studienhaus empowered female university students through academic community, and the 1912 exhibition rewrote urban narratives of mastery and subjecthood. Yet the making and taking of space by middle-class women involved broaching more than gendered spatial boundaries. As they carved out new territory for themselves in the city's commercial centers and elegant residential districts, bourgeois women also looked to its slums as a field of intervention.

Although German women's engagement in philanthropic work predated the imperial period, the turn of the twentieth century witnessed a remarkable growth in such activity. A survey in 1908 found that of all women's social welfare and charitable associations then in existence, half had been founded after 1900.[1] The repeal of the Law of Association in 1908, which previously barred women from "political" assemblies, further spurred membership in organizations devoted to the public good. In addition, a more diverse pool of women expressed the desire to participate in community life. As Nancy Reagin notes in her study of the women's movement in Hannover, women's philanthropic groups, which initially attracted married and widowed volunteers, experienced a dramatic increase in single members after the turn of the century, perhaps because newer organizations shifted from benefiting primarily married women to addressing the needs of single women.[2] Beyond expanding their membership and clientele, women's charitable and social welfare associations also widened the scope of their projects. As bourgeois women's spatial needs changed in response to novel social roles, their heightened awareness of their place (or placelessness) in the built environment extended to other women as well. In Berlin, attempts by middle-class women to erect homes, clubs, and other urban institutions for themselves occurred alongside similar efforts on behalf of poorer women.

Motivated by a genuine desire to improve the lives of working-class women, as well as by feelings of female solidarity, such incursions into the space of others nonetheless often asserted the superiority and authority of bourgeois women. Historians of English and American cities have shown how middle-class women promoted their values and bolstered their presence in public life through the creation of settlement houses, day cares, soup kitchens, and other urban institutions for the poor.[3] Berlin, with its wave of feminist building campaigns before the First World War, affords a broad perspective on the various and interlocking strategies used by bourgeois women to extend their dominion over urban space. This chapter explores the pursuit of architecture as social work, focusing on three distinct forms: social welfare institutions, clubs for working-class women, and the campaign for female housing inspectors. These projects highlight the power struggles—between poor and wealthy Berliners, bourgeois men and women, officials and housewives, as well as among middle-class women—to define and control the redemption of urban space.

From Feudal Might to the Rational Mind: The Competing Architectural Strategies of the Cecilienhaus and the Social School for Women

In her study of German social work, Young Sun Hong recounts how middle-class women staked a claim to the profession on the basis of their gender and class. Drawing on an ideology of motherhood that posited woman's nature as essentially nurturing, compassionate, and self-sacrificing, moderate bourgeois feminists portrayed social work as a feminine calling. The charity reform movement provided women with an important opening into the field. Deeming the punitive approach to poor relief (*Armenpflege*) inadequate to modern conditions of poverty, bourgeois social reformers at the end of the nineteenth century sought to rationalize charity and shift the focus to preventive social services such as maternity and infant care, which in turn permitted a greater role for women. Replacing traditional forms of poor relief with the "rational" and "scientific" approach of modern social work also reasserted the legitimacy of such efforts in the face of the lower classes' opposition to "bourgeois charity." Appealing to an ethos of education and professionalism, bourgeois feminists argued for the superiority of trained female social workers to less qualified men. The first professional social work schools in Germany were women's schools and drew their members from the privileged classes. Women were enjoined to fulfill the moral obligation of their class through social work and to perform "a 'feminine service duty' parallel to the male obligation to compulsory military service." In claiming social work as an exclusive realm of public feminine intervention, bourgeois feminists argued that it would benefit women, the poor, and the greater social good.[4] Some also believed it would lead to suffrage.[5]

Male administrators and volunteers responsible for *Armenpflege* opposed recruiting women, which they disparaged as "promoting a 'sport' for women." Furthermore, they claimed that the immorality that attached itself to the poor would rub off and tarnish the reputations of upstanding women. Arguing that men's objectivity and rationality better suited them to the job, they insisted that "women inherently lacked the toughness and authority necessary to deal with the deceptive and demoralizing poor." Support for female social workers was limited to those activities associated with their roles as housekeepers and mothers, namely, teaching poor women and girls how to better manage their households by inculcating "the basic bourgeois virtues of frugality, order, and industry."[6] Within this matrix of competing ideologies of femininity, social work, and charity, the jostling for hegemony played itself out on multiple fronts: science versus tradition, the professional versus the dilettante, the bourgeoisie versus the working class, and women versus men. As we will see later in the chapter, similar tensions shaped the debate over female housing inspectors.

Written by and for educated middle-class women, it is not surprising that *What a Woman Must Know about Berlin*, the 1913 guidebook discussed in chapter 1, incorporated a good deal of material on social welfare issues. Indeed, the image of the city presented by the authors was, to a considerable degree, constructed through the perspective of bourgeois women's engagement with such concerns. Among the chapters devoted to social welfare, Alice Salomon wrote on women's social work in Berlin; Rahel Hirsch, the first female doctor to hold a professorship in Prussia (at the Royal Charité Hospital), reported on institutions serving the sick; and jurist Annie Lehr de Waal tried to make sense of the city's maze of social services—a bewildering and poorly coordinated array of private and public agencies, some of which had overlapping and competing aims—that resulted from the lack of any centralized authority.[7] By way of an introductory survey, Lehr de Waal sketched out the diverse services available to the city's needy residents, from hungry children to "fallen women." Writing with an eye to what she thought would be most interesting to women, Lehr de Waal described resources for poor mothers and orphans while also addressing the needs of educated single women, such as for housing or job placement. Thus, social welfare was broadly defined to include the "disenfranchised" of both the lower and middle classes, namely, the urban poor and bourgeois women struggling to make it on their own. While both could be subjects of social welfare, the latter were also its agents.[8]

Lehr de Waal distinguished between the new social work schools described
by Salomon, which trained "women for pure social work, more or less with a bias
toward educating them for full citizenship," and traditional women's charities far
removed from such emancipatory interests. Yet even the latter, she acknowledged,
were changing to meet the times.[9] The oldest and most conservative of these was
the Prussian Patriotic Women's Association (Vaterländische Frauenverein), an affili-
ate of the Red Cross. Founded in 1866 to train women to care for wounded soldiers,
the association soon expanded into peacetime social service, with a focus on sick
wards, infant care, children's homes, and housekeeping courses. Although its board
of directors included men, it was run chiefly by aristocratic and upper-middle-class
women. With half a million members in 1913, it represented the largest and most
powerful women's organization in Germany.[10]

From 1907 to 1909, the Patriotic Women's Association, in cooperation with
municipal authorities, erected one of the most imposing landmarks of women's
social work in Berlin: the Cecilienhaus, in Charlottenburg (Figure 5.1). In order
to obtain a prime location near the city hall, the association selected an oddly
shaped site that offered ample space at an affordable price. With minimal frontage
on costly Berliner Strasse, the property extended backward from the street in a long,
narrow strip for a full city block and then turned westward to incorporate a large,
inexpensive back lot (Figure 5.2).[11] Walther Spickendorff, a municipal architect and
association board member, created a series of connected buildings and courtyards
that developed a sense of fluid movement from front to rear. The buildings hugged
the western and northern boundaries of the lot, a layout that maximized direct
sunlight to the interiors. A municipal report described the facilities as technically
and hygienically modern, boasting an immense central kitchen equipped with industrial machinery for preparing food and refrigerating milk, an electrically powered
laundry, and multiple elevators.[12] Among its facilities, the Cecilienhaus included a
sanatorium (which could be converted into a military hospital during wartime),
a lung disease clinic, a women's clinic (with delivery facilities), an infant care clinic,
a nursery, a soup kitchen (serving up to five hundred people a day), and an outdoor
playground.[13]

In addition to housing its own departments, the Patriotic Women's Association
rented space to municipal social welfare programs as well as to private organizations,
thus uniting diverse social services under one roof and making the Cecilienhaus the
center of social welfare administration for Charlottenburg.[14] Centralization achieved
more efficient use of resources and better coordination, as well as greater control
over the clientele. Mothers who gave birth here were encouraged to bring their
babies for monitoring twice weekly. Along with advice on proper care and nutrition,
they received "hygienic" milk for their infants. If they returned to work, they could

FIGURE 5.1. The imposing façade of the Cecilienhaus, on Berliner Strasse, designed by
Walther Spickendorff. Photograph taken in 1910 by Hermann Rückwardt. From *Bericht über
die Verwaltung und den Stand der Gemeinde-Angelegenheiten der Stadt Charlottenburg für das Verwaltungsjahr
1909*, 1910.

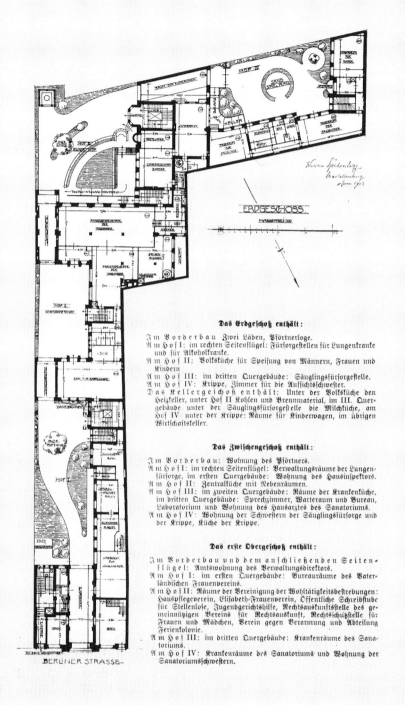

FIGURE 5.2. Ground-floor plan of the Cecilienhaus by Spickendorff, 1908. From *Bericht über die Verwaltung und den Stand der Gemeinde-Angelegenheiten der Stadt Charlottenburg für das Verwaltungsjahr 1909*.

place their children in day care from infancy until school age. Eventually, the children might participate in the lunch program for needy schoolchildren or, later on, benefit from youth and employment services.[15]

Rising high above street level to dwarf its neighbors, the Cecilienhaus visually declared its far-reaching powers. Erich Ritter, a journalist, described the impact of the building's physical presence:

> Anyone strolling beneath the pleasant trees that line the main street of Charlotten-burg, Berlin's flourishing neighbor–city, in the direction of the centuries-old royal palace, glimpses to his left . . . at a towering height, a mighty copper turret, from which the sign of the Red Cross on a brilliant white field calls down greetings. It surmounts a powerful, broad pediment that crowns a massive portal structure whose narrow, simply arranged sandstone façade—with the magnificent pillared gallery on the top floor and the castle-gate-like entry reaching above the second floor—produces a proud, monumental effect.[16]

This forceful impression continued at closer inspection, as visitors passed through the enormous gateway. Wrapped around the portal like a chain, the name of the association was engraved in thick letters (Figure 5.3). Directly above, a large crown hovered over a cross, and on either side, the solemn faces of two women watched over those who entered. Spickendorff brought stylistic unity to the various historical motifs (part Renaissance palazzo, part medieval fortress) by filtering the whole through a Jugendstil sensibility.

The adjectives employed to capture the physical qualities of the Cecilienhaus—*towering, mighty, powerful, massive, magnificent, castle-gate-like, proud,* and *monumental*—suggest an architecture designed to intimidate. Such an approach would seem to accord poorly with the activities occurring inside, which Ritter described repeatedly in terms of love: the building was "a landmark of working love," encapsulating "all the love that is shown to the weary and burdened within the rooms of this house."[17] The milk kitchen, which daily dispatched hundreds of bottles of sterilized milk to the city's babies, most clearly symbolized this nurturing aspect.

Yet this imposing stance, which strikes the passerby even today, served other purposes, too. Most obviously, it reflected the military origins of the Patriotic Women's Association, which remained ever-ready to nurse wounded soldiers. Allusions to medieval fortifications underscored the strength of its members' duty to the fatherland. Perhaps more important, the masonry forms and unified plan of the Cecilienhaus bespoke permanence and centralized authority. To the clientele, the architecture sent a message affirming the legitimacy of the association's claim to regulate their lives. Like a beacon on a rock, the Cecilienhaus promised protection

FIGURE 5.3. Cecilienhaus main entrance. The name of the association wraps around the inside of the doorway.

from the storms of destitution. Inside the flowing, interconnected complex, the chaos of life took on a linear, controlled order that began with the cradle and ended at the grave. Royal and castlelike imagery reminded all who entered that the association's charitable activities, though thoroughly modern in their technological and scientific rationalism, rested on older assumptions about the feudal obligation of the mighty toward the poor and about the appropriate humility and gratitude expected of the latter. But the building-as-message was also directed toward other social workers: The Cecilienhaus symbolized the association's attempt to consolidate power over rival organizations. With its dominant, phallus-shaped turret, perhaps evoking the father of its name, it made clear that it was the central organ to which others must cede. Finally, and at the broadest level, the building boldly asserted women's hegemony in the realm of social welfare. By echoing the monumentality of Charlottenburg's town hall, just a short distance away, the Cecilienhaus presented itself as an institution of comparable authority and power. And, indeed, its importance was recognized and sanctioned by state officials, who granted the Cecilienhaus permission to display the character of a public building.[18]

Built in the same period as the Cecilienhaus, the Social School for Women in Schöneberg resorted to a radically different representational strategy to make similar hegemonic claims. It, too, employed architecture to assert a particular vision of social work, which in form and substance largely repudiated the Cecilienhaus. Although both institutions promoted a central role for women and science, Alice Salomon, the school's founder and principal, rejected the lingering feudalism of the aristocratic Patriotic Women's Association in favor of her middle-class faith in the authority of the educated professional. Where the Cecilienhaus proffered the anchoring bulk of tradition, the school building appealed to the emancipating lightness of reason.

In 1893, twenty-one-year-old Salomon answered the call to take up her moral duty as a woman with time and money on her hands and help her less fortunate sisters. She was one of about fifty young women who responded to an appeal issued by prominent Berliners, who sought to recruit daughters of the educated middle classes for volunteer work among the city's poor. Together they formed the Girls' and Women's Groups for Social Assistance (Mädchen und Frauengruppen für Soziale Hilfsarbeit), an organization that trained its members in the new forms of social work. Salomon thereby escaped the boredom that had plagued her since her schooling ended at the age of fourteen. Like other "young ladies" of her generation, she was expected to "feed the canary, embroider dollies, and wait for marriage."[19] The Girls' and Women's Groups offered an active and socially conscious definition of the female experience, and it was here that Salomon discovered the redemptive power of serving the greater good.[20]

Influenced by social reformers who emphasized the need for educated intervention, the groups' founders organized lectures by academics, including the sociologist Max Weber, and onsite study of social welfare organizations and places of labor. They sought to yoke the "moral energies of young women" to the discipline and reason of science. In this manner, they hoped to create morally engaged social workers capable of planning effective programs based on an understanding of the root causes of social problems. Sympathy and "aimless almsgiving" would be replaced by a deeper moral and rational foundation. Young women responded enthusiastically to the program, and within a decade the organization had hundreds of volunteers working in a broad range of social services.[21]

From a naïve young woman who had once presumed (erroneously) that women had no right to enter city hall because they were not "citizens," Salomon emerged as an astute leader, rising within the ranks to become president of the Girls' and Women's Groups in 1899.[22] That same year she instituted a regular course of study for the volunteers that combined theoretical preparation with practical experience. With the help of influential mentors, Salomon furthered her own education at the Friedrich Wilhelm University, where she audited courses in economics and history, earning a doctorate in 1906 (against the wishes of the dean, who opposed female students).[23] Although Prussian universities remained legally closed to women until 1908, new attitudes toward women's education were beginning to take hold.[24] In this same period, women were also making gains, if slowly, in integrating municipal poor relief and other communal social services. (The case of female housing inspectors is examined later in the chapter.) Their activity prompted social reformers, both male and female, to urge better training for women as they assumed roles of greater public responsibility.[25] In response to these new possibilities and expectations, Salomon established the Social School for Women (Soziale Frauenschule) in 1908. The school was among the first in the nation to train social workers systematically, whether they intended to practice as volunteers or as paid professionals.

At the opening ceremonies, Salomon spoke of her desire to give young women "a modern education" that would enable them to engage concretely with contemporary life: "not useless knowledge (Luxuswissen), but instead an education that empowers them to serve humanity in some form, whether within the family or in a broader sphere."[26] While appealing to a woman's sense of duty and the ethical virtues of serving society, Salomon emphasized grounding action in objective knowledge of social problems, not sentiment. This was to be achieved through an intensive two-year curriculum that combined theoretical studies, in areas such as public health and family law, with practical work. Training in home economics and child pedagogy demonstrates that more traditional branches of women's work were not overlooked.[27]

Femininity was not to be discarded for scientific methodology but rather integrated into the pursuit of rationality and truth.

For the first few years, the Social School for Women rented classrooms and offices from the Pestalozzi-Fröbel-Haus, an institution for kindergarten teachers. These facilities soon proved inadequate, however, and in the summer of 1913, Salomon decided to build her own "house." The Pestalozzi-Fröbel-Haus, which owned most of a city block, granted her a thirty-year lease for one of its back lots.[28] Like the school itself, the new building was privately funded. In her autobiography, Salomon laughed at the ignorance and optimism she brought to the project. To finance construction, she donned her various "hats" as school principal, president of the Girls' and Women's Groups, and private individual and loaned money to and from herself, drawing up contracts that bore only her signatures (as both lender and borrower)—documents that she later learned had no legal value. Looking back at her funding strategies, she admitted, "No one except myself could understand this confusing hodgepodge of contracts." Fortunately, nobody tried, and the school building was completed within a year. Salomon confessed, "I had always disliked red tape and was convinced that institutions grow better and become stronger with a moving force behind them rather than a large endowment and a legal constitution. . . . If I had bothered about legal securities and waited for formal contracts, a move that would make the heart of every good civil servant rejoice, I should never have got the house."[29]

And the house she built was very much the one *she* wanted, according to Dora Peyser, Salomon's personal secretary and later biographer. The red brick structure, completed by September 1914, was exceptionally simple (Figure 5.4). Small window boxes and the stylized floral motifs of the windows on the ground floor, which echoed the garden they overlooked, formed the only ornament. Peyser thought the garden softened "the sobriety" of the building's "*sachlich* style"—an effect produced, one assumes, not only by its organic forms but also through its associations with femininity and domesticity.[30] Moreover, the garden enhanced the more intimate, human scale of the building, in comparison to the dwarfing effect of the Cecilienhaus. In the upper stories, large multipane windows flooded the spartan classrooms with light (Figure 5.5). The asymmetry of the bay window added a ripple of visual excitement to the otherwise flat façade without disturbing its pleasing regularity. With its glass-paneled doors and wall of windows directly above, the entrance permitted views of the interior as one approached, fostering a sense of transparency that contrasted sharply with the scopic regime of the Cecilienhaus (with its statuary that inspected visitors and its towering gallery that allowed administrators to look down on people). On the roof, a garden "with wisteria and crimson ramblers and real grass plots" encouraged students to reconnect with nature (Figure 5.6).[31]

Such rooftop gardens, then almost unknown in Berlin, would later become a common feature of modernist houses built in the Weimar era.

According to Peyser, Salomon incorporated (unspecified) features into the building that were inspired by her encounters with architecture abroad.[32] The most important influences, however, were clearly homegrown. In its *sachlich* sobriety, the school aligned itself with the design reform movement and its valorization of scientific and middle-class values as the basis for a new German culture. Both patron and architect contributed to this direction. Salomon's personal taste, class values, and feminist beliefs predisposed her toward a functional simplicity already evident in

FIGURE 5.4.
Façade of the Social
School for Women,
designed by Hans
Jessen, photograph
c. 1915. Alice-Salomon-
Archiv, Alice Salomon
Fachhochschule, Berlin.

FIGURE 5.5. The spartan, light-filled interior of a classroom at the Social School for Women, c. 1915. Alice-Salomon-Archiv, Alice Salomon Fachhochschule, Berlin.

FIGURE 5.6. The rooftop garden with members of the Social School for Women, 1932. Alice-Salomon-Archiv, Alice Salomon Fachhochschule, Berlin.

her female workers' clubs (Figure 5.7). Hans Jessen's architectural projects and membership in the German Werkbund expressed his commitment to reform principles.[33] By applying the movement's aesthetic concepts to her school building, Salomon signaled the institution's own middle-class reform impulses. The school's functional, but also "feminine," design promoted social work as a scientific endeavor to be undertaken by educated bourgeois women. The architecture's spare rectilinear geometry, measured proportions, and open expanses conveyed rationality, balance, and lightness, and its restrained decorative touches signified a sensible femininity. Ornament associated with the "irrational" aspects of female nature, particularly the love of luxury, was assiduously avoided. This building celebrated the rational mind of the New Woman and the disciplined energies she brought to social reform. As Peyser later wrote, the building was a "true expression of modern female culture."[34]

Although both claimed social work for women, Salomon and the Patriotic Women's Association publicized their ideological differences through their institutional architecture. Where the Cecilienhaus evoked castles and kings to defend aristocratic privilege, the Social School for Women wore its middle-class modernity on its sleeve. As these two projects reveal, women's struggle to establish a public presence in imperial Berlin played itself out not only against men but also among women. The political fractures that divided progressive and traditionally minded women also found expression in their architecture. At the same time, reformers looked to physical structures to heal social and spatial cleavages, as demonstrated by Salomon's *Arbeiterinnenheime*, an institution designed to bring bourgeois and working-class women together in the city's slums.

FIGURE 5.7.
Alice Salomon at work at the Social School for Women, c. 1915. Alice-Salomon-Archiv, Alice Salomon Fachhochschule, Berlin.

Salomon's pragmatic activism, evident in her aversion to red tape, bore the mark of the Girls' and Women's Groups' philosophy. Rejecting traditional church charity as well as the apparatus of modern bureaucracy, the groups understood social work as "practical politics" and "direct help from women to women."[35] One of Salomon's earliest projects applied this approach to the built environment, thereby launching a new form of urban space. In 1898, she and a small circle of friends began a social club for female factory workers, which they staffed with volunteers from the Girls' and Women's Groups. Their site was a modest apartment on Brückenstrasse in one of the city's manufacturing districts. Initially, the club was conceived as an *Abendheim*, a place to relax and meet others after work.[36] The clientele was mostly "very young girls" in search of "an ersatz parental home" and older single women who had little taste for dance halls.[37] Women who could claim only a *Schlafstelle* as home—often nothing more than a corner of someone else's apartment where they could bed down for the night, although sometimes not until 10 P.M.—could pass the evening hours in comfort and company (and not, pointedly, in pubs).[38] Services soon expanded to include an inexpensive lunch (the main meal of the day), educational courses, lectures, and evening entertainment. Demand for the midday meal increased sharply, and by 1906 up to two hundred lunches per day were served in the club's small dining room. A participant had no obligation to become a member (for a nominal monthly fee of fifteen pfennig), and all were encouraged to use the club's resources.[39] The success of this experiment prompted the opening of three more branches in 1903, 1906, and 1912 in an ever-widening arc through the city's industrial neighborhoods.[40] Those of 1906 and 1912 also offered lodging (to twenty-five and sixty women, respectively), which the founders intended to make a standard feature of all future clubs (Figures 5.8 and 5.9).[41] In addition to these facilities, a rural retreat was established in 1905 for female factory workers in need of fresh air, exercise, and hearty meals. (An annual club report boasted of the guests' weekly weight gains.)[42] By the First World War, the *Arbeiterinnenheime* had achieved a high public profile in Berlin and served as the model for similar initiatives.[43]

From Salomon's perspective, the clubs stood apart from other types of social organizations for Berlin's working poor. Social Democratic associations served as a gathering point for factory workers (male and female) but excluded people on a political basis. Moreover, the relaxed atmosphere of the *Arbeiterinnenheime*—women who entered were welcomed without queries about political or religious affiliation or about name—contrasted sharply with the stifling supervision and regimentation of charitable institutions, which the freedom-loving *Arbeiterin* avoided at all costs.[44] Salomon credited foreign influences with inspiring the creation of the clubs.

Members of the Girls' and Women's Groups, she recounted, had been deeply impressed by Arnold Toynbee's ideas of living among London's poor, and some had
personally experienced the English settlement movement initiated by his friends.[45]
Canon Samuel Barnett, the movement's founder, envisioned nonsectarian missions
of educated, genteel individuals elevating the lives of East London workers through
culture and friendship. Although Barnett recruited male students from Oxford and
Cambridge for his project, women soon began their own parallel settlements.[46]

To German audiences, Salomon presented the clubs as mutually beneficial: Factory workers were uplifted by the presence of cultured women, and the latter were
enriched through the experience of befriending and assisting their less fortunate sisters. "We must get to know one another through social work," Salomon wrote, "in
order to help others better their living conditions and to liberate ourselves from the
guilt of carefree indulgences." Friendship, not charity, would help heal class hatred
and bridge the gulf between the haves and the have-nots.[47] Socialist Lily Braun pro-
tested that the "object of these clubs was purely selfish; namely, to alienate the girls
from the labor movement by satisfying their needs and thus stave off the collapse of

FIGURE 5.8. Interior of the third *Arbeiterinnenheim*, which had just opened in 1906 (at Kottbuser
Ufer 33), with guests and "lady" volunteers. Alice-Salomon-Archiv, Alice Salomon
Fachhochschule, Berlin.

FIGURE 5.9. A resident's room in the third *Arbeiterinnenheim* (Kottbuser Ufer 33). The rent, including coffee, cost twelve Marks monthly. From Elsa Herzog, "Arbeiterinnenheime," *Die praktische Berlinerin*, no. 16 (1906): 282.

the capitalistic system." Discussing Braun's criticism decades later, Salomon admitted it had stirred doubts about social work as "a palliative, a compromise."[48]

Like the founders of the English settlements, Salomon and her friends chose to encounter working-class women in their own neighborhoods. As historian Martha Vicinus has noted, the missions of women in the English settlements resembled urban homes, whereas those of men recalled university college buildings—differences that reiterated, in architectural form, gendered ideologies of Victorian society that associated women with nurturing and domesticity and men with higher learning and public service.[49] In Berlin, the *Arbeiterinnenheime* similarly employed a domestic type, the apartment dwelling, to signal the creation of a public space that harnessed feminine values for the greater good. The press portrayed the club as a familial home for rootless migrant workers as well as a nurturing refuge after a long day of work.[50] Converting apartments into public space also made strategic sense, for it allowed the clubs to be located amid factories and tenement buildings. Moreover, the founders could not have afforded more luxurious facilities: Early fundraising attempts earned them only "objections and warnings." As a result of this demoralizing resistance, Salomon and her friends resolved to realize the project entirely from their own pockets. Salomon recalls poaching objects from her own house, over her mother's objections, to furnish the first club. Although donors emerged once the clubs became a success, the clubs owed their existence to the penny pinching and long hours of labor on the part of these determined young women.[51]

If wealthy Berliners initially expressed reservations about the venture, working-class women were no different. Visitors were slow to come, and early exchanges did not always conform to the founders' expectations:

> We had invited our younger sisters to one carefully prepared party in order to interest them in the work. The program was proceeding nicely when a textile worker, apparently a well-mannered girl, stunned us with the most vulgar catch-song I have ever heard. It was not quite so easy to teach "culture."[52]

By the time of the club's tenth anniversary in 1908, however, Salomon could pronounce the experiment a great success. The easy amiability she observed among "women and girls from such different circles" proved that friendship could surmount class barriers. The merit of the volunteers' "cultural work," sharing the benefit of their middle-class *Bildung* with others, was also confirmed by the fine performances, ranging from operetta to plays, staged by female factory workers. The workers' ability to rise from "vulgar" ditties to Offenbach and Goethe demonstrated "the great talent that lies within our people and that can be developed—although only through laborious, patient care."[53]

Yet if friendships had been sown across the chasm of class and lives on both sides had thereby been enriched, a divide still existed. When Salomon asserted that social work would bring women from different classes together, she did not specify where they would meet. The *Arbeiterinnenheime* occupied the territory of female workers but were organized and run by women from distant, elegant neighborhoods. Unlike settlers in London's slums, Salomon and her covolunteers returned to their own worlds at the end of the night. There was no reciprocal encroachment as rapprochement: Working-class women were not invited to join the ladies' clubs then forming in the genteel Tiergarten district. Vicinus argues that a colonizing mentality underlay the English settlement movement, particularly evident in its metaphors of "conquering territory" and civilizing "the natives."[54] Whether similar attitudes informed the *Arbeiterinnenheime* is difficult to say; the limited literature on hand does not contain overt references of this sort, although a patronizing tone does occasionally surface. Thus, Salomon claimed that the clubs' achievement lay foremost in convincing female workers "that women of our classes look after them, that they mean well by them, that they can trust us." In this way, she concluded, the clubs prepared the ground for other organizations by making poor women less suspicious of social intervention.[55]

Without doubt, the working women who frequented the clubs did so because they profited in some way. In her autobiography, written in a period of isolation and disillusionment in the United States, where the Nazis had forced her to flee in 1937, Salomon wondered whether that gain had been chiefly material.[56] Contemporary accounts, however, suggest broader advantages. In addition to satisfying basic needs for food and shelter, the clubs provided valued companionship, entertainment, and opportunities for self-improvement. Social events were so well attended, it became difficult to accommodate the number of guests. Instructional offerings, particularly courses on dressmaking and millinery, met with equal enthusiasm. Working women felt sufficiently engaged to attend the monthly members' meetings and voice their opinions on the club's program or to make suggestions about "new furnishings, excursions and other matters." Although workers were encouraged to assume more of the running of the clubs themselves in order to build self-reliance, management remained in the hands of middle-class volunteers. The hierarchy was evident even at member meetings, which were chaired by a "lady" from the board of directors while a worker oversaw the protocol.[57] Still, the workers' participation in decision making and their freedom of choice in the use of club resources (for example, whether to become a member or remain a casual visitor, participate in a lecture or simply chat with friends) distinguished the club from less democratic religious institutions.

Nonetheless, the role of agency in the conception of the *Arbeiterinnenheime* was far different from that in the *Frauenklubs* that bourgeois women created for themselves.

Whereas the latter were defined in terms of an expansive empowerment, the workers' clubs offered limited development. Both types of clubs appealed to the transformative power of *Frauengeselligkeit,* the good company of women. But the potential of such growth in community was determined by class status. No one expected a factory worker's attainment of "culture" to entitle her to the same role in public affairs that educated bourgeois women claimed for themselves. Nor did spatial horizons expand on equal terms. As Vicinus writes of the English settlements, "Charitable work gave women freedom to walk and move in areas that were previously forbidden."[58] In Berlin, reformers coaxed female workers off the streets and into safe, homelike clubs, even as the reformers themselves gained access to "dangerous" districts. It is difficult to imagine workers being comparably licensed to take and regulate space in their mentors' neighborhoods. Although Salomon's *Arbeiterinnenheime* were progressive relative to other such organizations, the workers' clubs were not envisioned as sites of agency on par with the *Frauenklubs.* The similarities and differences between the two types of clubs suggest the flexibility of the idea of *Frauengeselligkeit* while also revealing the ways in which class divided women.

The Campaign for Female Housing Inspectors

As women expressed the desire for more control over the built environment, the issue of authority was inevitably raised. Who would regulate urban space? Should women administer female domains? If so, what were they? The problem of policing urban space, particularly in relation to sexual activities, such as prostitution, vexed Wilhelmine Germans, whose cities—above all Berlin—exploded in population and size after national unification in 1871. Recent scholarship on these discourses has concentrated on the search for ordered streets.[59] Here, I turn the focus inward, to the control of "private" space. I examine efforts by the bourgeois women's movement to intervene in the regulation of what they considered a feminine realm: the homes of the urban poor. The *Wohnungsinspektorin* campaign, led by bourgeois feminists after the turn of the century, pressured government agencies to hire educated women as female housing inspectors. In staking their claim, women argued for the surveillance of women by women and of the working classes by the bourgeoisie.

A centralized system of housing inspection began to appear in Germany at the end of the nineteenth century, when some state governments, seeking to alleviate overcrowded housing conditions in urban areas, passed legislation mandating and regulating inspection of tenement dwellings. Hesse was the first to pass such laws in 1893, which became more common in the first decade of the twentieth century. Other states, including Prussia, declined to legislate housing inspection, leaving it instead to municipal initiative.[60] Below, I chronicle the *Wohnungsinspektorin* campaign at both the state and municipal levels, with special attention to the case of Charlottenburg, which instituted a bureau for housing inspection in 1910.

In England, which preceded Germany in instituting government housing inspection, women successfully lobbied for the hiring of "women sanitary inspectors," whose numbers among the staff of public health departments, although small, were growing by the turn of the century. A leaflet from 1902 that advocated hiring many more female housing inspectors described their function as primarily educational. On the basis of the duties already assigned to women in such roles, the pamphlet's authors envisioned female inspectors conducting house-to-house visits for the purpose of improving the standard of cleanliness in the homes of the urban poor. Change would be effected both through immediate action—women inspectors were told "to carry disinfectant powder and use it where required"—and by inculcating bourgeois notions of housekeeping and childcare. Among their prescribed duties, female inspectors were instructed to make note of everything from the dirtiness of the walls and floors to "the general mode of living, particularly with regard to personal and general cleanliness" of the occupants. Women were needed for this particular work because "in making such inspections it is the *woman* of the house with whom the inspector will come in contact, and on *her* cleanliness and intelligence depend the healthiness of the home and the well-being of the family."[61] The English campaign for female housing inspectors thus employed a twofold strategy: It exalted the female-to-female bond between inspector and inspected and emphasized the role of the housewife as both problem and solution.

As German states and municipalities developed housing inspection offices, German women, who had followed the progress of female inspectors in England, demanded they be hired for the new positions.[62] Hesse became the first state to put a woman on its payroll in 1908, hiring Dr. Else Conrad, a political economist, as housing inspector for the county of Worms.[63] By 1914, fifteen cities had salaried female housing inspectors, and another twenty-two recruited them as volunteers.[64] Advances did not come easily, however, and male resistance to female colleagues slowed appointments. In Mannheim, for example, volunteer positions created for women in housing offices remained vacant because the men in charge refused to fill them.[65] Between the turn of the century and the end of the imperial period, the women's press gave voice to a strong campaign for female inspectors, which subsided only temporarily in the first years of the war. The German debate on their necessity repeated some of the English arguments concerning the roles of gender and the housewife but was also shaped by a larger issue, namely, disagreement over the nature of housing inspection.

No one, however, doubted the pressing need for intervention. Deplorable housing conditions among Germany's urban poor aggravated human suffering: Between

1908 and 1910, infant mortality rates in Berlin's northern working-class district, where many families crowded into one- or two-room apartments, reached 42 percent (Figure 5.10).[66] More than a localized problem, slums appeared to breed tuberculosis and crime, social ills that threatened the entire city. The spread of disease was blamed on the unsanitary living conditions of worker tenements caused by structural deficiencies, such as a lack of indoor plumbing and windows, bad housekeeping due to the ignorance or laziness of the housewife, and overcrowding, which prevented the isolation of the sick and increased contagion. Along with germs, immorality seemed to fester in this unhealthy environment. The practice of subletting a bed for a night, usually to a male *Schlafgänger* (overnight lodger), particularly troubled reformers, who worried about the effect of the unwholesome presence of male strangers on adolescent girls. Finally, the misery of housing conditions was thought to drive men to the haven of taverns, resulting in alcoholism and gambling.

A 1911 handbook by the new Charlottenburg housing office detailed its plans for treating these social ills. The office limited housing inspection to the "smaller and

FIGURE 5.10. Heinrich Lichte, "Möckernstrasse 115," 1904. A family of eight, as well as a *Schlafgänger*, occupied this one-room apartment. The kitchen, shown here, was also used for sleeping. Bildarchiv Preussischer Kulturbesitz/Art Resource, New York.

smallest" of dwellings, encompassing one to three rooms, as well as to all homes that sublet to *Schlafgänger*. Commercial accommodations, including flophouses, also fell under its surveillance. Because of their larger size, middle- and upper-class residences were effectively excluded, although worker, servant, and apprentice quarters located in an employer's house were subject to inspection. This provision, which recognized the homes of wealthy families as potential contributors to the problem, distinguished the Charlottenburg office from those of other municipalities. For the most part, however, the Charlottenburg office focused its activities on the homes of the working poor. The handbook depicted regulation of this group as a benevolent form of encroachment: "Over and above the well-being of the individual, housing inspection serves the welfare of the state: general health conditions, especially of the urban population, will improve."[67]

Charlottenburg's authorities envisioned the ideal inspector as a paid male official (*Beamte*) who had graduated from a building trade school and possessed some training in hygiene. Additionally, he should be "a man with rich life experiences and moral maturity." Although a handful of women occupied (largely advisory) positions on housing councils, Charlottenburg declined to "experiment" with women inspectors until housing inspection had established itself.[68] In 1912, however, the housing office relented and hired Marie-Elisabeth Lüders, a social worker with a doctorate in political science (and later, one of Germany's first female parliamentarians). She was paid half the salary of male inspectors and given the most difficult cases—cases that her colleagues had dismissed as "hopeless." Her contemporary reports for the housing office reveal that she embraced the work and its challenges. In her later autobiography, however, she spoke candidly about the ineffectualness of housing inspection in the face of dire poverty and inequality. How could she prevent several people from sharing a bed, for example, if there was no money to buy more beds?[69]

An inspector's duties, as outlined in the handbook, encompassed a broadly defined field of intervention that stretched from the apartment walls to the occupant's body. The inspector employed his diagnostic skills to establish "deficiencies manifest either as unhealthy building conditions or as dwelling practices that endanger health or are morally suspect." If he identified such shortcomings, he "amiably" encouraged the tenant (or landlord) to take appropriate steps to eliminate the problem and, if that failed, turned to the police or courts to enforce compliance. On his structural checklist, the inspector noted humidity within the apartment, ventilation, light, insulation, exits (for basement apartments), ceiling height, floor covering, the condition of walls, coal oven construction, drinking water, the quality of gas piping, the availability and condition of toilets, and the removal of waste water. Concerning dwelling practices, he checked for adherence to zoning regulations, dirtiness (which necessitated peeking under furniture), dampness (for example, from hanging laundry to dry), unclean air due to a lack of airing or noxious sources (including unwashed occupants, who were directed to the public baths), poor housekeeping, intentional destruction of property by the tenant, insufficient garbage removal, overcrowding, insufficient sleeping space, "improper" room usage (no one should be sleeping in the kitchen), and the functional use of space (the vanity of a "for-show" salon was particularly discouraged). Housing inspection paid particular heed to sleeping conditions, which were considered the foundation of healthy and moral living. Beyond adequate space and fresh air, proper sleeping arrangements separated the sexes over fourteen years of age, preferably even earlier. The *Schlafgänger* was a pressing concern, in terms of both protecting the family and according the "sleeper" his or her rights (including a room with a door that locked).[70]

In creating their housing office, Charlottenburg authorities were influenced by and contributed to a national discourse that sought to define a new field of public intervention. Charlottenburg's program balanced two opposing viewpoints to emerge from these broader discussions, which I term the technical and the behavioral (or cultural). The first pursued a legal and technical solution: enforcing building bylaws in order to compel landlords to make structural improvements to their buildings, particularly with regard to sanitation. The second aimed at internal reform, focusing on improving living conditions by modifying the occupant's use of the apartment. Here, educating or "cultivating" the tenant held the key to success. These two approaches envisioned different roles for the housing inspector, with the question of gender forming a focal point of dissent.

Those who emphasized the importance of technical expertise in housing inspection tended to argue that women did not have the requisite skills for the job. In their view, housing inspection was best carried out by a *Bautechniker* or a *Baumeister*, a building technician or an architect (without a diploma). These were not college-trained professionals, who aspired to more prestigious jobs as government architects, but rather men who had been educated at a trade school. Throughout the imperial period, German women were strongly discouraged (and, for decades, legally prevented) from seeking a technical education. Prussia did not permit women to matriculate in college architectural programs until 1909, and the building trade schools, which fiercely opposed female students, took even longer to integrate.[71] The objection to women inspectors was thus founded, at least in part, on the assumption that they simply did not have the opportunity to acquire the necessary technical expertise.

Even after technical schools admitted women, however, this point of view continued to hold sway. Removing the legal barriers to women's education did not eliminate the deep-seated prejudice that held "technical" thinking to be foreign to the feminine mind. Otto Schulze, a Werkbund member and advocate of female inspectors, dismissed questions about their competence by pointing out that "female architects, building enthusiasts, and technical experts" already existed.[72] Lüders went a step further, suggesting that "a woman architect with social work practice and a knowledge of political economy would be the ideal" housing inspector.[73] Like her contemporaries, Lüders seemed to assume that a woman architect was naturally attuned to the domestic realm. Margarete Pochhammer expressed this view in her essay on Berlin's housing conditions for the guidebook *What a Woman Must Know about Berlin:* Where male architects had mishandled some of the basic needs of the housewife and domestic servant, women architects would complete the task of practical housing reform.[74]

Auguste Lange, one of Germany's most outspoken advocates of female housing inspectors and herself a housing inspector in Halle with a doctorate in political economy, countered the objection that women lacked technical expertise by arguing that the heart of the housing crisis lay outside the technical sphere. Specifically, she believed that many of the worst problems in worker tenements could be substantially alleviated, if not outright eliminated, by reforming the dwellers. Lange asserted that the housing question was foremost a cultural issue: Rather than blame buildings for debasing their occupants, she argued that it was people who must be elevated in order to learn how to appreciate and use a good dwelling. "Human reform and housing reform must go hand in hand—or better yet, the first should precede the latter."[75]

From this perspective, the inspector's ability to educate the tenant was more important than technical proficiency: "What use is cross-ventilation if the windows remain shut and a 'draft' is regarded first and foremost as dangerous?" Lange did not deny the need for physical improvements but refused to see them as the whole solution. She also warned against the dangers of overzealous interventions. Making substantial improvements to older tenement buildings required wholesale renovations. If the landlord passed these costs on to tenants, the higher rents would force the eviction of the very people the inspector claimed to help. And smaller technical problems that were easily remedied, such as a defective oven or a loose step, hardly required a diploma to identify. In Lange's opinion, the technical dimension of housing inspection had been vastly overrated.[76]

Even in those rare cases in which Lange was willing to cede "the technical, external, even manly side" of inspection to a *Techniker,* or male technician—whose input she disparaged as "a brief stride across the apartment"—she insisted on the indispensable collaboration of the female inspector: "To her must and will remain the warmer, living concerns, the actual care of the dwelling, the feminine, the educational side."[77] The distinction between *Wohnungsinspektion* and *Wohnungspflege,* inspection and care, was a common theme among supporters of female housing inspectors. Some even argued for a division of housing duties along gender lines: *Wohnungsin-spektoren* (male housing inspectors) would perform the technical aspects of the job, and *Wohnungspflegerinnen* (female housing caretakers) would tend to the inhabitants.[78] In this arrangement, inspection rendered the diagnosis, and care provided the cure: "Where inspection stops, care begins; where the man stops, the woman begins."[79] The proposed separation of functions mirrored "natural" gender roles in broader society, whereby men took care of technical and external matters, and women, as caretakers, tended to the personal and internal. While such distinctions often served as an argument to keep women out of public affairs, here they could be used to women's advantage: "People always reproach us women for feeling and doing things too personally to be good civil servants. But isn't this precisely the quality that helps us think innovatively about social work and that will enable us to find new ways and means to alleviate housing needs?"[80]

Efforts to claim housing inspection as a feminine prerogative repeated some of the arguments made by English women. Lange pointed out that the housing inspec-tor most often encountered the wife on his rounds. By the very nature of his mas-culine persona, he appeared to her as an arm of the law, "a policeman and housing warden."[81] Striking fear in the heart of the housewife, from Lange's perspective, undermined the pedagogical goals of housing inspection. A reporter for the family magazine *Daheim* similarly warned against a punitive approach. Instead of an enforcer, "people must see in the inspector's personality a helper and adviser, a friend."[82] But this amicable tone, Lange asserted, was far more difficult for a man to establish than a woman. Alone in her apartment with a male inspector, a housewife would undoubtedly misinterpret such efforts as sexual advances.[83]

Stymied in his efforts to establish bonds of trust, the argument continued, the inspector struggled ineffectually to observe and modify the inhabitants' behavior. As Lange implied in the following description, effective inspection demanded the intimate exposure of life within the home: "The housing question is to a large extent a question of correct usage and treatment of the dwelling, a question of per-sonal hygiene, cleanliness, health maintenance, budgeting one's means (alcohol!), bringing up the children." Lange, like other advocates of female inspectors, mocked the idea of a male official discussing bodies and babies with a housewife: "Negoti-ating all of these questions with a woman is a woman's business."[84] As a skillful negotiator of this realm, the female inspector was expected to possess appropriate expertise in all matters domestic, beyond her natural ability to communicate with other women. In her capacity as teacher, she was to act as a role model and not "confuse those to be educated with sermons and dead theory, but rather to persuade by active example."[85]

Housing officials in Bavaria thereby recommended hiring female inspectors with hands-on experience. In particular, they suggested recruiting housewives and mothers who had managed a household and raised children; nurses; and health workers in the fields of maternal, infant, and tuberculosis care.[86] Ideally, the female housing inspector—here described in a 1908 article—combined all these roles:

> A woman effortlessly discovers an apartment's deficiencies and can give advice on cleanliness, airing of the rooms, infant care, and bringing up adolescents, for whom poor housing conditions present a special moral danger. In cases of illness she can provide counsel and active service. . . . She can help effectively in the battle against alcohol and tuberculosis, the two worst enemies of the national body.[87]

In actual practice, female hiring patterns in housing inspection favored single professional women with advanced academic degrees. Despite advocates and experts promoting a woman's special expertise in domestic affairs, academic credentials carried greater weight in securing those coveted positions, a point I return to below.

A journalist who wrote extensively on women and careers, Käthe Schrey, added the keen female gaze to the list of inherent advantages the female inspector brought to her work: "The oft-praised female eye for details benefits housing inspection."[88] Lange argued that the female inspector's gaze was more penetrating than the male's: She "manages to go there, where people very rarely let themselves be seen; she sees into every nook and cranny and is, therefore, in a position to see people as they really are."[89] Through the gaze, Lange evoked the female inspector's psychic access to this realm and her ability to unlock its secrets.

Having uncovered the dirty truth, the female inspector was poised to cultivate proper bourgeois values. Serving as a moral compass, "she awakened in [the housewives] a sense of the great ethical significance of a good, bright, and airy apartment as well as for order and cleanliness, and made them realize the consequences of a woman's housekeeping competence for family life as a whole."[90] Drawing on her own bourgeois thriftiness, the inspector taught the housewife how to stretch the family's meager income so as to avoid the morally dangerous practice of subletting to strangers.[91] A good dose of "feminine practicality" also helped in making do with less. Anticipating Lange's pessimism about relying on physical improvements, housewife advocate Martha Voss-Zietz wrote: "It is easy to declare an apartment unlivable, but it is very difficult to produce a good replacement instantly in cities, above all Berlin, as well as in mid- and small-sized towns. Woman's practical sense often helps wonderfully to make such objectionable apartments reasonably livable again."[92]

The "feminine" pragmatism advanced by Voss-Zietz and others could be criticized for inadvertently undermining the larger goals of housing reform. Making miserable tenement dwellings tolerable potentially defused the pressure to improve the housing stock and ultimately prolonged the housing crisis. Conversely, one could argue that their position was a more realistic one. While maintaining the desirability of long-term structural change, they rejected an instant technical solution as unlikely, looking instead to the material at hand to improvise a more immediate, if admittedly less profound, respite from suffering.

The case thus having been made that women were right for the job, the question remained as to their might. By what means would a female housing inspector persuade a housewife to listen to her? There were hints that some did not: Marie Kröhne, housing inspector for the county of Worms, mentioned women who considered themselves "too smart" for advice.[93] Female inspectors' self-declared preference for guidance over enforcement presumed that they would not seek to win converts through coercion. In his book on housing policy in Essen, political scientist Erich Enke argued that the female inspector was undermined and perhaps endangered by her gender because

in many circles of the lower classes, a woman is mostly regarded as a creature of her sex. A female official would have to struggle with completely unforeseeable difficulties. As much as I am sympathetic to developing new careers for the female sex, I would like to see the field of housing inspection, as far as it concerns activities outside the office, reserved for men. The fact that a woman is a woman does not help her. And precisely in industrial cities with their motley collection of people . . . I hold women's participation to be completely out of the question. In the interest of their reputation and dignity, I would not like to see positions in housing inspection wasted on women.[94]

Enke thus sidestepped the issue of women's special abilities for the work by focusing on the gender politics of public space. Supporters of female inspectors recognized potential difficulties in dealing with "motley" groups but argued that a woman was marked by more than her gender in such encounters. Specifically, she bore other badges of authority earned on the basis of her class, education, and professional status.

A female inspector's social status constituted a powerful source of authority. Female housing inspectors, culled from the educated middle classes, almost always carried out their inspections in poor working-class neighborhoods. Except in the case of Charlottenburg, which also investigated servants' quarters, one could usually assume that the inspector's clients possessed a lower social background than her own. In executing her work, the inspector claimed her right as a member of an entitled class to intrude in the lives of the poor. Needless to say, a working-class woman

would never be granted the right to poke and pry in the house of her social supe-
riors. Calling the female inspector a friend or a co-sister of the housewife did not
erase class differences. Nor did sharing "feminine" interests and concerns imply
equality: No one considered the possibility, for example, that an inspector would
take advice from her client. Their relationship was clearly one of patronage. Among
other comments made by inspectors, Lange's dismay at the lack of toothbrushes
among poor families and the "hair-raising ignorance of women about the simplest
things" suggests the patronizing tone of such encounters.[95]

Education represented another means for a woman to acquire authority. Conrad,
who earned her doctorate before being hired as an inspector, remarked, "The practical value of the doctor title is not to be underestimated. There is no doubt that
the title considerably enhances [the female inspector's] influence on the people
and gives emphasis to her orders and suggestions."[96] Kröhne, Conrad's colleague,
insisted on a doctorate in political economy or a degree in law.[97] Other commentators preferred training in social work, and, in the discourse on female housing inspectors, an undercurrent of competition emerges between those claiming it as a
field for university-trained women, particularly the political economists, and those
who envisioned it as a field for women trained in the social work schools.[98] Which-
ever academic path an inspector followed, education validated her housewifery skills,
making her advice to "the often quite distrustful and stubborn working-class woman"
presumably more persuasive and, because it was coming from a so-called expert, also
more palatable.[99]

Ideally, the inspector's authority also derived from her position as a government
official (*Beamtin*). Many female inspectors, however, could not claim this status.
Their actual employment was perhaps the most contentious demand in the campaign for female housing inspectors. Even as municipal authorities warmed to the
idea of women's participation, they were reluctant to put them on their payroll.
Rather, the majority of women who engaged in housing inspection did so as volunteers. Drawing on the experience in Worms, Conrad warned that women must
be hired on equal terms with men. Without official backing, female volunteers in
Worms suffered "such unpleasant experiences in performing housing inspection,
that gradually all but one of them withdrew."[100] Advocates of female housing inspectors thus lobbied for full bureaucratic support.[101] In so doing, they denied
that the authority of the *Beamtin* would suggest to the working-class housewife the
negative aspects of the male official, "in whom the policeman will all too readily
be seen."[102] In their eyes, the *Beamtin*'s femininity tempered her official persona:
"A woman always finds her way to another woman, and so she achieves in milder
form much more, even in her capacity as an official, than a 'Herr Beamter' ever
could."[103] At the same time, her official status qualified her gender—a viewpoint

that challenged Enke's assertion that a woman was first and foremost marked by her sex. Lange argued that no discomfort occurred when a female inspector found herself alone in an apartment with a man. In such cases, the man understood that the office took precedence over the bearer and her sex.[104]

Authority was not simply an issue between inspector and client. Female inspectors were equally concerned about their status vis-à-vis male colleagues. An academic education, and preferably a *Doktor* title, represented an important advantage. Conrad believed that a woman entering a government agency without an academic education would run a high risk of being regarded as less than fully official. "It will greatly ease her position if she has training comparable to that of her educated male coworkers. Similarly, this gives her more authority over subordinate officials (building technicians and so forth), on whose advice she often relies."[105] These factors and the desire to expand professional opportunities for female academics compelled some advocates of female housing inspectors to argue for highly educated women as the best candidates for the job, a position that drew criticism from men in the field. At a time when the housing inspector's training and credentials were under debate, academically trained women threatened less-educated men.

The issue came to a head at the 1913 Conference for Housing Supervision and Care in Charlottenburg. In her speech, Lange boldly argued for hiring female political economists to run housing inspection offices.[106] The heated discussion that followed produced no consensus on issues of women's status and pay.[107] Some male respondents derided such demands as "egoism, ambition, and pure suffragism."[108] Lamenting the uproar, a writer for the feminist journal *Die Frau* commented on the paradoxical male reaction to women entering new professional fields: Demands for appropriate pay were labeled "tremendously arrogant," yet accepting lower wages was deemed a threat to (male) salaries.[109]

Questions about the professional scope of the female inspector proved equally contentious. Reflecting on the outcome of the gathering, Kröhne remarked, "As much as the conference strongly recognized the care of the dwelling as particularly feminine and almost universally supported men consulting women, one nonetheless sensed that a woman would be welcome in housing reform only as long as she confined herself to teaching and advising the housewife, tending to the family's health and morality, practical care, and detail work." Kröhne defended a greater role for female inspectors and warned against splitting housing inspection into male supervision (*Aufsicht*) and female caretaking (*Pflege*).[110] She even envisioned a participatory role for female inspectors in planning new building.[111]

Even within the more limited *Pflege* category, female inspectors defined their intervention in the broadest terms. Conrad portrayed the housing inspector as a social agency unto herself: "Noticing the dubious cough of a woman, she advises her to be examined at a tuberculosis clinic; noting a youth roaming about aimlessly, she persuades his parents to direct him toward a trade or at least a training course; if a mother complains about her miserable child, she tries to interest the community doctor in sending the girl or boy to a fresh-air camp; if a man is unemployed, she gives him the name of an employment office or perhaps approaches the authorities on his behalf."[112] In her own work, Kröhne attempted "to make housing inspection a kind of center for social welfare in the county."[113] Other advocates reiterated this image of the female housing inspector as a mediator and unifier of social welfare services.[114]

In pursuing housing reform from the point of view of the social worker instead of the building technician, some female inspectors raised issues rarely addressed by their male counterparts, such as the abuse of children and women. Lange described seeing children "with open wounds all over their bodies from floggings" and women who were "convinced that beatings from their husbands were prescribed by the emperor." Lange's conception of the housing problem thus extended to all human misery contained within four walls:

> Do not say that all of this no longer has anything to do with the dwelling—be it only that housing inspection offers an opportunity to approach people. But precisely, we must come nearer to the people if we want to improve something. Of all things, we have forgotten people, and that must change! Let us help fight the boundless ignorance of the populace, which lectures and public reading halls outside the home do not adequately overcome. Let us make people more demanding, more enlightened, let us awaken their needs. Then housing conditions will also change.[115]

Lange's emphasis on *Menschenreform*, which elsewhere seems ideologically conservative, reveals here a certain radical potential. It suggests that people were not simply subservient to their environment but could act on it. In other words, living differently could change the world. Consciously desiring, knowing, and needing were the first steps to bringing about reform. While the bourgeois female inspector played a critical role as instigator, Lange recognized that people themselves must remake their world. In the importance placed here on consciousness raising as a means of acquiring agency over the built environment, one could argue that the political economist struggling to make a place for herself in the city and the female factory worker seeking a dignified home for her family were not so distant from one another.

EPILOGUE

What a Woman Must Know about Berlin,
Twenty Years Later

IN 1932, A SECOND EDITION OF *What a Woman Must Know about Berlin* went on sale in the German capital. Fully revised but faithful to the format of the 1913 edition, the guidebook once again explored the city from the point of view of the New Woman. By 1932, however, both the city and the New Woman had changed dramatically from the prewar period. The collapse of global markets devastated an already weak German economy, and from 1928 to 1932 unemployment in Berlin soared from 133,000 to 600,000. In addition to joblessness, political chaos confronted city residents, as communist and Nazi paramilitary forces battled for control of the streets.[1] The general outlook in 1932 was unavoidably, desperately grim and profoundly shaped the tone of the women's guidebook. Whereas in 1913 women faced formidable legal and social hurdles in their quest for meaningful lives, the barriers in 1932 seemed, in some instances, even greater, as women, along with men, struggled simply to exist.

The intervening years, by contrast, had been full of promise. The establishment of a politically progressive republic in 1919, following four years of war and a bloody revolution, augured well for women. In an effort to eradicate prejudices and hierarchies entrenched under monarchical rulers, the Weimar Constitution guaranteed all citizens equal rights. Women acquired full access to schools and employment, which, along with the vote, placed them, at least theoretically, on an equal footing with men. The state appeared to sanction the New Woman, and over the next decade government and industry invested considerable resources to meet her needs and desires as a worker and a consumer. With her bobbed hair, athletic body, and social and economic freedoms, the New Woman dominated the mass media as the symbol of the Weimar Republic's radical modernity.

Despite these advances, a large discrepancy emerged between legal rights awarded in principle and their attainment in practice. Women discovered that other barriers, often less tangible and therefore more difficult to overcome, replaced the legal ones that kept them from competing fairly with men. At the Bauhaus, for example, the embrace of the new republic's egalitarian goals, glorified in the school's inaugural program of 1919, proved less than comprehensive. Director Walter Gropius reacted to the influx of female students by covertly raising the admission standards for women, despite the illegality of such a measure, and by refusing to admit them to programs other than weaving, regardless of their academic intentions or talents. His fear that a sizable female presence would threaten the school's academic integrity and reputation found echoes in the architectural profession, among others, which continued to question the ability of women to function in "masculine" fields.[2] By 1932, the economic crisis strongly compounded such forms of social discrimination. Discussions of career opportunities for women explored in the revised version of *What a Woman Must Know about Berlin* sometimes verged on hopelessness, as contributors acknowledged the dearth of job openings due to layoffs, rationalization, and continued bias toward hiring men. Alice Salomon's optimistic outlook on the professional prospects for academically trained women expressed in the 1913 guidebook completely vanished in her revised essay for the second edition, in which she discouraged women from pursuing university study altogether.[3]

Attesting to women's diminished expectations vis-à-vis the public sphere, the 1932 guidebook placed a greater emphasis on domesticity, echoing broader social and economic trends. Despite the constitution's declaration of sexual equality, efforts to reestablish traditional gender roles began immediately after the war and continued throughout the Weimar period. Demobilization, which returned six million soldiers to the workforce, created enormous tensions between men who wanted women's jobs and women who were determined to keep them. As historian Claudia Koonz recounts, "Trade unions, best-selling authors, politicians, government ministers, and industrialists (who could not agree on policy in any other area), cooperated to expel the women they had lured into 'men's work.'"[4] Disunity, indifference, and the marginalization of radical voices hindered women's ability to resist their forced repatriation to the domestic sphere. Conservative women's groups, some of which actively promoted an antifeminist agenda, gained the upper hand in the bourgeois women's movement, which after the war was severely weakened by the struggle to find a raison d'être, internal political struggles, empty coffers, and a lack of interest among younger women.[5] The National Federation of German Housewives' Associations (Reichsverband Deutscher Hausfrauenvereine, RDH), formed during wartime to distribute food and rally support for the war among German women, emerged after the revolution as a powerful advocate for women's "place" in the home.[6] Frustrated by the half-fulfilled promises of the constitution and exhausted by their double burdens as housewives and wage workers, many German women by the early 1930s yearned for the security and comfort of traditional domestic life as it was idealized by conservative politicians.[7] Changes to the 1932 Berlin guidebook captured this turn inward and toward the political right. In the place of a chapter in the 1913 edition that had explored women's organizations across the political spectrum, from conservative Christians to socialist suffragettes, the 1932 version substituted an essay on the increasingly right-wing RDH, written by its president.[8] It was followed by a chapter titled "What Must the Housewife Know about Berlin?" a topic not included in 1913. The essay's author, the politically conservative housewife advocate Charlotte Mühsam-Werther, discussed the Central Office of the Housewives' Associations of Greater Berlin (Zentrale der Hausfrauenvereine Gross-Berlin) and its institutions, such as the popular Heibaudi (Hauswirtschaftlicher Einkaufsberatungs- und Auskunftsdienst), on Potsdamer Strasse, a showroom filled with kitchen displays, furnishings, and textiles where Berlin housewives could test out appliances and consult experts before making purchases.[9] In a chapter on the professionalization of housework, an aging Hedwig Heyl glorified the return to traditional female strengths, claiming that as other "women's professions" stagnated in the Depression, the professional housewife could emerge triumphant and save the German people in their hour of need.[10] Taken together, these chapters encouraged a shift in women's relationship to the city, emphasizing urban life viewed from the traditional perspective of the marital home.

The movement to place housework on a rational and scientific basis, begun in the imperial period, gained the support of state agencies during the 1920s under pressure from housewives' organizations and as part of a broad campaign to persuade women to return to the hearth. Through the elimination of drudgery and the conferment of professional status on housework, proponents of redomestication hoped to convince women to embrace the home as their workplace. The construction of over two million new dwellings in Germany between 1920 and 1932 provided an opportunity for professional housewives and architects to collaborate on the rationalization of the home, creating hygienic, modernist spaces for the housewife's labors.[11] Housewives' representatives also occupied important positions in government bureaus, such as the Federal Research Agency (Reichsforschungsgesellschaft, RFG), which exhaustively studied all aspects of efficient domestic design, from building materials to the movements of the housewife's body. Such efforts owed a heavy debt to Christine Frederick, a leading figure in the prewar home economics movement in the United States, who applied the scientific management techniques developed for American industry by the engineer Frederick Taylor to domestic labor. American ideas on rationalization found an eager audience in economically devastated postwar Germany, where efficiency gurus such as Henry Ford acquired an almost godlike status. Publications, conferences, and exhibitions popularized the ideas and designs of rationalized housekeeping and encouraged all women, even those who could not afford the new technologies, to think of themselves as domestic managers.[12]

No project better exemplifies the impact of the New Housekeeping on modernist design than the "scientific" kitchen created by Grete Lihotzky in 1927 for the Frankfurt am Main housing developments (Figure E.1). Ernst May, the powerful director of municipal construction, assembled a staff of progressive architects to produce low-cost dwellings that provided a maximum of comfort within a minimum of space. Lihotzky, the only woman architect on May's design team, was asked to create a fully rationalized kitchen. Based on commercial models, such as ship and train galleys, Lihotzky's tiny kitchen represented the ultimate meal-making machine, calculated with mathematical precision to streamline operations and reduce them to the smallest possible space. As Susan Henderson has argued, Lihotzky transformed the traditional German *Wohnküche*, or "living kitchen," a multiuse family space that encompassed not only housework activities but also social interaction, into a spatially isolated niche for a single cook. A sliding door sealed the niche from the rest of the dwelling, further rendering the housewife's labor invisible to the home's other occupants, whose relaxation remained undisturbed by clanging pots and cooking odors. Although Lihotzky's design generated much attention and praise, some critics expressed concern about its rigidity and the inability for two people to work together. In their eyes, the housewife paid for her new professionalism with a loss of creativity and segregation.[13]

The processes involved in manufacturing the Frankfurt Kitchen—from the ergonomic analyses of movement and space conducted by Lihotzky, through the mass-production of prefabricated parts, to the delivery of factory-assembled modules to the construction site and their installation by crane into ten thousand dwellings in Frankfurt[14]—point to the enormous differences between experimental design created for women in the imperial and Weimar periods. Without state support, female patrons and architects in the Wilhelmine era worked on a much smaller scale, which allowed them to create designs attentive to difference. Indeed, and as demonstrated by the built projects discussed in previous chapters, difference (as defined by gender, class, age, and profession) stood at the center of the conception of the New Woman and her architecture. Far more eclectic, this architecture supported the expression and fulfillment of individual desires in the search for a room of one's own. Cast as a misfit by the broader society, the New Woman in imperial Berlin seized the possibilities of nonconformity when she built, inventing forms that catered specifically to her needs. By contrast, the quest for typologies and standards (as tools of a broader policy of redomestication) drove the architecture for the New Woman in the 1920s. She was studied exhaustively by scientists, architects, and professional housewives, and the common denominator that emerged, the generically modern

FIGURE E.1. Grete Lihotzky's rationalized kitchen for the Frankfurt am Main housing settlements, 1927. University of Applied Arts Vienna; copyright by Dorothea Stransky.

housewife, represented an abstraction. Rather than express the New Woman's modernity as an individual, the New Architecture symbolized her function as a highly efficient cog in a larger social and economic system geared to maintaining the gendered status quo. While purporting to create design that empowered women, mass-produced modernist architecture of the 1920s standardized gender roles along with its prefabricated concrete panels, eliding the needs of the female individual and those of the state. The aesthetic modernity of such projects often disguises their reactionary potential. This emerges all the more clearly in comparison to modernist houses produced by and for individual women interested in exploring the new in a more nuanced relation to the female self, such as the Rietveld-Schröder house (1923–24) or Eileen Gray's E.1027 (1926–29).[15] From the perspective of challenging gender norms, the architecture of the New Woman in Wilhelmine Berlin proved to be far more radical than the mass-produced housing of the Weimar Republic.

Few of the modernist building projects of the 1920s addressed unmarried men and women, despite the continuing need for such housing in the Weimar period. Housing chapters in *What a Woman Must Know about Berlin* suggest that the range of alternatives for single women decreased from 1913 to 1932. In her 1913 essay on Berlin's housing conditions, journalist Margarete Pochhammer surveyed the limited but growing options available to single women, from privately run homes for "ladies" to the rise of self-help ventures such as the Women's Apartment Cooperative Limited and the Haus in der Sonne. Maria Hessberger, former president of the Berlin branch of the League of Catholic German Women (Katholischer Deutscher Frauenbund Berlin), wrote the comparable chapter on housing for the 1932 edition. Denying the existence of earlier precedents, she noted the appearance of a new "dwelling type," "the bachelor and bachelorette home," revealing once again the typological emphasis of Weimar architecture. Hessberger further limited her discussion of residences for single women in Berlin to the modernist apartment building for single career women constructed in 1931 by the Catholic league. Thoroughly rationalized, the 190-unit residence applied the lessons of minimalist living to the spaces of single women, offering tiny but technologically advanced self-enclosed dwellings.[16] This narrow focus reflects in part the author's interest in promoting both the New Architecture and the league's work. At the same time, it also speaks to the disappearance of many of the small-scale housing experiments created and funded by single women in the prewar period.

How might we account for such losses in an era that seemed, at least on paper, to offer women more, not fewer, possibilities? Economic circumstances are part of the story. The hyperinflation of 1923 eradicated the financial capital of the German middle class, devastating women's ability to act as architectural patrons. Women's associations struggled to survive the crisis with depleted treasuries and members unable to pay their dues. Many older women who occupied leadership positions in these organizations lost their financial independence as the value of their pensions and annuities plummeted. Focused on feeding themselves, they had little to spare in terms of time, energy, or resources for other projects.[17] More broadly, hyperinflation and political tensions after the revolution splintered the social alliances and financial networks that women activists depended on to achieve their goals.[18] Building initiatives suspended during wartime as a result of the reorientation of women's activities and the lack of construction materials, and then once again during the economic chaos that followed peace, rarely regained their momentum after the German economy stabilized. Among the architectural casualties was a private hospital for female patients to be run entirely by female doctors, an idea initiated in 1908 by the Berlin surgeon Agnes Hacker along with one of the city's first female physicians, Franziska Tiburtius. Eliza Ichenhaeuser, the editor of the first guidebook, chaired a committee at the Lyceum Club to promote and fundraise for the project. Although by 1913, its supporters had raised sufficient capital to negotiate a location with municipal authorities and to ask Emilie Winkelmann to draw up plans, war and inflation set back the project, and by the time of the 1932 guidebook, it had yet to be completed.[19] In a few instances, architectural projects planned before the war found fruition after economic stabilization, especially where the need continued to be pressing: The Haus in der Sonne, confronting a tidal wave of female retirement in the 1920s, added a second residence to its site in Potsdam in 1927; and in 1928, female university students obtained a long-awaited day home, the Helene-Lange-Heim, where they could rest between classes and meet their friends (Figure E.2).[20] More commonly, prewar institutions struggled to adapt to changed circumstances. The Lyceum Club continued to operate in its Lützowplatz clubhouse, but membership declined from the prewar years as a result of the club's failure to entice younger women. This lack of interest compelled the closure of several other women's clubs by 1930, including the German Women's Club, which was the first to have opened in Berlin, in 1898.[21]

Economic pressure alone, however, cannot account for the declining support for communal, women-centered spaces in postwar Berlin. In the transition between the two eras, a profound generational shift occurred, redefining how women imagined their urban identities. Berlin in the Weimar years was identified in the popular imagination more than ever with female modernity, but the idea of *the city as woman* differed vastly from the notion of *a women's city*, which had found architectural expression in the imperial period.[22] Despite their nearly identical structure and chapter topics, the two guidebooks reveal a profoundly different relationship between Berlin's female residents and their city. One looks in vain in the 1932 edition for the conception of a women's Berlin articulated in the prewar era. Gone is the emphasis on an urban female community that expressed its modernity in women's social clubs, political organizations, housing cooperatives, and so forth. The strong female "we" that enabled women to establish a gendered presence in an often hostile urban environment once again reverted to a singular "I." In the pages of the 1913 guide-book, the New Woman rallied publicly with others to block laws that violated her body; in 1932, she visited Heibaudi for expert shopping advice on the latest kitchen appliance. This shift from civic activism to consumerism is mirrored in the women's exhibitions discussed in the two guidebooks. The spirit of Die Frau in Haus und Beruf, which displayed a self-sufficient women's cosmos in the heart of Berlin for four weeks in 1912, permeated the pages of the 1913 edition. By contrast, readers of the 1932 guidebook were encouraged to visit commercial exhibitions with titles such as the Culture of Bridge, Country House and Garden, and Chintz.[23] Older femi-nists who had dedicated their lives to building female solidarity in conceptual and material terms felt abandoned by a "selfish" younger generation, who in turn com-plained that these aging activists were hopelessly out of touch.[24] Young women in Berlin no longer needed a supportive community to realize their ambitions of a modern life, which they defined in terms of individual freedoms and pleasures.

FIGURE E.2. Women in the Helene-Lange-Heim gazing at the Berliner Dom, c. 1929. The day home for female university students was located in the apothecary wing of the Royal Palace on Unter den Linden. From *1 Jahr Studentinnen-Tagesheim (Helene-Lange-Heim), 1928–1929* (Berlin: Studentenwerk, c. 1930), 16.

Being a modern woman, as popularly imagined, meant bobbed hair, short dresses, and a night at the movies, not fundraising for a home for retired career girls.[25] Although most women did not interpret the constitution's promise of sexual equality to mean they were the same as men, they increasingly viewed their experience of modernity as one that united them with, rather than distinguished them from, men.[26] Tellingly, the 1932 guidebook included a few male authors in its roster of experts; the above-cited recommendation to visit exhibitions on chintz and bridge, which the author insisted "must be of particular interest to every woman," appeared in a chapter on contemporary domestic culture written by a man.[27] In the imperial period, women perceived their urban modernity to be defined by and crucially tied to other women, to being part of a larger female collective in the metropolis. As this understanding frayed, so, too, did the vision of a women's Berlin. The pursuit of an affirmative urban experience that necessitated separate female spaces in the city was ultimately undermined in the 1920s by a different notion of self and modernity.

In "The Art of Being Prominent in Berlin," a new chapter in the 1932 edition, Renate Müller, the popular film actress best known for her role in *Viktor und Viktoria* (1933), wrote of the "uncanny" attraction of the metropolis for a girl seeking fame as an actress.[28] Müller, like contributors to the earlier guidebook, treated Berlin as a stage to enact a modern female self, which more than ever necessitated a highly visible presence. One must be glimpsed in nightclubs, written up in gossip columns, photographed, and set fashion trends. But a spotlight shines only on one, and the desire, voiced by Müller, to be a "star" in the metropolis betrays the hegemony of seeing other people as masses over the older ideal of a female collective. Müller counterposed her aspiring starlet to *das Publikum* (the public), a binary opposition that construed urban modernity as either a singular or a mass experience: One either rose above the crowd or melted into it. Müller did not pretend that becoming a Berlin celebrity would be easy: A woman would find herself, the author cautioned, one of many pursuing this dream. Being one of many suggested, in this instance, futility at worst, a challenge at best: how to rise above these other women? In the 1913 guidebook, by contrast, being one of many was not a reason for discouragement or competition but rather a source of indissoluble strength.

Why reissue the guidebook in 1932? Unlike the original edition, which included an introduction by Ichenhaeuser explaining the aims of the book, the 1932 version lacked an overview or an accounting of its purposes. Clearly, the information from 1913 was outdated and no longer conformed to the image that many women held of the German metropolis or themselves. Perhaps the upcoming twentieth anniversary of the book's publication stimulated the desire to rethink the relationship between women and the city. Reflecting on this period with the benefit of hindsight, one might also imagine that women attempted to hold on to something they sensed was about to be lost. Despite the sometimes bleak portrayal of urban life in these pages, however, the 1932 guidebook as a whole does not suggest an incipient awareness of doom. Women confronted renewed hardships, and many possibilities that had blossomed in the prewar period had failed to come to fruition. Nonetheless, the city remained a focus for the exploration and realization of a modern female self. Women had established their presence in Berlin, and the 1932 guidebook made clear that they planned to stay.

NOTES

INTRODUCTION

1. In recent years, feminist scholars in Berlin have begun to link women's histories to urban topography through walking guidebooks. Particular individuals, events, and organizations are associated with landmarks such as a building or marketplace. Although these accounts do not provide a framework for analyzing women's physical interventions in the built environment (most of the sites included were neither commissioned nor designed by women), they emphasize more broadly the importance of incorporating women's stories into a sense of place. See Gélieu, *Frauengeschichte entdecken in Berlin;* Carstens, Höver, Ow, Stange, and Wolters, eds., *Frauen an der Spree;* Carstens and Luikenga, eds., *Immer den Frauen nach!*

2. Ichenhaeuser, ed., *Was die Frau von Berlin wissen muss.* This guidebook is the subject of chapter 1.

3. For a brief overview, see Frevert, *Women in German History,* 107–30.

4. Baedeker, *Berlin and Its Environs,* 50.

5. Eloesser, "Die neue Strasse" (1910), in *Die Strasse meiner Jugend,* 63–70.

6. Baedeker, *Berlin and Its Environs,* 52.

7. On women's architectural education, see Stratigakos, "'I Myself Want to Build.'" For a discussion of women's admittance to applied arts schools, see Droste, "Women in the Arts and Crafts and in Industrial Design, 1890–1933."

8. Stratigakos, *Skirts and Scaffolding,* 355. On Winkelmann, see also Schmidt-Thomsen, "Frauen in der Architektur," 19–23; and Dörhöfer, *Pionierinnen in der Architektur,* 14–37.

9. For example, see Jessen, ed., *Angewandte Kunst;* and the businesses listed in the exhibition catalog *Die Frau in Haus und Beruf.* "Jarno Jessen" was the pseudonym for Anna Michaelson. A prolific writer on art and other topics, Michaelson published extensively under her pen name, which is retained here in the text and notes. On Michaelson's career, see "Jarno, Jessen [*sic*] (Anna Michaelson)," in Wininger, *Grosse jüdische National-Biographie,* 269.

10. Kay, *The Social Condition and Education of the People in England and Europe,* vol. 2, 110.

11. Kuhn, *Familienstand ledig,* 63–68.

12. See, for example, Flanagan, *Seeing with Their Hearts;* Rappaport, *Shopping for Pleasure;* Deutsch, *Women and the City;* and Enstam, *Women and the Creation of Urban Life.*

13. Lamping, "Ein Frauenhotel in Neuyork"; "Ein Haus der Frauen."

14. In addition to the authors listed in note 12, see also Parsons, *Streetwalking the Metropolis;* and Ryan, *Women in Public.*

15. Glassie, *Vernacular Architecture,* 20–21.

16. Spain, *How Women Saved the City,* 2.

17. "A Building for Women's Clubs."

18. Bohlmann, "Our 'House Beautiful.'"

19. Wolff, "The Invisible *Flâneuse:* Women and the Literature of Modernity," in *Feminine Sentences,* 34–50; Simmel, "The Metropolis and Mental Life," in *Simmel on Culture,* 175–76; Scheffler, *Berlin—ein Stadtschicksal,* 219; Fritzsche, "Vagabond in the Fugitive City," 390–97.

20. On the problematic relationship of antiurbanism to antimodernism, see Lees, *Cities, Sin, and Social Reform in Imperial Germany,* 23–48.

21. Jessen, "Das Kunstgewerbe in Berlin," 44. Unless otherwise noted, all translations from the original language are my own.

22. Kerber, "Separate Spheres, Female Worlds, Woman's Place: The Rhetoric of Women's History" (1988), in Kerber, *Toward an Intellectual History of Women,* 159–99; Helly and Reverby, eds., *Gendered Domains;* Weintraub, "The Theory and Politics of the Public/Private Distinction."

23. Allen, *Feminism and Motherhood in Germany, 1800–1914.*

24. Anthony, *Feminism in Germany and Scandinavia,* iii. On the association of Germany's maternally based feminist politics with conservatism, see Allen, "Feminism and Motherhood in Germany and in International Perspective, 1800–1914."

25. On the spaces occupied by the Association of Berlin Female Artists, see Meyer, "Auf der Suche nach den historischen Stätten des 'Vereins der Berliner Künstlerinnen.'"

26. Scheffler, *Berlin—ein Stadtschicksal,* 219.

1. REMAPPING BERLIN

1. Jessen, "Das Kunstgewerbe in Berlin," 44.

2. Ichenhaeuser, "Einleitung."

3. Erdmann, "Berlins wissenschaftliche Anstalten," 61.

4. Jessen, "Das Kunstgewerbe in Berlin."

5. Salomon, "Soziale Frauenarbeit in Berlin."

6. Kissel, "Gymnastik und Sport in der Reichshauptstadt," 280; Ichenhaeuser, "Berliner Ausflüge und Spaziergänge," 288–89.

7. Baedeker, *Berlin and Its Environs.* 55–63.

8. Grünert, "Die Mode in Berlin."

9. Müller, "Berlin als Musik- und Konzertstadt," 118–19, 117, 120, 114–15, 127–28, 122–23. On women's music salons in Berlin, see Beci, *Musikalische Salons,* 101–29; and Wilhelmy-Dollinger, *Die Berliner Salons.*

10. "Frauen als Baumeister."

11. See Rowe, *Representing Berlin,* 81–129.

12. On the diary, see Evans, *Tales from the German Underworld,* 166–69, 210–12; and Richards, "Sense and Sentimentality?"

13. Rowe, *Representing Berlin*, 111.

14. Evans, *Tales from the German Underworld*, 204–5.

15. Spiekermann, "Theft and Thieves in German Department Stores, 1895–1930"; Dehn, *Die Grossbazare und Massenzweiggeschäfte*, 33; Rowe, *Representing Berlin*, 114–21.

16. Fritzsche, "Vagabond in the Fugitive City," 389; Rowe, *Representing Berlin*, 90.

17. Rowe, *Representing Berlin*, 81, 90–91, 96.

18. Walkowitz, *City of Dreadful Delight*, 191–228. For American examples, see Ryan, *Women in Public*, 68–76.

19. Pappritz, "Feuerbestattung und Virginität"; "Am 6. Januar ist die Wissenschaftliche Deputation . . ." See also "Protest preussischer Frauen gegen die Ausführungsbestimmungen zum preussischen Feuerbestattungsgesetz"; and Marg., "Feuerbestattung und Virginität."

20. "Feuerbestattung und Virginität," *Die Frau im Osten*.

21. Plothow, "Frauenbewegung und Frauenvereine," 173.

22. Ichenhaeuser, "Vorwort."

23. On connections between dress reform and women's architecture, see Stratigakos, "Women and the Werkbund."

24. For a history of the dress reform movement in Germany, see Welsch, *Ein Ausstieg aus dem Korsett*.

25. "Eine Sensation im Berliner Tiergarten."

26. Parsons, *Streetwalking the Metropolis*, 82.

27. Roberts, *Disruptive Acts*, 6. See also Wilson, "The Invisible *Flâneur*," chapter 7 in *The Contradictions of Culture*, 72–89.

28. Parsons, *Streetwalking the Metropolis*, 82–83.

29. Showalter, *Sexual Anarchy*, 38–58; Roberts, *Disruptive Acts*, 25–27; Ehrenpreis, "Cyclists and Amazons."

30. Ehrenpreis, "Cyclists and Amazons," 26–27.

31. Ibid., 28–30.

32. Reuter, *From a Good Family*, 166–69.

33. Arnold, "Die alleinstehende Frau," 7.

34. Weber, "Die alte Jungfer von einst und das reife Mädchen von heut." On shifting views of the "old maid," see Dollard, "The *alte Jungfer* as New Deviant"; and Göckenjan and Taeger, "Matrone, alte Jungfer, Tante."

35. As an unmarried daughter, Reuter's protagonist, Agathe Heidling, suffers many deprivations. Among them, her parents do not heat her room. Reuter, *From a Good Family*, 166.

36. "Diplomingenieur Dieter," "Die Wohnung einer selbständigen Dame."

37. The Women's Bank was first named the Genossenschaftsbank selbständiger Frauen, or the Independent Women's Credit Union. It changed its name in 1913 to the Women's Bank (Frauenbank) to emphasize its broader appeal. For a history of the bank, see Dölle, *Die (un)heimliche Macht des Geldes*, 193–220.

38. Marie Raschke in a speech quoted in "Die Besichtigung der Frauenbank," 7.

39. "Women's Financial Daily."

40. Dölle, *Die (un)heimliche Macht des Geldes*, 213.

41. Raschke, as quoted in "Die Besichtigung der Frauenbank," 6–7.

42. "Women Would Join the Boerse"; Falk, "Die rückständige Börsenordnung" (parts I–II).

43. Horwitz, "Frauen an der Börse," 4.

44. Dölle, *Die (un)heimliche Macht des Geldes*, 216.

45. "Attack Women's Bank"; Dölle, *Die (un)heimliche Macht des Geldes*, 201; "Die erste Genossenschaftsbank selbständiger Frauen," 5.

46. "Attack Women's Bank."

47. "Women's Bank a Failure."

48. The women's hospital is briefly discussed in the Epilogue.

49. Aschhoff, *Das deutsche Genossenschaftswesen*, 27–28.

50. For example, see Gustav Nieritz's warning tale of an innocent mountain girl's moral descent when she leaves her family for Paris. She is rescued, on the brink of death, by her brother. *Mutterliebe und Brudertreu.* See also Johnson, *Urbanization and Crime*, 95.

51. Evans, *The Feminist Movement in Germany, 1894–1933*, 10–11.

52. Fritzsche, "Vagabond in the Fugitive City," 390–97.

2. FROM PICCADILLY TO POTSDAMER STRASSE

1. Reuter, "Ein Frauenwerk."

2. Stropp, "Berliner Frauenklubs," 257. See also Plothow, "Berliner Frauenklubs."

3. Katscher, *Berliner Klubs*, 61–62.

4. Rappaport, *Shopping for Pleasure*, 92–93. On similar criticisms of women's clubs in the United States, see Blair, *The Clubwoman as Feminist*, 70–71.

5. Barry, "The Tea Rooms, Where Society and Business Meet."

6. Linton, *The New Woman in Haste and at Leisure*, 52; quoted in Rappaport, *Shopping for Pleasure*, 92.

7. Rappaport, *Shopping for Pleasure*, 85.

8. Smedley, *Crusaders*, 54–56.

9. Ibid., 57, 62–68.

10. "A New Club for Women Workers," 382.

11. Smedley, *Crusaders*, 94, 68–69. The press itself remarked on the attention received by the club. See "E. M. E.," "What the Lyceum Club Is Doing." The clubhouse at 128 Piccadilly was sold to the Royal Air Force Club in 1919, and the Lyceum Club relocated to even more sumptuous quarters at 138 Piccadilly.

12. Smedley, *Crusaders*, 59, 67, 70.

13. "A New Club for Women Workers," 382.

14. Smedley, *Crusaders*, 61.

15. "A New Club for Women Workers," 382. In addition to an entrance fee of one guinea, annual membership dues were three guineas for town members and two guineas for all others. See "Women's Club in London."

16. On this point, see Sinha, "Britishness, Clubbability, and the Colonial Public Sphere," 520.

17. "E. M. E.," "What the Lyceum Club Is Doing."

18. "Women's Club in London"; "A. P.," "Der Internationale Lyceumsklub"; "The Lyceum Club of London," 137.

19. Smedley, *Crusaders*, 79–80.

20. Reprinted ibid., 91.

21. "E. M. E.," "What the Lyceum Club Is Doing."

22. For an account of how the club instigated a practice debate group on the basis of the realization that women needed to learn to speak in public, see Smedley, *Crusaders*, 94–95.

23. Nevill, *London Clubs*, 135–36.

24. Rendell, *The Pursuit of Pleasure*, 63, 66–71.

25. Smedley, *Crusaders*, 73.

26. "A New Club for Women Workers," 382. The illustrated weekly the *Graphic* ran a series on women's clubs from March 7 through April 25, 1908, featuring a new club each week. The introduction to the series referred to the social opprobrium attached to the clubs when they first appeared but stated that they had since become "a very firmly rooted institution" in London. See "B. T.," "Our Ladies Clubs."

27. Rappaport, *Shopping for Pleasure*, 86.

28. D'Espaigne, "The Lyceum Club for Ladies," 602.

29. Rappaport, *Shopping for Pleasure*, 100.

30. Rendell, *The Pursuit of Pleasure*, 74.

31. Smedley, *Crusaders*, 55, 58; Marie von Bunsen, "Einiges über den Lyceum-Club," in *Lyceum-Club Berlin* (Berlin: Lyceum Club Berlin, 1905), 7. The latter is a brochure that lists founding members and describes the organization and goals of the Berlin club. It is located in the archive of the Deutscher Staatsbürgerinnen-Verband, Berlin. I thank Isabel Bauer for bringing it to my attention.

32. Maier-Dependorf, "Constance Smedley," 15. On the European social clubs, see Sinha, "Britishness, Clubbability, and the Colonial Public Sphere."

33. "Women's Club in London."

34. Smedley, *Crusaders*, 132.

35. Heyl, *Aus meinem Leben*, 74.

36. Smedley, *Crusaders*, 78, 92, 116.

37. Rappaport, *Shopping for Pleasure*, 106. Although the clubhouse and most members were lost when the club went into liquidation in 1933, the London Lyceum Club has continued to function under the shelter and auspices of other organizations since that time. See Seton Veitch, "London Lyceum Club."

38. Brockington, "'A World Fellowship,'" 19.

39. Smedley, *Crusaders*, 79–84. While the token participation of male designers in the Wertheim show increased public interest, it also somewhat shifted the focus. Thus, reviewer Curt Stoeving, although favorably impressed by the women designers, emphasized their artistic dependence on their male colleagues. He also gave the male judges credit for the "firm impression" of the exhibition. Stoeving, "Ausstellung des Londoner Lyceum-Club in Berlin."

40. Stoeving, "Ausstellung des Londoner Lyceum-Club in Berlin," 509.

41. Smedley, *Crusaders*, 83.

184Notes to Chapter 2Reuter, "Ein Frauenwerk."Stratigakos, "Women and the Werkbund"; Lewis, *Art for All?* 214ff.Clubs were concentrated in the government district, although not on particular streets, as in London.Walter, "Berliner Klubs," 4. For a discussion of the exceptional clubs, see Katscher, *Berliner Klubs*, 15, 21–27, 70–71.*Berlin und die Berliner*, 252.In 1905, the Berliner Frauenklub von 1900 was located at 125 Potsdamer Strasse, next door to the Deutscher Frauenklub at 126. See *Berlin und die Berliner*, 255. On the nature of these two clubs, see Plothow, "Berliner Frauenklubs."Rappaport, *Shopping for Pleasure*, 101.Kirchner's ambiguous representation of the women on Potsdamer Platz suggests a double reading: the woman as consumer and as commodity (i.e., prostitute). See Haxthausen, "'A New Beauty.'"Reuter, "Ein Frauenwerk."Reuter, "Ein Klubhaus für Frauen in Berlin."Elsa Schulhoff, "Über die Arbeiten des Lyceum-Bureaus," in *Lyceum-Club Berlin* (Berlin: Lyceum Club Berlin, 1905), 10, brochure, archive of the Deutscher Staatsbürgerinnen-Verband, Berlin."Auszug aus den Satzungen," in *Lyceum-Club Berlin* (Berlin: Lyceum Club Berlin, 1905), 15–16, brochure, archive of the Deutscher Staatsbürgerinnen-Verband, Berlin; "Der Lyzeumklub," 755.Deutscher Lyceum-Klub, *Satzungen* (Berlin: Deutscher Lyceum Club, 1910), 4, brochure in "Beschickung von Kunst- und Gewerbeausstellungen," Rep. 120E, 16, 1.8, vol. 9 (1911–12), Geheimes Staatsarchiv Preussischer Kulturbesitz, Berlin.On professionalism and Germany's middle classes, see Cocks and Jarausch, eds., *German Professions, 1800–1950*.Reuter, "Ein Frauenwerk."Jessen, "Der Lyceumklub."The building no longer stands. The plans are preserved under the postwar address 61 Potsdamer Strasse: B Rep. 202, no. 3153, at the Landesarchiv Berlin."Im Lyzeumklub."Jessen, "Der Lyceumklub." For a description of the club's facilities, see also "Der Lyzeumklub," 755; and Marelle, *Die Geschichte des Deutschen Lyceum-Clubs*, 11.Heyl, *Aus meinem Leben*, 75–76. Heyl served together with the countess Helene Harrach, whom Heyl invited to act as copresident in an effort to integrate influential aristocratic circles.Smedley, *Crusaders*, 172, 60, 66–67, 189–90; Rendell, *The Pursuit of Pleasure*, 67."Im Lyzeumklub."Heyl, *Aus meinem Leben*, 75.Quoted in "Im Lyzeumklub."Marelle, "Berliner Frauenklubs," 164.Koschwitz-Newby, "Hedwig Heyl."
eheaders noted

68. Constance Smedley to William T. Smedley, n.d. [after November 7, 1906], private collection.

69. Heyl, *Aus meinem Leben*, 76.

70. Ibid., 76–77. Building plans at the Landesarchiv Berlin indicate the club left the Potsdamer Strasse clubhouse in April 1908 and, after a brief stay in temporary quarters (mentioned in Heyl's autobiography), relocated to new premises at Am Karlsband 12–13 in the summer or fall of 1908. See B Rep. 202, no. 3153, and B Rep. 202, no. 6681, Landesarchiv Berlin.

71. Glinga, *Legacy of Empire*, 7.

72. Breckman, "Disciplining Consumption."

73. Bode, "Vom Luxus," 493; quoted and translated in Breckman, "Disciplining Consumption," 488.

74. Breckman, "Disciplining Consumption," 489.

75. Ibid., 490ff.

76. *Der Deutsche Lyceum-Klub* (Berlin: Deutscher Lyceum Club, 1911), 4, brochure in "Beschickung von Kunst- und Gewerbeausstellungen," Rep. 120E, 16, 1.8, vol. 9 (1911–12), Geheimes Staatsarchiv Preussischer Kulturbesitz, Berlin.

77. The four-story house was designed by Gropius and his partner Heino Schmieden. The spacious ground floor was occupied by the Gropius family and the architectural firm's offices. Upper floors contained rental units. The Lyceum Club occupied the ground floor (with its terrace and garden) in 1908, expanding to the second story in 1911. The building was destroyed in the Second World War. Building plans are preserved at the Landesarchiv Berlin (B Rep. 202, no. 6681). See also Architekten Verein zu Berlin, ed., *Berlin und Seine Bauten*, 472.

78. Klinkott, "Martin Gropius und die Berliner Schule," 98.

79. In 1911, when the club expanded to the second floor of the Gropius house, the total number of guest rooms increased to nine. *Deutscher Lyceum-Club* 7, no. 10 (1911): 215.

80. For a description and images of the club's facilities, see *Der Deutsche Lyceum-Klub*, brochure. The best men's clubs in Berlin similarly offered their members bathing facilities. Katscher, *Berliner Klubs*, 22.

81. Heyl, *Aus meinem Leben*, 77.

82. Glinka, *Legacy of Empire*, 7.

83. Lejeune, *The Gentlemen's Clubs of London*, 59.

84. Marelle, *Die Geschichte des Deutschen Lyceum-Clubs*, 11.

85. Melton, *The Rise of the Public in Enlightenment Europe*, 219–23; Wilhelmy-Dollinger, *Die Berliner Salons*.

86. Bilski and Braun, "The Power of Conversation," 2, 17.

87. *Der Deutsche Lyceum-Klub*, 3, brochure. See also "Der Lyzeumklub," 752–53.

88. Ichenhaeuser, "Frauenklubs," 727; Salomon, "Frauenklubs," 125–26; Stropp, "Berliner Frauenklubs," 264.

89. On the women's hospital, see the Epilogue.

90. Ichenhaeuser, "Frauenklubs," 728–29.

91. Stropp, "Berliner Frauenklubs," 256–57.

92. Ichenhaeuser, "Frauenklubs," 727.

93. Ibid. For an American example of women's clubs and their civic engagement, see Flanagan, *Seeing with Their Hearts.*

94. Levy-Rathenau, "Unsre deutschen Frauenklubs und ihre Leistungen"; Salomon, "Frauenklubs," 125. See also Stropp, "Berliner Frauenklubs," 264.

95. *Deutscher Lyceum-Club* 5, no. 6 (1910): 74.

96. Salomon, "Frauenklubs," 125.

97. Groddeck, *Hin zu Gottnatur,* 115–47.

98. Danneel, "Nachrichten von den Mitgliedern."

99. "Bericht über die 6. ordentliche Generalversammlung des Deutschen Lyceum-Clubs," 337, 339.

100. Heyl, *Aus meinem Leben,* 135. The clubhouse, destroyed in the Second World War, was located at Lützowplatz 8. Building plans are preserved at the Landesarchiv Berlin under the address Lützowplatz 15 (B Rep. 202, nos. 3082 and 3083).

101. "Orte der Mütterlichkeit: Tiergartenviertel."

102. *Deutscher Lyceum-Club* 10, no. 6 (1914): 232–33; *Deutscher Lyceum-Club* 10, no. 7 (1914): 271, 275–76; and Wiese, "Inneneinrichtung des neuen Hauses." On Knobelsdorff, see Stratigakos, "'I Myself Want to Build'"; and Stratigakos, "The Professional Spoils of War"; on Kirschner, see Günther, "International Pioneers," 50–53.

103. See, for example, Gutman, "Inside the Institution."

104. Jessen, "Der Deutsche Lyzeumklub und seine bildenden Künstlerinnen," 165.

105. Schwartz, *The Werkbund,* 39–43. See also Jarzombek, "The *Kunstgewerbe,* the *Werkbund,* and the Aesthetics of Culture in the Wilhelmine Period"; and Jarzombek, "The Discourses of a Bourgeois Utopia, 1904–1908, and the Founding of the Werkbund."

106. Boetticher, "Das neue Heim des Deutschen Lyzeumklubs," 16.

107. Ibid., 15.

108. Ibid.

109. Jessen, "Der Deutsche Lyzeumklub und seine bildenden Künstlerinnen," 166.

110. On the club's role as a venue for its designers, see Jessen, "Das Kunstgewerbe in Berlin," 52.

111. *Deutscher Lyceum-Club* 5, no. 6 (1910): 74. For further discussion of the *Einküchenhaus,* see chapter 3.

112. For example, on January 6, 1913, suffragist Adele Schreiber-Krieger spoke on the topic "Humankind and Housing"; and on February 14, 1914, Elisabeth von Knobelsdorff delivered a slide lecture on the theme "How Should We Live?" See *Deutscher Lyceum-Club* 9, no. 1 (1913): 25; *Deutscher Lyceum-Club* 10, no. 2 (1914): 72.

113. *Deutscher Lyceum-Club* 9, no. 6 (1913): 210; *Deutscher Lyceum-Club* 10, no. 6 (1914): 236. The two associations are discussed, respectively, in chapters 3 and 5.

3. A Home of Our Own

1. Lengefeld, *Der Maler des glücklichen Heims,* 84.

2. Pochhammer, "Berliner Wohnungsverhältnisse," 234–36. For a thorough discussion of women as landlords and boardinghouse operators in Berlin, see Gunga, *"Zimmer frei."*

3. Beaulieu, *Das weibliche Berlin*, 144.

4. Mensch, "An Damen wird nicht vermietet." Similar reasons for refusing to rent to women were cited by Stropp, "Die Wohnungsnot der gebildeten Frau." See also Gunga, *"Zimmer frei,"* 93–96.

5. Schmidt, "Die 'möblierte Dame.'" See also the unsympathetic response to this article, "Nochmals die 'möblierte Dame.'"

6. Schrey, "Die Wohnungsfrage der alleinstehenden Berufsfrau."

7. Roloff, "Rat an alleinstehende Frauen," 177.

8. Ohlert, "Das Lehrerinnenheim in Hamburg," 238.

9. Schrey, "Die Wohnungsfrage der alleinstehenden Berufsfrau."

10. See, for example, Hayden, *The Grand Domestic Revolution.*

11. Terlinden, Grieser, and Ross, *Wohnungspolitik in der alten Frauenbewegung;* and Mentner, "Lebensräume für Frauen zwischen Fremdbestimmung und Selbstverwirklichung."

12. Albisetti, *Schooling German Girls and Women,* 117–18, 157.

13. "Das Kultusministerium und die Hansemann-Stiftung." See also Albisetti, *Schooling German Girls and Women,* 285.

14. Sonnenschein, *Wie Studenten Wohnen;* Temming, *Sturmfreie Buden,* 13–16. For a discussion of the problem from a "concerned mother's" point of view, see Schulze-Brück, "Die Budenfrage."

15. "A. P.," "Das Viktoria-Studienhaus," 142. The article was reprinted from the *Berliner Tageblatt.*

16. See Huerkamp, *Bildungsbürgerinnen,* 31–40.

17. "A. P.," "Das Viktoria-Studienhaus," 142.

18. Velsen, "Die Wohnungsverhältnisse der Studentinnen."

19. Kiehm, "Das Wohnungsproblem der Studentin." For further discussion of the housing problems of female students in Berlin, see Gunga, *"Zimmer frei,"* 96–99.

20. "Das Studentinnenheim in der Berliner Strasse."

21. Lange, "Das Berliner Victoria-Studienhaus," 339–40.

22. Jordan, "Im Studentinnenheim"; Zunk, "Die Töchter der Alma mater," 56.

23. Fleer, "Das Werden des ersten Studentinnenheims in Deutschland," 2–3. Fleer was active in the movement for women's education and taught in a higher girls' school in Göttingen before becoming director of the Victoria Studienhaus in 1911. She remained in that position until her retirement in 1934.

24. Albisetti, *Schooling German Girls and Women,* 285 n. 32.

25. Stratigakos, *Skirts and Scaffolding,* 128–35, 307–15.

26. On these projects, see Stratigakos, "Building for Women: Emilie Winkelmann and the Patronage of the Women's Movement," chapter five, *Skirts and Scaffolding,* 256–303.

27. Stratigakos, "Architects in Skirts," 96–98.

28. Stratigakos, "'I Myself Want to Build,'" 736–40.

29. Fleer in a speech quoted by Friedlaender, "Die Direktorin des 'Studentinnenheims des Viktoria-Studienhauses,'" 13; "Victoria-Studienhaus," 38. The street address was then Berliner Strasse 37–38, today Otto-Suhr-Allee 18–20.

30. According to Fleer, additional funding from Hansemann made it possible to

continue building during the war. She also notes that even though all the rooms were rented, only sixty could be occupied when the residence opened, because the war had caused delays in the delivery of the furniture. By the end of the first semester, however, the house was fully occupied. Friedlaender, "Die Direktorin des 'Studentinnenheims des Viktoria-Studienhauses,'" 14.

31. Harder, "Ein Heim für studierende Frauen in Berlin," 564–65.

32. Lange, "Das Berliner Victoria Studienhaus," 341.

33. Emilie Winkelmann, "Erläuterungsbericht zum Neubau Berlinerstrasse 37–38," 1–2. This was a narrative report submitted with drawings and plans to the municipal building authorities in March 1914 (archive of the Bau- und Wohnungsaufsichtsamt, Bezirksamt Charlottenburg-Wilmersdorf). I am grateful to Helga Schmidt-Thomsen for sharing her copy with me.

34. Velsen, "Die Wohnungsverhältnisse der Studentinnen."

35. Lange, "Das Berliner Victoria Studienhaus," 342.

36. Winkelmann, "Erläuterungsbericht zum Neubau Berlinerstrasse 37–38," 2; report in the archive of the Bau- und Wohnungsaufsichtsamt, Bezirksamt Charlottenburg-Wilmersdorf. In 1916, Fleer still expected this goal to be realized in the future. See "Das Heim unsrer Studentinnen," 23.

37. Winkelmann, "Erläuterungsbericht zum Neubau Berlinerstrasse 37–38," 1; report in the archive of the Bau- und Wohnungsaufsichtsamt, Bezirksamt Charlottenburg-Wilmersdorf.

38. Wirz, "Frau und Qualität," 198.

39. For a discussion of the gendering of classical orders, see Forty, *Words and Buildings*, 44–50.

40. Harder, "Ein Heim für studierende Frauen," 563–64; "A. P.," "Das Viktoria-Studienhaus," 143; Lange, "Das Berliner Victoria Studienhaus," 341; "Das Heim unsrer Studentinnen," 23.

41. Bergdoll, *European Architecture 1750–1890*, 43.

42. Jefferies, *Politics and Culture in Wilhelmine Germany*, 128, 131. See also Anderson, *Peter Behrens and a New Architecture for the Twentieth Century*, 129–64.

43. Riess, "Schaffende Frauen," 37.

44. Faubel, "Das Viktoria-Studienhaus in Berlin," 2.

45. Habermas, *The Structural Transformation of the Public Sphere*, 31–43. For feminist critiques of Habermas, see Meehan, ed., *Feminists Read Habermas*; and Ryan, "Gender and Public Access."

46. Wilhelmy-Dollinger, *Die Berliner Salons*, 2.

47. Schwarzer, *German Architectural Theory and the Search for Modern Identity*, 165.

48. "Das Heim unsrer Studentinnen," 23.

49. Faubel, "Das Viktoria-Studienhaus in Berlin," 2.

50. Harder, "Ein Heim für studierende Frauen," 564.

51. "Das Heim unsrer Studentinnen," 23; Harder, "Ein Heim für studierende Frauen," 564.

52. Spickernagel, "Wohnkultur und Frauenrolle im Biedermeier," 26–28.

53. Faubel, "Das Viktoria-Studienhaus in Berlin," 2.

54. Velsen, "Die Wohnungsverhältnisse der Studentinnen."

55. Ibid.; "Das Heim unsrer Studentinnen," 23; Harder, "Ein Heim für studierende Frauen," 564.

56. Bullock and Read, *The Movement for Housing Reform in Germany and France, 1840–1914*, 96–98.

57. Spickernagel, "Wohnkultur und Frauenrolle im Biedermeier," 30.

58. Ibid.

59. See Vickery, *Buildings for Bluestockings.*

60. Irmer, "Zur Wohnungsfrage der Studentinnen," 10.

61. Lange, "Das Berliner Victoria-Studienhaus," 341; Faubel, "Das Victoria-Studienhaus in Berlin," 2.

62. Irmer, "Zur Wohnungsfrage der Studentinnen," 10; Lange, "Das Berliner Victoria-Studienhaus," 341.

63. "Das Heim unsrer Studentinnen," 23.

64. Ibid., my emphasis.

65. Harder, "Ein Heim für studierende Frauen," 565.

66. "Vorträge im Viktoria-Studienhaus."

67. "A. P.," "Das Viktoria-Studienhaus," 142.

68. Friedlaender, "Die Direktorin des 'Studentinnenheims des Viktoria-Studienhauses,'" 14.

69. Faubel, "Das Viktoria-Studienhaus in Berlin," 2.

70. Harder, "Ein Heim für studierende Frauen," 566.

71. "A. P.," "Das Viktoria-Studienhaus," 142. See also Albisetti, "American Women's Colleges through European Eyes, 1865–1914," 447–48.

72. A German woman studying at Bryn Mawr College in 1914 remarked on the much greater emphasis on communal life at American women's colleges in comparison to German universities. Beermann, "Erinnerungen an Bryn Mawr," 5.

73. For an analysis of the masculinity of German academic culture, see Mazón, *Gender and the Modern Research University.*

74. Harder, "Ein Heim für studierende Frauen," 566; Maier, "Begleitworte des Vorsitzenden des Kuratoriums Oberpräsidenten i. R. Dr. Maier," 15.

75. "Das Heim unsrer Studentinnen," 23.

76. See Vickery, *Buildings for Bluestockings*, 6, 9–12, 19; Horowitz, *Alma Mater*, 32–33, 57.

77. Friedlaender, "Die Direktorin des 'Studentinnenheims des Viktoria-Studienhauses,'" 13–14.

78. Harder, "Ein Heim für studierende Frauen," 566.

79. See, for example, Broecker, "'Dank' und 'Wilkommen.'"

80. Friedlaender, "Die Direktorin des 'Studentinnenheims des Viktoria-Studienhauses,'" 14.

81. Velsen, "Die Wohnungsverhältnisse der Studentinnen."

82. Grimm, "Ein Studentinnenheim in Charlottenburg," 8.

83. Haemmerling, *Charlottenburg*, 77–78, 102.

84. Postwar administrative records for the Verein Victoria-Studienhaus are housed at the Landesarchiv Berlin (under B Rep. 232–05).

85. Interview with Dr. Ella Barowsky, Berlin, Germany, November 6, 1996.

86. Enzelberger, *Sozialgeschichte des Lehrerberufs*, 110.

87. "Die Vereinigung für Frauenwohnungen," *Die deutsche Frau*, no. 30; "Eine 'Vereinigung für moderne Frauenwohnungen,'" *Die Frau im Osten*.

88. "Die Vereinigung für moderne Frauenwohnungen," *Die deutsche Frau*, no. 43.

89. Pochhammer, "Berliner Wohnungsverhältnisse," 236.

90. "Die Vereinigung für moderne Frauenwohnungen," *Die deutsche Frau*, no. 30.

91. Pochhammer, "Berliner Wohnungsverhältnisse," 236.

92. "Vereinigung für moderne Frauenwohnungen," *Frauen-Rundschau*.

93. A similar concept, "co-flatting," emerged simultaneously among single independent women in American cities, although without the institutional support represented by the Association for Modern Women's Apartments. See Cromley, *Alone Together*, 225 n. 22.

94. "Vereinigung für moderne Frauenwohnungen," *Frauen-Rundschau*.

95. "Die Vereinigung für Frauenwohnungen," *Die deutsche Frau*, no. 43; Haupt, "Moderne Frauenwohnungen."

96. "Die Vereinigung für Frauenwohnungen," *Frauenkapital-eine werdende Macht*. I have been unable to locate illustrations or surviving examples of the stamps.

97. Henderson, "A Revolution in the Woman's Sphere." See also the Epilogue.

98. "Die Vereinigung für Frauenwohnungen," *Frauenkapital-eine werdende Macht*.

99. Bullock and Read, *The Movement for Housing Reform in Germany and France, 1840–1914*, 235–38.

100. "Die Genossenschaft 'Die Frauenwohnung' E.G.m.b.H," *Frauenkapital-eine werdende Macht*.

101. Behnisch-Kappstein, "Wohnung und Frau," 381.

102. Crawford, *Enterprising Women*, 206–17; Pearson, *The Architectural and Social History of Cooperative Living*, 45–55; Vicinus, *Independent Women*, 295–97.

103. The promotional stamp series mentioned above was sold at the Frauenbank. The association's headquarters were also located in the bank. "Die Vereinigung für Frauenwohnungen," *Frauenkapital-eine werdende Macht*.

104. On issues of women dining alone, see Glock, "Die Dame im Restaurant"; and the response by Bram, "Die Dame im Restaurant!?"

105. Uhlig, *Kollektivmodell "Einküchenhaus,"* 25–70.

106. Eichler, "Die Frauenwohnung."

107. Pochhammer, "Berliner Wohnungsverhältnisse," 237–38.

108. Schrey, "Die Wohnungsfrage der alleinstehenden Berufsfrau."

109. Behnisch-Kappstein, "Wohnung und Frau," 381.

110. "Das Damenheim zu Potsdam."

111. "Damen-Wohnungen," advertisement.

112. Friedheim, "Aus unserer Bildermappe."

113. "Damen-Wohnungen," advertisement.

114. Zepler, "Frauenheime," 214–15.

115. Pochhammer, "Berliner Wohnungsverhältnisse," 237.

116. Gildemeister, "Das Einküchenhaus," 754.

117. The housing cooperative was called the "Female Teachers' Home" Building and Savings Association ("Lehrerinnenheim" Bau- und Sparverein). The current address of the former Lehrerinnenheim is Wisbyer Strasse 43–44a. Original building plans are held by the Pankow Bauaktenarchiv.

118. Enzelberger, *Sozialgeschichte des Lehrerberufs*, 111–15.

119. Heeren, "Lehrerinnenheim in Berlin," 332.

120. "K. H.," "Unser Lehrerinnenheim."

121. Enzelberger, *Sozialgeschichte des Lehrerberufs*, 115.

122. "Die Einweihung des Lehrerinnenheims," 217.

123. "'Lehrerinnenheim,' Bau- und Sparverein," 111.

124. Ohlert, "Das Lehrerinnenheim in Hamburg," 238.

125. Heeren, "Lehrerinnenheim in Berlin," 332.

126. "Das Lehrerinnenheim des Vereins Berliner Volkschullehrerinnen."

127. "Die Einweihung des Lehrerinnenheims," 217.

128. Heyer, "'Lehrerinnenheim,'" 13; "Die Einweihung des Lehrerinnenheims," 216.

129. Meyer, *Paul Mebes*, 22–55.

130. Ibid., 15–18.

131. Heyer, "'Lehrerinnenheim,'" 13; "Geschäftsbericht für das Jahr 1913."

132. The name was chosen by Dora Martin, director of the Pestalozzi-Fröbel-Haus II, a domestic science institute for women. A leading member of the Cooperative for Women's Homesteads, she was instrumental in the successful completion of the Haus in der Sonne. See "Fest-Zeitung zum 25 jährigen Jubiläum von Fräulein Martin," September 8, 1917, 11–12, archive of the Pestalozzi-Fröbel-Haus, Berlin.

133. Lengefeld, *Der Maler des glücklichen Heims*, 5.

134. "Frauenheimstätten," *Die Frauenwacht*, 181; Boetticher, "Heimstätten für Frauen," 5.

135. "Genossenschaft für Frauenheimstätten: Sitz Berlin," 46.

136. "Frauenheimstätten," *P. F. H. II Zeitung*, 9. This journal is available at the archive of the Pestalozzi-Fröbel-Haus. See also "Genossenschaft für Frauenheimstätten," *Die Lehrerin*, 6.

137. Boetticher, "Heimstätten für Frauen," 5.

138. Martin, "Heim der Genossenschaft für Frauenheimstätten," 9.

139. "Fest-Zeitung zum 25 jährigen Jubiläum," 11. See also Sprengel, "'Die Frau in Haus und Beruf,'" 17, no. 6: 49–50.

140. On the school's history, see Meckel, ed., *Das Pestalozzi-Fröbel-Haus*.

141. "Fest-Zeitung zum 25 jährigen Jubiläum," 11.

142. Albisetti, *Schooling German Girls and Women*, 85. For a guide to retirement homes for female teachers in Germany, see Münsterberg, ed., *Die Anstaltsfürsorge in Deutschland*, 232–38.

143. Sprengel, "'Die Frau in Haus und Beruf,'" 17, no. 6: 50–51.

144. "Genossenschaft für Frauenheimstätten: Sitz Berlin," 46. The cooperative was founded at a meeting held on September 16, 1912, at the Pestalozzi-Fröbel-Haus, according to "Genossenschaft für Frauenheimstätten," *Die Lehrerin*, 7.

145. "Mitglieder der Heimgenossenschaft für Frauen." Although the size and number of the intended houses varied in different reports, the emphasis on the model of the single-family home remained constant.

146. "Mitteilung, betreffend die Vorarbeiten zur Gründung einer Heimgenossenschaft für aus dem Beruf geschiedene gebildete Frauen."

147. Boetticher, "Heimstätten für Frauen," 6.

148. "Frauenheimstätten," *P. F. H. II Zeitung,* 9; "Genossenschaft für Frauenheimstätten," *Die Frau.*

149. "Genossenschaft für Frauenheimstätten: Sitz Berlin," 47; Boetticher, "Heimstätten für Frauen," 7.

150. Mensch, "Das Haus in der Sonne," 19.

151. "Fest-Zeitung zum 25 jährigen Jubiläum," 11, archive of the Pestalozzi-Fröbel-Haus, Berlin.

152. "A. S.," "Das Haus in der Sonne," 19.

153. "Mitteilung, betreffend die Vorarbeiten zur Gründung einer Heimgenossenschaft," 24.

154. "Frauenheimstätten," *P. F. H. II Zeitung,* 9; Skladny, "Genossenschaft für Frauenheimstätten E.G.m.b.H.," 102.

155. "A. S.," "Das Haus in der Sonne," 19.

156. "Mitteilung, betreffend die Vorarbeiten zur Gründung einer Heimgenossenschaft," 24.

157. *Die Frau in Haus und Beruf,* 152–53.

158. "A. S.," "Das Haus in der Sonne," 19. The current address of the building is Hermann-Maass-Strasse 18–20 in Potsdam. Building plans are located at the Amt für Denkmalpflege, Potsdam.

159. "Die Frauenheimstätten in Neu-Babelsberg-Nowawes," 1.

160. "A. S.," "Das Haus in der Sonne," 20.

161. Ibid., 19; Schulze, "Das Haus in der Sonne," 8; "Genossenschaft für Frauenheimstätten: Neubabelsberg-Nowawes, Heimdalstrasse," 159.

162. Schulze, "Das Haus in der Sonne," 8.

163. Ibid., 9.

164. "Genossenschaft für Frauenheimstätten: Neubabelsberg-Nowawes, Heimdalstrasse," 159.

165. "Genossenschaft für Frauenheimstätten: Sitz Berlin," 46.

166. Mensch, "Das Haus in der Sonne," 18.

167. Schulze, "Das Haus in der Sonne."

168. Martin, "Heim der Genossenschaft für Frauenheimstätten," 9; Mensch, "Das Haus in der Sonne," 18. The original windows have been replaced.

169. Schulze, "Das Haus in der Sonne," 9.

170. Lengefeld, *Der Maler des glücklichen Heims,* 67ff.; Lane, *National Romanticism and Modern Architecture,* 114.

171. Boetticher, "Heimstätten für Frauen," 6.

172. Mensch, "Das Haus in der Sonne," 18.

173. "Frauenberufe"; "Die Frauenheimstätten in Neu-Babelsberg-Nowaves," 2. The address of the former vacation home, called the Dora-Martin-Haus, is Heinestrasse 24. I am grateful to Andreas Kirschning for generously sharing his research with me.

174. "Fest-Zeitung zum 25 jährigen Jubiläum," 12, archive of the Pestalozzi-Fröbel-Haus.

175. Stropp, "Die Wohnungsnot der gebildeten Frau," 286; "Frauenberufe."

176. Dölle, *Die (un)heimliche Macht des Geldes,* 221–20.

177. Weinberg, "Ein neues Frauenheim." Constructed adjacent to the first residence, it was designed by a male architect, Friedrich Lüngen. The address is Hermann-Maass-Strasse 22–22a. Plans are at the Amt für Denkmalpflege in Potsdam. Why Winkelmann, or another woman architect, was not given the commission is unknown. The shift may reflect the new status and authority of male architects in the Weimar Republic as housing reformers for all social groups.

178. The complex was sold to the Bauverein Babelsberg (a building cooperative) in August 1942. Letter from Jörg Limberg to the author, March 10, 1998.

4. EXHIBITING THE NEW WOMAN

1. Radel, "Von der Berliner Ausstellung 'Die Frau in Haus und Beruf.'" The Hamburg State Archive has an extensive collection of local press clippings on the 1912 exhibition and women's congress: Staatsarchiv Hamburg, Bestand 111-1 Senat, Cl. I, Lit. Sd, no. 2, vol. 10, fasc. 4, inv. 55.

2. "Woman's Work in Many Fields."

3. The total number of visitors was 500,231 as reported in "Bericht über die 6. ordentliche Generalversammlung des Deutschen Lyceum-Clubs," 338.

4. Heyl, *Aus meinem Leben,* 114; Salomon, *Character Is Destiny,* 93–94.

5. "Frau Hedwig Heyl Dead in Berlin, 83."

6. *Deutscher Lyceum-Club* 7, no. 1 (1911): 1; and *Deutscher Lyceum-Club* 7, no. 2 (1911): 29.

7. Greenhalgh, "Education, Entertainment and Politics," 89.

8. Salomon, "Zur Eröffnung der Ausstellung 'Die Frau in Haus und Beruf,'" *Der Tag.* Although neither the German politician nor the event is named, the comments Salomon cites were probably made in relation to the Berlin Trade Exhibition of 1896. An international women's conference was held in the capital to coincide with the event, which likely prompted the politician's statement. See Spitzer, "Zwei Veranstaltungen, ein Zeitpunkt."

9. Greenhalgh, *Ephemeral Vistas,* 23.

10. "Ansprache von Frau Hedwig Heyl." See also Salomon, "Zur Eröffnung der Ausstellung 'Die Frau in Haus und Beruf,'" *Der Tag.*

11. Salomon, "Zur Eröffnung der Ausstellung 'Die Frau in Haus und Beruf,'" *Der Tag.*

12. "Bericht über die 6. ordentliche Generalversammlung des Deutschen Lyceum-Clubs," 336. On this same theme, see Plothow, "Die Ausstellung die Frau in Haus und Beruf," *Berliner Tageblatt.*

13. Heuss, "Die Frauenausstellung in Berlin," 171.

14. Lange, "Ausstellung und Kongress 'Die Frau in Haus und Beruf,'" 300–301. On the

"Yellow Brochure" and Lange's role in promoting women's education in the later nineteenth century, see Albisetti, *Schooling German Girls and Women.*

15. Colze, *Berliner Warenhäuser,* 14.

16. "'Die Frau in Haus und Beruf': Zur Eröffnung der Ausstellung," *Berliner Tageblatt.*

17. The exhibition building was damaged in the war and demolished in the 1950s to make way for a new business and entertainment complex. Some of the original plans are preserved at the Landesarchiv Berlin (B Rep. 207, no. 225).

18. Streich, "Franz Heinrich Schwechten."

19. Heyl, *Aus meinem Leben,* 113; Cecil, *Wilhelm II,* vol. 2, 7.

20. "P. B.," "Die Frau in Haus und Beruf."

21. Gottschalk, "Bildungs- und Erziehungsfragen auf dem Deutschen Frauenkongress in Berlin," 230; Goldschmidt, "Die Damenausstellung," 395.

22. Ratzka-Ernst, "Die Ausstellung 'Die Frau in Haus und Beruf,'" 38.

23. Plothow, "Die Ausstellung 'Die Frau in Haus und Beruf' I," *Frauenwirtschaft,* 26; Grube, "Rundgang durch die Ausstellung 'Die Frau in Haus und Beruf,'" 115; Lorm, "'Die Frau in Haus und Beruf.'"

24. "Aus dem Reiche."

25. "F. E.," "Die Frau in Haus und Beruf."

26. "Festkantate," 72.

27. Williams, *Dream Worlds,* 85.

28. Rowe, *Representing Berlin,* 43, 32.

29. James, "From Messel to Mendelsohn," 262–63.

30. "F.-T.," "Frauenindustrie."

31. See Bennett, "The Exhibitionary Complex"; Clausen, *Frantz Jourdain and the Samaritaine;* and Friedberg, *Window Shopping,* 79–83.

32. On the contemplative gaze of the shopper, see Friedberg, *Window Shopping,* 57–58. For a discussion of the "comprehensive feminine glance" as developed in London shopping guides for women, see Rappaport, *Shopping for Pleasure,* 128–29.

33. "Die Frau in Haus und Beruf," *Der Tag;* "O. T. Sch.," "Die Frau in Haus und Beruf."

34. "Tietz und Wertheim," 541–42. For similar criticisms pertaining to France and England, see Tiersten, "Marianne in the Department Store," 124; and Rappaport, *Shopping for Pleasure,* especially chapter 2.

35. Salomon, "Zur Eröffnung der Ausstellung 'Die Frau in Haus und Beruf,'" *Central-blatt des BDF,* 173.

36. Friedberg, *Window Shopping,* 37, 42.

37. "Acta des Polizei-Präsidii zu Berlin, betreffend den Königlichen Commerzienrath und Fabrikbesitzer Georg Friedrich Heyl und Frau Hedwig Heyl," Landesarchiv Berlin, A Pr. Br. Rep. 30, no. 10564, 170.

38. Salomon, "Zur Eröffnung der Ausstellung 'Die Frau in Haus und Beruf,'" *Central-blatt des BDF,* 174; "Die Frau in Haus und Beruf," *Die Woche,* 322; Radel, "Von der Berliner Ausstellung."

39. Salomon, "Zur Eröffnung der Ausstellung 'Die Frau in Haus und Beruf,'" *Central-blatt des BDF,* 174.

40. On women's pavilions, see Grever and Dieteren, eds., *A Fatherland for Women*; Barth-Scalmani and Friedrich, "Frauen auf der Wiener Weltausstellung von 1873"; Cordato, *Representing the Expansion of Woman's Sphere*; and Greenhalgh, "Women: Exhibiting and Exhibited," in *Ephemeral Vistas*, 174–97.

41. On the conception of women's work developed at the Philadelphia Centennial Exhibition of 1876, see Cordato, *Representing the Expansion of Woman's Sphere*, 80ff.

42. "E. H.," "Die Frau in Haus und Beruf," 475.

43. *Die Frau in Haus und Beruf*, 11, 13, 71.

44. On Wille, see Günther, "International Pioneers," 54–55; on Oppler-Legband, see Droste, "Women in the Arts and Crafts and in Industrial Design 1890–1933," 185; "Else Oppler-Legband"; and Wigley, *White Walls, Designer Dresses*, 138–40; on Reich, see McQuaid and Droste, *Lilly Reich*; and Günther, *Lilly Reich, 1885–1947*. For additional information and sources on these three designers, see Stratigakos, "Women and the Werkbund"; and Stratigakos, *Skirts and Scaffolding*, chapters 4 and 7.

45. Harder, "Die Frau in Haus und Beruf," 24.

46. *Die Frau in Haus und Beruf*, 13.

47. Stropp, "Die Ausstellung 'Die Frau in Haus und Beruf,'" *Illustrirte Zeitung*, 447.

48. *Die Frau in Haus und Beruf*, 13. The title in German was *Der Weg des Weibes*.

49. Ibid., 14, 42–43.

50. An image of the interior of the reception hall is reproduced in Stropp, "Die Ausstellung 'Die Frau in Haus und Beruf,'" *Illustrirte Zeitung*, 447.

51. On the impact of Hahn's work, see Harder, "Unsere Kunstgewerblerinnen," no. 34: 6. See also Stephani-Hahn, *Schaufenster Kunst*.

52. Plothow, "Rundgang durch die Ausstellung," 8, no. 2a: 86.

53. "Ausstellung 'Die Frau in Haus und Beruf,' Berlin 1912: Ausstellungs-Bedingungen für Industrie und Gewerbe," 7, regulations for exhibitors, private collection.

54. Gertrud Bäumer quoted in Consbruch, "Die Ausstellung," 707–8.

55. Scholtz, "Die Frau in Haus und Beruf." One of the most popular displays in the second hall was a sow with her piglets housed in a "hygienic" stall.

56. "Von der Ausstellung."

57. Stropp, "Die Ausstellung 'Die Frau in Haus und Beruf,'" *Illustrirte Zeitung*, 449. See also Hirschfeld, "Die Ausstellung 'Die Frau in Haus und Beruf' in Berlin," 314.

58. *Die Frau in Haus und Beruf*, 129–32.

59. "Die Frau in Haus und Beruf," *Berliner Tageblatt*.

60. Die Frau in Haus und Beruf was not the first women's exhibition or pavilion to integrate the idea of the machine or industrial hall. The most important precedent was probably the 1898 National Exhibition of Women's Labor, held at The Hague, because it focused on a similar national theme and included a substantial industrial section. For most Berliners, however, the Berlin Trade Exhibition of 1896 would have been the more familiar precursor, an association further reinforced by the iron and glass aesthetic exploited by Oppler-Legband and Reich. (The Hague show, by contrast, took place in wooden buildings.) On the Dutch exhibition, see Grever, "Reconstructing the Fatherland," 20–25.

61. Osborn, "Frauenarbeit in Kunst und Kunstgewerbe."

62. Heuss, "Die Frauenausstellung in Berlin," 171.

63. See, for example, Ratzka-Ernst, "Die Ausstellung 'Die Frau in Haus und Beruf,'" 38; and Radel, "Von der Berliner Ausstellung."

64. On the gendering of design values, see Stratigakos, "Architects in Skirts"; and Stratigakos, "Women and the Werkbund."

65. Plothow, "Die Ausstellung 'Die Frau in Haus und Beruf' I," 26.

66. Westheim, "Von der Frauen-Ausstellung-Berlin," 89; Westheim, "Die Frauenausstellung," 274.

67. Westheim, "Berlin," 142.

68. See Stratigakos, "Women and the Werkbund."

69. Ibid.

70. Ibid., 493–94. For the theorization of the female kleptomaniac and her destructive economic impact, see Spiekermann, "Theft and Thieves in German Department Stores, 1895–1930." On the "problem" of women's work in Wilhelmine discourses, see Franzoi, *At the Very Least She Pays the Rent*, 61ff.

71. Westheim, "Von der Frauen-Ausstellung-Berlin," 88.

72. Kraus, "Mir schwirrt der Kopf," 2. On the eroticized representation of women in *Die Fackel*, see Henderson, "Bachelor Culture in the Work of Adolf Loos," 129.

73. Heller, "Die Frau in Beruf," 1.

74. In 1910, 13.5 percent of Berlin apartments had a private bathroom. Teuteberg and Wischerman, *Wohnalltag in Deutschland 1850–1914*, 138.

75. Heyl, *Aus meinem Leben*, 114.

76. Hagen, "Zimmereinrichtungen von der Ausstellung," 715; Bäumer, "Ein Rückblick auf die Ausstellung," 388. On the luxury debates, see Breckman, "Disciplining Consumption."

77. Muthesius, *Style-Architecture and Building-Art*, 79; Muthesius, "Die Bedeutung des Kunstgewerbes," 181.

78. Schwartz, *The Werkbund*, 42–43.

79. Oppler-Legband, Wille, Hahn, and Baczko were Werkbund members by the spring of 1912. Lilly Reich's work for the School for Display Art brought her into Werkbund circles, and she was invited to join the organization later in 1912.

80. Breckman, "Disciplining Consumption," 492. Gertrud Bäumer, defending the show from allegations of elitism, argued that it heralded a new form of restrained female luxury. Bäumer, "Ein Rückblick auf die Ausstellung," 388.

81. Hagen, "Zimmereinrichtungen von der Ausstellung," 715.

82. Westheim, "Von der Frauen-Ausstellung-Berlin," 89; Westheim, "Berlin," 142.

83. Stratigakos, "Women and the Werkbund," 497–506.

84. *Die Frau in Haus und Beruf*, 77–85, 103; Hirschfeld, "Die Ausstellung 'Die Frau in Haus und Beruf' in Berlin," 314.

85. *Die Frau in Haus und Beruf*, 79.

86. Ibid., 102.

87. Droste, "Lilly Reich," 48. See also Bullock and Read, *The Movement for Housing Reform in Germany and France, 1840–1914*, 123ff.

88. Plothow, "Rundgang durch die Ausstellung," no. 3: 115; Bullock and Read, *The Movement for Housing Reform in Germany and France, 1840–1914*, 151–52.

89. *Die Frau in Haus und Beruf*, 102.

90. Urbach, "Bilder aus der Ausstellung," 94; Droste, "Lilly Reich," 48.

91. "Fr.," "Aerztliche Tagesfragen."

92. "L.," "Bürgerliche Innen-Räume," 223–24.

93. "E. S.," "Die Frau und die Wohnungskunst."

94. Westheim, "Die Frauenausstellung," 273–74; Westheim, "Berlin," 143.

95. Westheim, "Die Frauenausstellung," 274.

96. For a discussion of these debates, see Stratigakos, "Women and the Werkbund."

97. "D. W.," "Momentbilder von der Frauenausstellung."

98. Harder, "Unsere Kunstgewerblerinnen," 5.

99. "Pavillon für Jugendpflege," in *Die Frau in Haus und Beruf*, 108–15.

100. Jessen, "Das Reich der Frau," 415.

101. Westheim, "Die Frauenausstellung," 269.

102. Ibid., 269–70.

103. Heyl, "Die Ausstellung 'Die Frau in Haus und Beruf,'" *Die Woche*, 129. See also Heyl, "Die Ausstellung: Die Frau in Haus und Beruf," *Frauenwirtschaft*, 263.

104. Szczesny-Heyl, "Die Ausstellung," 65.

105. My use of this term is inspired by Matei Calinescu's description of kitsch as "aesthetic inadequacy." See Calinescu, *Five Faces of Modernity*, 236. See also Stratigakos, "Women and the Werkbund," 498, 509 n. 61.

106. Westheim, "Die Frauenausstellung," 271–73.

107. Westheim, "Berlin" 142.

108. Westheim, "Von der Frauen-Ausstellung-Berlin," 88.

109. Westheim, "Die Frauenausstellung," 270.

110. "Die Frau in Haus und Beruf," *Der Sturm*.

111. Lewis, *Art for All?* 212–16.

112. Much like Paul Westheim, Paul Fechter situated the accomplishments of the best exhibiting female artists in relation to the lingering "horrors" of "ladies' painting." Fechter, "Die Frau in der Kunst."

113. Salomon, "Zur Eröffnung der Ausstellung 'Die Frau in Haus und Beruf,'" *Centralblatt des BDF*, 175.

114. Why so few women architects participated is unclear. Other women were active in the field by this time, but they may have been unknown to Winkelmann. The three women who exhibited were connected personally or professionally, and all had studied at technical colleges (*technische Hochschulen*). Moreover, in keeping with the national focus of the exhibition, all three were German. The catalog entry, probably written by Winkelmann, suggests that she limited her selection of participants to practicing German women architects who had trained at a technical college; in 1912, this pool was small indeed. See *Die Frau in Haus und Beruf*, 152; and Stratigakos, "'I Myself Want to Build.'"

115. Urban, "Die Frau als Architektin," 16.

116. Heyl, "Die Ausstellung 'Die Frau in Haus und Beruf,'" *Die Woche*, 131.

117. *Die Frau in Haus und Beruf*, 168, 170–71. For a description of the contents and displays of one of the rooms (within the social work section) that featured images and models of various kinds of homes for female teachers, see Sprengel, "Die Frau in Haus und Beruf," 17, no. 5: 34–35.

118. Abeking, "Die Ausstellung 'Die Frau in Haus und Beruf.'" For a discussion of these homes, see Stratigakos, *Skirts and Scaffolding*, chapter 6.

119. Thoma, "Zur Ausstellung."

120. *Die Frau in Haus und Beruf*, 153. For a detailed discussion of Mogger's education and career, see Stratigakos, *Skirts and Scaffolding*, chapters 3 and 6.

121. Fechter, "Die Frau in der Kunst."

122. "Fest-Zeitung zum 25 jährigen Jubiläum von Fräulein Martin," September 8, 1917, 11, archive of the Pestalozzi-Fröbel-Haus, Berlin. On the talk and its context, see Sprengel, "'Die Frau in Haus und Beruf,'" 17, no. 6. Winkelmann's model was also on display at the exhibition in the room featuring homes for female teachers. See Sprengel, "Die Frau in Haus und Beruf," 17, no. 5: 35.

123. Announcement of lecture schedule in *Deutscher Lyceum-Club* 8, no. 3 (1912): 109.

124. "Der deutsche Frauenkongress"; Plothow, "Der Deutsche Frauenkongress in Berlin," 53; Gottschalk, "Bildungs- und Erziehungsfragen," 225; "Die Frau in Haus und Beruf," *Vossische Zeitung*; Arndt, "Zur Einführung," 1.

125. Stöcker, "Ein Nachwort zum Berliner Frauenkongress," 164.

126. "Die 'purpurne Revolution' der Suffragetten"; and "Schlusssitzung des Frauenkongresses."

127. "Die Frauen im Reichskanzlerpalais."

128. Urbach, "Bilder aus der Ausstellung," 93.

129. Cauer, "Gedanken zur Ausstellung."

130. Stöcker, "Ein Nachwort zum Berliner Frauenkongress."

131. Goldschmidt, "Die Damenausstellung," 394–95. For further criticism of the show's class elitism, see "Die Ausstellungen der Frauen"; and "A. C.," "Die Frau in Haus und Beruf: Ein Epilog," *Neue badische Landeszeitung*, no. 141 (1912), newspaper clipping in the Helene-Lange-Archiv, Landesarchiv Berlin.

132. The German text reads: "Ich? Ich habe die Totenscheine meiner ersten drei Männer ausgestellt." "Die Frau in Haus und Beruf," *Simplicissimus*.

133. "E. H.," "Die Frau in Haus und Beruf," 475.

134. "W. T.," "Die Frau in Haus und Beruf."

135. Lehmann, "Die 'Damenausstellung.'"

136. Heuss, "Die Frauenausstellung in Berlin," 171. The problem of class bias was not unique to the women's exhibition in Berlin. For further readings, refer to essays in Grever and Dieteren, eds., *A Fatherland for Women*, on Dutch and Danish women's exhibitions, which also discuss the interrelated issues of race.

137. Heuss, "Die Frauenausstellung in Berlin," 171.

138. Lehmann, "Die 'Damenausstellung,'" 10.

139. "Die Ausstellungen der Frauen."

140. Goldschmidt, "Die Damenausstellung," 395.

141. Lehmann, "Die 'Damenausstellung,'" 10.

142. Heuss, "Die Frauenausstellung in Berlin," 171.

143. According to Hans Ostwald, the area of the Tiergarten north of the Zoological Garden was known for its illicit evening trade. Ostwald, *Prostitutionsmärkte*, 27.

144. Urbach, "Bilder aus der Ausstellung," 93.

145. "Acta des Polizei-Präsidii zu Berlin, betreffend den Königlichen Commerzienrath und Fabrikbesitzer Georg Friedrich Heyl und Frau Hedwig Heyl," Landesarchiv Berlin, A Pr. Br. Rep. 30, no. 10564, 170.

146. Goldschmidt, "Die Damenausstellung," 395.

147. "E. H.," "Die Frau in Haus und Beruf," 479; "O. T. Sch.," "Die Frau in Haus und Beruf."

148. "F. E.," "Die Frau in Haus und Beruf."

149. Planert, *Antifeminismus im Kaiserreich*, 113.

150. Evans, *The Feminist Movement in Germany, 1894–1933*, 90.

151. Planert, *Antifeminismus im Kaiserreich*, 113.

152. Monsterberg, "Die Frau in Haus und Beruf."

153. Heyl, *Aus meinem Leben*, 135.

154. Hopffgarten, "Die Ausstellung: Die Frau in Haus und Beruf," 115.

155. Salomon, *Character Is Destiny*, 94.

5. The Architecture of Social Work

1. *Statistik der Frauenorganisationen im Deutschen Reich*, 17.

2. Reagin, *A German Women's Movement*, 36–37.

3. Vicinus, *Independent Women*, 211–46; Flanagan, *Seeing with Their Hearts*; Haar, "At Home in Public"; Spencer-Wood, "Utopian Visions and Architectural Designs of Turn-of-the-Century Social Settlements"; Gutman, "Adopted Homes for Yesterday's Children"; Spain, *How Women Saved the City*; Deutsch, *Women and the City*.

4. Hong, "Femininity as Vocation," 232–37. See also Schröder, "Soziale Frauenarbeit als bürgerliches Projekt."

5. Levy-Rathenau, "Soziale Berufsarbeit in der öffentlichen und privaten Wohlfahrtspflege," 8.

6. Hong, "Femininity as Vocation," 234–35.

7. Salomon, "Soziale Frauenarbeit in Berlin"; Hirsch, "Was Berlin für seine Kranken tut"; Lehr de Waal, "Die Wohlfahrtspflege in Berlin."

8. Lehr de Waal, "Die Wohlfahrtspflege in Berlin."

9. Ibid., 142.

10. Süchting-Hänger, "'Gleichgrosse mut'ge Helferinnen' in der weiblichen Gegenwelt"; Frevert, *Women in German History*, 137; Riemann, "Die Rolle der Frauenvereine in der Sozialpolitik."

11. Ritter, "Das Cecilienhaus des Vaterländischen Frauenvereins Charlottenburg," 26; *Bericht über die Verwaltung und den Stand der Gemeinde-Angelegenheiten der Stadt Charlottenburg für das Verwaltungsjahr 1909*, 153. The building, which was extensively damaged in the Second World War, is located at Otto-Suhr-Allee 59.

12. *Bericht über die Verwaltung*, 153; Ritter, "Das Cecilienhaus des Vaterländischen Frauen-vereins Charlottenburg."

13. Ritter, "Das Cecilienhaus des Vaterländischen Frauenvereins Charlottenburg."

14. *Bericht über die Verwaltung*, 152–53.

15. Ritter, "Das Cecilienhaus des Vaterländischen Frauenvereins Charlottenburg." Barba, Bergler, Dominik, Neugebauer, and Wohlauf, *"O Charlottenburg, du frauenfreundlichste unter den Städten . . ."*? 30–32.

16. Ritter, "Das Cecilienhaus des Vaterländischen Frauenvereins Charlottenburg," 26. The façade was actually composed of limestone. *Bericht über die Verwaltung*, 153.

17. Ritter, "Das Cecilienhaus des Vaterländischen Frauenvereins Charlottenburg," 26.

18. *Bericht über die Verwaltung*, 154.

19. Peyser, "Alice Salomon," 17–18.

20. On the history of the Girls' and Women's Groups, see Lees, *Cities, Sin and Social Reform in Imperial Germany*, 298–305; Sauer, "Den Zusammenhang zwischen der Frauenfrage und der sozialen Frage begreifen"; and Peyser, "Alice Salomon," 19–46.

21. Lees, *Cities, Sin and Social Reform*, 299; Salomon, *Zwanzig Jahre soziale Hilfsarbeit.*

22. Peyser, "Alice Salomon," 20, 29, 35.

23. Salomon, *Character Is Destiny*, 44–46.

24. See Albisetti, *Schooling German Girls and Women*, 238–73.

25. Lees, *Cities, Sin and Social Reform*, 305–6.

26. Salomon, "Zur Eröffnung der Sozialen Frauenschule," 105.

27. Sachsse, *Mütterlichkeit als Beruf*, 143–44.

28. The address is Barbarossastrasse 65 in Schöneberg.

29. Salomon, *Character Is Destiny*, 74–76.

30. Peyser, "Alice Salomon," 68.

31. Salomon, *Character Is Destiny*, 77. The building still stands. Original building plans (under the address Barbaraossa 64–65) are held by the building archive of Tempelhof City Hall.

32. Salomon, *Character Is Destiny*, 77.

33. Examples of Jessen's work were published in *Moderne Bauformen* 11 (1912): 431–33. Salomon was familiar with Jessen's architecture through a previous building he had designed for the Pestalozzi-Fröbel-Haus in 1905.

34. Peyser, "Alice Salomon," 68.

35. Kaplan, *The Making of the Jewish Middle Class*, 215–16; Sauer, "Den Zusammenhang zwischen der Frauenfrage und der sozialen Frage begreifen," 88.

36. *Bericht über das erste Arbeiterinnenheim in Berlin SO, Brückenstrasse 81* (Berlin, 1902), 1, STA Rep. 00-02/1 2454, Landesarchiv Berlin.

37. "Das erste Arbeiterinnenheim in Berlin."

38. Herzog, "Arbeiterinnenheime," 281. For a description of *Schlafstelle* conditions, see Trott, "Die Wohnungsfrage eine brennende Frauenfrage," 139.

39. Das Comité zur Errichtung von Arbeiterinnenheimen, *3. Tätigkeitsbericht über die Arbeiterinnenheime* (Berlin: Sommer, 1906), 4–5, HA-I, Rep. 77, Tit. 1072, no. 63, Geheimes Staatsarchiv Preussischer Kulturbesitz, Berlin.

40. The addresses of the Arbeiterinnenheime were: Brückenstrasse 8 (House I, 1898); Usedomstrasse 7 (House II, 1904); Kottbuser Ufer 33 (House III, 1906); Greifswalder Strasse 225 (House IV, 1912).

41. "Ein neues Arbeiterinnenheim in Berlin."

42. Das Comité zur Errichtung von Arbeiterinnenheimen, 3. *Tätigkeitsbericht über die Arbeiterinnenheime*, 13.

43. Roth, "Das Arbeiterinnenheim in der Greifswalder Strasse als Zufluchtsstätte." The home opened by Mathilde Kirschner in 1908, mentioned in chapter 3, was clearly influenced by their example. See Kirschner, "Ein Heim für Arbeiterinnen."

44. Salomon, "Zehn Jahre Arbeiterinnenheime," 132; Zepler, "Heimstätten für Arbeiterinnen," 683–84. For a survey of charitable homes for female workers in Berlin, see Zepler, "Frauenheime." Although Salomon encouraged less regimentation, she nonetheless believed that female workers needed discipline, particularly in relation to their excessive love of pleasure. See Salomon, "Ein Arbeiterinnen-Klub in Berlin."

45. Salomon, "Zehn Jahre Arbeiterinnenheime," 132.

46. Vicinus, *Independent Women*, 214.

47. Salomon, "Zehn Jahre Arbeiterinnenheime," 132–33.

48. Salomon, *Character Is Destiny*, 30. For similar criticisms that *Arbeiterinnenheime* retarded social change, see Mentner, "Bürgerliche Frauenbewegung und Arbeiterinnenheime," 32–33.

49. Vicinus, *Independent Women*, 216.

50. "Das Zweite Arbeiterinnenheim in Berlin."

51. Salomon, "Zehn Jahre Arbeiterinnenheime," 132–33; Salomon, *Character Is Destiny*, 29; Das Comité zur Errichtung von Arbeiterinnenheimen, 3. *Tätigkeitsbericht über die Arbeiterinnenheime*, 14.

52. Salomon, *Character Is Destiny*, 29.

53. Salomon, "Zehn Jahre Arbeiterinnenheime"; Salomon, *Character Is Destiny*, 29.

54. Vicinus, *Independent Women*, 216.

55. Salomon, "Zehn Jahre Arbeiterinnenheime," 133.

56. Salomon, *Character Is Destiny*, 29.

57. Das Comité zur Errichtung von Arbeiterinnenheimen, 3. *Tätigkeitsbericht über die Arbeiterinnenheime*, 5–8.

58. Vicinus, *Independent Women*, 220.

59. See, for example, Evans, *Tales from the German Underworld*, 166–212; and Rowe, *Representing Berlin*, 81–129.

60. Seydel, *Das Charlottenburger Wohnungsamt*, 11–12.

61. National Council of Women of Great Britain, *Women as Sanitary Inspectors*, 1–4; emphasis in the original. On women housing inspectors in England, see Adams, *Architecture in the Family Way*, 98–99.

62. "Weibliche Gesundheitsinspektoren"; "Weibliche Sanitätsinspektion in England."

63. "E. D.," "Die Wohnungsinspektorin." Conrad's later married name was Kester-Conrad.

64. "Die Frau in der Wohnungspflege."

65. Kester-Conrad, "Weibliche Wohnungsinspektion," 71.

66. Voss-Zietz, "Die Arbeit der Frau in der Wohnungsfürsorge," 9.

67. Seydel, *Das Charlottenburger Wohnungsamt,* 34–35, 20.

68. Ibid., 37–39, 80–82.

69. Lüders, *Fürchte Dich Nicht,* 50–52.

70. Seydel, *Das Charlottenburger Wohnungsamt,* 25, 29–33. See also *Die gesundheitlichen Einrichtungen der Königl. Residenzstadt Charlottenburg,* 68–75.

71. Stratigakos, "'I Myself Want to Build.'"

72. Schulze, "Wohnungsaufsicht."

73. Lüders, "Probleme der städtischen Wohnungspflege und die weibliche Wohnungsinspektion," 134.

74. Pochhammer, "Berliner Wohnungsverhältnisse," 233. On contemporary views of women architects, see Stratigakos, "Architects in Skirts."

75. Lange, "Die Frau in der Wohnungsinpektion," nos. 11 and 12: 43.

76. Ibid., 42–43.

77. Ibid., 43.

78. Debates about what to call housing inspection reflected the struggle to define a new field of government intervention. Proponents of a more authoritarian approach favored *Wohnungsinspektion* or *Wohnungsaufsicht* (housing supervision), whereas others prefered the gentler *Wohnungspflege.* The Charlottenburg housing office chose the latter, calling its male inspectors *Wohnungspfleger.*

79. Lüders, "Der Entwurf zum Berliner Wohnungsamt," 178.

80. "E. D.," "Die Wohnungsinspektorin."

81. Lange, "Die Frau in der Wohnungsinspektion," nos. 11 and 12: 42.

82. "E. D.," "Die Wohnungsinspektorin."

83. Lange, "Die Frau in der Wohnungsinspektion," nos. 11 and 12: 42.

84. Auguste Lange, quoted in "Wohnungsaufsicht: Die Frau in der Wohnungsinspektion."

85. "Wohungsaufsicht: Ausbau der Wohnungsaufsicht," 285.

86. Ibid.

87. "E. D.," "Die Wohnungsinspektorin."

88. Schrey, "Soziale Berufe."

89. Lange quoted in "Wohnungsbeaufsichtigung," 162.

90. H[eller], "Noch einmal die Wohnungsinspektorin."

91. "Wohungsaufsicht: Ausbau der Wohnungsaufsicht," 285.

92. Voss-Zietz, "Die Arbeit der Frau in der Wohnungsfürsorge," 11.

93. Marie Kröhne quoted by Bäumer, "Aus der Arbeit der hessischen Wohnungsinspektorin," 106.

94. Enke, *Private, genossenschaftliche und städtische Wohnungspolitik in Essen a/R. vom Anfang des 19. Jahrhunderts bis zur Gegenwart,* 138–39.

95. Lange quoted in "Wohnungsbeaufsichtigung," 163.

96. Kester-Conrad, "Weibliche Wohnungsinspektion," 72.

97. Kröhne, "Wohnungsaufsicht." See also Apolant, "Kommunal-soziale Frauenberufe," 311.

98. "Die Mitwirkung der Frau in der Wohnungspflege und Wohnungsaufsicht," 114.

99. "Wohungsaufsicht: Ausbau der Wohnungsaufsicht," 285.

100. Kester-Conrad, "Weibliche Wohnungsinspektion," 71.

101. Kröhne, "Eindrücke vom Wohnungskongress in Berlin," 2. See also Franken, "Die Tätigkeit einer Wohnungsinspektorin," 327; and Kröhne, "Ehrenamtliche Wohnungsfürsorge," 115.

102. Auguste Lange, quoted in "Wohnungsaufsicht: Die Frau in der Wohnungsinspektion."

103. Schulze, "Wohnungsaufsicht," 261.

104. Lange, "Die Frau in der Wohnungsinspektion," nos. 11 and 12: 42.

105. Kester-Conrad, "Weibliche Wohnungsinspektion," 72.

106. Lange quoted in "Kongress für 'Wohnungsaufsicht und Wohnungspflege,'" 97. On pay and professional status issues, see also Gottberg, "Die Wohnungsaufsicht in Bayern," 3; Lüders, "Probleme der städtischen Wohnungspflege," 135; and Lüders, "Der Entwurf zum Berliner Wohnungsamt," 178.

107. Kröhne, "Eindrücke vom Wohnungskongress in Berlin," 2.

108. "Die Frauen und die Wohnungsaufsicht," 247.

109. Ibid.

110. Kröhne, "Eindrücke vom Wohnungskongress in Berlin," 2.

111. Kröhne, "Ehrenamtliche Wohnungsfürsorge," 115; see also Kester-Conrad, "Weibliche Wohnungsinspektion," 72.

112. Kester-Conrad, "Weibliche Wohnungsinspektion," 72.

113. "Frauen in der Wohnungsinspektion," 136.

114. See, for example, Otto, "Die Frau in der Wohnungsinspektion," 188; and Apolant, "Die Frau im öffentlichen Leben," 107–8.

115. Lange, "Die Frau in der Wohnungsinspektion," nos. 13 and 14: 51.

EPILOGUE

1. Evans, *The Coming of the Third Reich*, 236, 270, 291.

2. Baumhoff, *The Gendered World of the Bauhaus*, 53–75; Maasberg and Prinz, *Die Neuen kommen!*

3. Salomon, "Das Frauenstudium und die wissenschaftlichen Frauenberufe"; Salomon, "Das Frauenstudium und die wissenschaftlichen Frauenberufe," 2nd ed.

4. Koonz, *Mothers in the Fatherland*, 26; see also Sneeringer, *Winning Women's Votes*, 20, 28–29.

5. Reagin, *A German Women's Movement*, 203–19.

6. Bridenthal, "'Professional' Housewives," 155.

7. Bridenthal and Koonz, "Beyond *Kinder, Küche, Kirche*," 33–65; Koonz, *Mothers in the Fatherland*, 21–49.

8. Plothow, "Frauenbewegung und Frauenvereine"; Jecker, "Aufbau und Aufgaben des Reichsverbandes Deutscher Hausfrauenvereine."

9. Mühsam-Werther, "Was muss die Hausfrau von Berlin wissen?"

10. Heyl, "Hausfrauenarbeit als Berufsarbeit."

11. Frevert, *Women in German History*, 176.

12. Beer, *Architektur für den Alltag;* Nolan, *Visions of Modernity,* 206–26; Bullock, "First the Kitchen—Then the Façade."

13. Henderson, "A Revolution in the Woman's Sphere."

14. Ibid., 232–37; Noever, ed., *Die Frankfurter Küche von Margarete Schütte-Lihotzky.*

15. Friedman with Casciato, "Family Matters"; Constant, *Eileen Gray,* 93–125; Bonnevier, "A Queer Analysis of Eileen Gray's E.1027."

16. Pochhammer, "Berliner Wohnungsverhältnisse"; Hessberger, "Wohnungswesen in Berlin." The building still stands at Wundtstrasse 40–44. Despite Hessberger's insistence on the building's novelty, its origins date to the Wilhelmine period. In 1913, the Catholic league began providing housing for women on a modest scale, initially renting a single apartment and later expanding to several floors of a building. In the early 1920s, the league acquired a villa and on adjacent property built the women's residence in 1931. Barba, Bergler, Dominik, Neugebauer, and Wohlauf, "Das Frauenbundhaus am Lietzensee," in *"O Charlottenburg, du frauenfreundlichste unter den Städten . . ."?* 13; Ehlert, "Das Frauenbundhaus in Berlin."

17. Reagin, *A German Women's Movement,* 218.

18. Dölle, *Die (un)heimliche Macht des Geldes,* 221–22.

19. Marelle, "Berliner Frauenklubs," 165. On the women's hospital, see Ichenhaeuser, "Weibliche Arzte [*sic*] und Frauenkrankenhäuser unter Leitung weiblicher Ärzte," 613; Hoesch, *Ärztinnen für Frauen,* 94–131, 142; and Stratigakos, *Skirts and Scaffolding,* 271–80.

20. Weinberg, "Ein neues Frauenheim"; "Genossenschaft für Frauenheimstätten," *Was die Frau von Berlin wissen muss; 1 Jahr Studentinnen-Tagesheim (Helene-Lange-Heim).*

21. Marelle, "Berliner Frauenklubs."

22. On representations of Berlin as a woman, see Rowe, *Representing Berlin;* Ankum, ed., *Women in the Metropolis;* and Tartar, *Lustmord.*

23. Clobes, "Möbelkunst und Wohnkultur im neuzeitlichen Berlin," 232.

24. Stoehr, "Neue Frau und Alte Bewegung?"

25. Meskimmon, *We Weren't Modern Enough,* 163–96; Sykora, Dorgerloh, Noell-Rumpeltes, and Raev, eds., *Die Neue Frau;* Petro, *Joyless Streets,* 68–78.

26. Frevert, *Women in German History,* 168–204.

27. Clobes, "Möbelkunst und Wohnkultur im neuzeitlichen Berlin," 232.

28. Müller, "Die Kunst, in Berlin prominent zu sein."

BIBLIOGRAPHY

Primary and Secondary Sources

Abeking, S. "Die Ausstellung 'Die Frau in Haus und Beruf.'" *Düsseldorfer General-Anzeiger*, no. 12, March 24, 1912, Frauen-Rundschau section.

Abrams, Lynn, and Elizabeth Harvey, eds. *Gender Relations in German History: Power, Agency and Experience from the Sixteenth to the Twentieth Century*. Women's History. London: University College London Press, 1996.

Adams, Annmarie. *Architecture in the Family Way: Doctors, Houses, and Women, 1870–1900*. Montreal and Kingston: McGill–Queen's University Press, 1996.

Agrest, Diana, Patricia Conway, and Leslie Kanes Weisman, eds. *The Sex of Architecture*. New York: Abrams, 1996.

Albisetti, James C. "American Women's Colleges through European Eyes, 1865–1914." *History of Education Quarterly* 32, no. 4 (1992): 439–58.

———. *Schooling German Girls and Women: Secondary and Higher Education in the Nineteenth Century*. Princeton, N.J.: Princeton University Press, 1988.

Allen, Ann Taylor. *Feminism and Motherhood in Germany, 1800–1914*. New Brunswick, N.J.: Rutgers University Press, 1991.

———. "Feminism and Motherhood in Germany and in International Perspective, 1800–1914." In *Gender and Germanness: Cultural Productions of Nation*, ed. Patricia Herminghouse and Magda Mueller, 113–28. Providence, R.I.: Berghahn Books, 1997.

"Am 6. Januar ist die Wissenschaftliche Deputation. . . ." *Centralblatt des Bundes Deutscher Frauenvereine* 13, no. 20 (1912): 158.

Anderson, Stanford. *Peter Behrens and a New Architecture for the Twentieth Century*. Cambridge, Mass.: MIT Press, 2000.

Ankum, Katherine von, ed. *Women in the Metropolis: Gender and Modernity in Weimar Culture*. Berkeley: University of California Press, 1997.

"Ansprache von Frau Hedwig Heyl." Special exhibition issue, *Deutscher Lyceum-Club* 8, no. 2a (1912): 72–73.

Anthony, Katharine. *Feminism in Germany and Scandinavia*. New York: Holt, 1915.

"A. P." [Anna Plothow?]. "Der Internationale Lyceumsklub." *Berliner Tageblatt*, no. 590, November 19, 1904, Frauen-Rundschau section.

——. "Das Viktoria-Studienhaus: Ein neues Studentinnenheim in Charlottenburg." *Neue Bahnen* 50, no. 18 (1915): 142–43.

Apolant, Jenny. "Die Frau im öffentlichen Leben: Die Frau in der Gemeinde." *Jahrbuch der Frauenbewegung* (1912): 101–11.

——. "Kommunal-soziale Frauenberufe." *Die Welt der Frau*, no. 20 (1911): 310–11.

Architekten Verein zu Berlin, ed. *Berlin und Seine Bauten.* Berlin: Architekten-Verein, 1877.

Arndt, Delia. "Zur Einführung." *Gartenlaube*, special issue, *Frauen-Kongress: Illustrierter Bericht der "Gartenlaube" mit "Welt der Frau"* (1912): 1–2.

Arnold, Hans [Bertha von Bülow]. "Die alleinstehende Frau." *Die deutsche Frau* 2, no. 52 (1912): 7–8.

"A. S." [Alice Salomon?]. "Das Haus in der Sonne." *P. F. H. II Zeitung* (January 1914): 19–20.

Aschhoff, Gunther. *Das deutsche Genossenschaftswesen.* 2nd ed. Frankfurt: Knapp, 1995.

"Attack Women's Bank." *New York Times*, June 14, 1914.

"Aus dem Reiche." *Hamburgischer Correspondent*, no. 101, February 24, 1912.

"Die Ausstellungen der Frauen." *Für die Frau Meisterin*, no. 8 (1912): 6.

Baedeker, Karl. *Berlin and Its Environs.* 5th ed. Leipzig: Baedeker, 1912.

Balfour, Alan. *Berlin: The Politics of Order, 1737–1989.* New York: Rizzoli, 1990.

Barba, Monika, Andrea Bergler, Annette Dominik, Eva Neugebauer, and Gabriele Wohlauf. *"O Charlottenburg, du frauenfreundlichste unter den Städten . . ."? Wege zur Frauengeschichte Charlottenburgs 1850–1930.* Berlin: Frauenforschungs-, -bildungs- und –informationszentrum, 1989.

Barry, Richard. "The Tea Rooms, Where Society and Business Meet: Where the Women from One Field Reach Up, and from the Other Down, Groping toward Each Other—the Drinking and the Intrigue—the Froth and the Earnest Purpose." *New York Times*, December 1, 1912.

Barth-Scalmani, Gunda, and Margret Friedrich. "Frauen auf der Wiener Weltausstellung von 1873: Blick auf die Bühne und hinter die Kulissen." In *Bürgerliche Frauenkultur im 19. Jahrhundert*, ed. Brigitte Mazohl-Wallnig, 175–232. Vienna: Bölhau, 1995.

Bartning, Otto. "Sollen Damen bauen?" *Die Welt der Frau*, no. 40 (1911): 625–26.

Baudissin, Eva Gräfin von. "Die Architektin." *Die Frauenfachschule*, no. 29 (1919): 598–601.

Bäumer, Gertrud. "Aus der Arbeit der hessischen Wohnungsinspektorin." *Neue Bahnen* 46, no. 14 (1911): 105–8.

——, ed. *Der deutsche Frauenkongress: Sämtliche Vorträge.* Leipzig: Teubner, 1912.

——. *Die Frau und das geistige Leben.* Die Kulturaufgaben der Frau, ed. Jakob Wychgram. Leipzig: Amelangs, 1911.

——. "Ein Rückblick auf die Ausstellung." *Die Frau* 19, no. 7 (1912): 385–89.

Baumhoff, Anja. *The Gendered World of the Bauhaus.* Frankfurt am Main: Peter Lang, 2001.

Beaulieu, Gertraut von. *Grossstadt-Originale: Humoristisch-satirische Skizzen.* Leipzig: Reclam, 1903.

——. *Neu-Berlin: Was Frau Guticke in der Reichshauptstadt erlebt.* Breslau: Schlesischer, 1890.

——. *Das weibliche Berlin: Bilder aus dem heutigen socialen Leben.* Berlin: Fischer, 1892.

Bechtold, F. "Die Frau in Haus und Beruf." *Für die Frau Meisterin*, no. 6 (1912): 2–4.

Beci, Veronika. *Musikalische Salons: Blütezeit einer Frauenkultur.* Düsseldorf: Artemis and Winkler, 2000.

Beer, Ingeborg. *Architektur für den Alltag: Vom sozialen und frauenorientierten Anspruch der Siedlungsarchitektur in den zwanziger Jahren.* Berlin: Schelzky and Jeep, 1994.

Beermann, Eugenie. "Erinnerungen an Bryn Mawr." *Die Studentin* 8, no. 1 (1919): 4–6.

Behnisch-Kappstein, Anna. "Wohnung und Frau." *Die Welt der Frau,* no. 24 (1916): 380–81.

Beier, Rosmarie. *Frauenarbeit und Frauenalltag im Deutschen Kaiserreich.* Frankfurt: Campus, 1983.

Bell, David, and Gill Valentine, eds. *Mapping Desire: Geographies of Sexualities.* London: Routledge, 1995.

Bennett, Tony. "The Exhibitionary Complex." *New Formations,* no. 4 (1988): 73–102.

Bergdoll, Barry. *European Architecture 1750–1890.* Oxford: Oxford University Press, 2000.

Berghahn, Volker R. *Imperial Germany, 1871–1914: Economy, Society, Culture, and Politics.* Providence, R.I.: Berghahn, 1994.

"Bericht über die 6. ordentliche Generalversammlung des Deutschen Lyceum-Clubs." *Deutscher Lyceum-Club* 8, no. 5 (1912): 335–41.

Bericht über die Verwaltung und den Stand der Gemeinde-Angelegenheiten der Stadt Charlottenburg für das Verwaltungsjahr 1909 (1910).

Berlin und die Berliner: Leute, Dinge, Sitten, Winke. Karlsruhe: Bielefelds, 1905.

"Die Besichtigung der Frauenbank." *Frauenkapital—eine werdende Macht,* no. 2 (1914): 5–9.

Betterton, Rosemary. "Women Artists, Modernity and Suffrage Cultures in Britain and Germany 1890-1920." In *Women Artists and Modernism,* ed. Katy Deepwell, 18–35. Manchester: Manchester University Press, 1998.

Bilski, Emily D., and Emily Braun. "The Power of Conversation: Jewish Women and Their Salons: Introduction." In *Jewish Women and Their Salons: The Power of Conversation,* ed. Emily D. Bilski and Emily Braun, 1–21. New York: Jewish Museum; and New Haven, Conn.: Yale University Press, 2005.

————, eds. *Jewish Women and Their Salons: The Power of Conversation.* New York: Jewish Museum; and New Haven, Conn.: Yale University Press, 2005.

Bingaman, Amy, Lise Sanders, and Rebecca Zorach. *Embodied Utopias: Gender, Social Change, and the Modern Metropolis.* London: Routledge, 2002.

Blackbourn, David. *The Long Nineteenth Century: A History of Germany, 1780–1918.* New York: Oxford University Press, 1998.

Blackbourn, David, and Richard J. Evans, eds. *The German Bourgeoisie.* London: Routledge, 1991.

Blair, Karen J. *The Clubwoman as Feminist: True Womanhood Redefined, 1868–1914.* New York: Holmes and Meier, 1980.

Bode, Wilhelm. "Vom Luxus." *Der Kunstwart* 19, no. 22 (1906): 493–503.

Boetticher, Else von. "Heimstätten für Frauen." *Berliner Frauenclub von 1900* 3, no. 10 (1915): 5–7.

————. "Das neue Heim des Deutschen Lyzeumklubs." *Die Welt der Frau,* no. 1 (1915): 14–16.

Bohlmann, Rachel E. "Our 'House Beautiful': The Woman's Temple and the WCTU Effort to Establish Place and Identity in Downtown Chicago, 1887–1898." *Journal of Women's History* 11, no. 2 (1999): 110–34.

Bonnevier, Katarina. "A Queer Analysis of Eileen Gray's E.1027." In *Negotiating Domesticity:*

Spatial Productions of Gender in Modern Architecture, ed. Hilde Heynen and Gülsüm Baydar, 162–80. London: Routledge, 2005.

Bram, Franziska. "Die Dame im Restaurant!?" *Die deutsche Frau* 3, no. 18 (1913): 17–18.

Breckman, Warren G. "Disciplining Consumption: The Debate about Luxury in Wilhelmine Germany, 1890–1914." *Journal of Social History* 24, no. 3 (1991): 485–505.

Bridenthal, Renate. "'Professional' Housewives: Stepsisters of the Women's Movement." In *When Biology Became Destiny: Women in Weimar and Nazi Germany,* ed. Renate Bridenthal, Atina Grossmann, and Marion Kaplan, 153–73. New York: Monthly Review Press, 1984.

Bridenthal, Renate, Atina Grossmann, and Marion Kaplan, eds. *When Biology Became Destiny: Women in Weimar and Nazi Germany.* New York: Monthly Review Press, 1984.

Bridenthal, Renate, and Claudia Koonz. "Beyond *Kinder, Küche, Kirche:* Weimar Women in Politics and Work." In *When Biology Became Destiny: Women in Weimar and Nazi Germany,* ed. Renate Bridenthal, Atina Grossmann, and Marion Kaplan, 33–65. New York: Monthly Review Press, 1984.

Brockington, Grace Ellen. "'A World Fellowship': The Founding of the International Lyceum Club." *Transnational Associations* 1 (2005): 15–22.

Broecker, Ludwine von. "'Dank' und 'Wilkommen.'" *Nachrichtenblatt Haus Ottilie von Hansemann, Victoria-Studienhaus,* no. 14 (1934): 5–6.

"B. T." "Our Ladies Clubs: I. The Alexandra." *Graphic* 77, no. 1997 (1908): 333.

Buddensieg, Tilmann, ed. *Berlin 1900–1933: Architecture and Design.* Berlin: Mann, 1987.

"A Building for Women's Clubs." *New York Times,* May 3, 1896.

Bullock, Nicholas. "First the Kitchen—Then the Façade." *Journal of Design History* 1, nos. 3–4 (1988): 177–91.

Bullock, Nicholas, and James Read. *The Movement for Housing Reform in Germany and France, 1840–1914.* Cambridge: Cambridge University Press, 1985.

Calhoun, Craig, ed. *Habermas and the Public Sphere.* Cambridge, Mass.: MIT Press, 1992.

Calinescu, Matei. *Five Faces of Modernity: Modernism, Avant-Garde, Decadence, Kitsch, Postmodernism.* Rev. ed. Durham, N.C.: Duke University Press, 1987.

Canning, Kathleen. *Gender History in Practice: Historical Perspectives on Bodies, Class, and Citizenship.* Ithaca, N.Y.: Cornell University Press, 2006.

Carstens, Cornelia, Stefanie Höver, Stephanie von Ow, Heike Stange, and Rita Wolters, eds. *Frauen an der Spree: Ein Spaziergang durch die Geschichte.* Berlin: be.bra, 1999.

Carstens, Cornielia, and Margret Luikenga, eds. *Immer den Frauen nach! Spaziergang am Landwehrkanal zur Berliner Frauengeschichte.* Berlin: Berliner Geschichtswerkstatt, 1993.

Cauer, Minna. "Gedanken zur Ausstellung: 'Die Frau in Haus und Beruf.'" *Die Frauenbewegung* 18, no. 5 (1912): 35–36.

Cecil, Lamar. *Wilhelm II,* 2 vols. Chapel Hill, N.C.: University of North Carolina Press, 1989.

Chapman, Dora D'Espaigne. "The Lyceum Club." *Girl's Own Paper* 26, no. 1312 (1905): 323–25.

Clausen, Meredith L. *Frantz Jourdain and the Samaritaine: Art Nouveau Theory and Criticism.* Leiden: Brill, 1987.

Clobes, W. "Möbelkunst und Wohnkultur im neuzeitlichen Berlin." In *Was die Frau von Berlin wissen muss: Ein praktisches Frauenbuch für Einheimische und Fremde,* 229–33. 2nd ed. Berlin: Loesdau, 1932.

Cocks, Geoffrey, and Konrad H. Jarausch, eds. *German Professions, 1800–1950.* New York: Oxford University Press, 1990.

Coleman, Debra, Elizabeth Danze, and Carol Henderson, eds. *Architecture and Feminism.* New York: Princeton Architectural Press, 1996.

Colomina, Beatriz, ed. *Sexuality and Space.* Princeton, N.J.: Princeton Architectural Press, 1992.

Colze, Leo. *Berliner Warenhäuser* [1908]. Ed. Detlef Bluhm, vol. 4 of Berliner Texte. Berlin: Fannei and Walz, 1989.

Consbruch, E. "Die Ausstellung: 'Die Frau in Haus und Beruf.'" *Der alte Glaube* 13, no. 30 (1912): 707–11.

Constant, Caroline. *Eileen Gray.* London: Phaidon, 2000.

Cordato, Mary Frances. *Representing the Expansion of Woman's Sphere: Women's Work and Culture at the World's Fairs of 1876, 1893, and 1904.* Ann Arbor, Mich.: UMI, 1989.

Crawford, Elizabeth. *Enterprising Women: The Garretts and Their Circle.* London: Francis Boutle, 2002.

Cromley, Elizabeth Collins. *Alone Together: A History of New York's Early Apartments.* Ithaca, N.Y.: Cornell University Press, 1990.

Crossick, Geoffrey, and Serge Jaumain, eds. *Cathedrals of Consumption: The European Department Store, 1850–1939.* Aldershot: Ashgate, 1999.

Dal Co, Francesco. *Figures of Architecture and Thought: German Architecture Culture, 1880–1920.* New York: Rizzoli, 1990.

Dalhoff, Jutta, Uschi Frey, and Ingrid Schöll. *Frauenmacht in der Geschichte: Beiträge des Historik-erinnentreffens 1985 zur Frauengeschichtsforschung.* Düsseldorf: Schwann, 1986.

"Das Damenheim zu Potsdam." *Das deutsche Landhaus* 10 (1906): 173–75.

"Damen-Wohnungen," advertisement. *Centralblatt des Bundes Deutscher Frauenvereine* 5, no. 7 (1903): 56.

Danneel, Margarete. "Nachrichten von den Mitgliedern." *Deutscher Lyceum-Club* 5, no. 4 (1910): 45–47.

Daussig, Fritz. "Ein weiblicher Architekt." *Daheim* 45, no. 48 (1909): 11–14.

Deepwell, Katy, ed. *Women Artists and Modernism.* Manchester: Manchester University Press, 1998.

Dehn, Paul. *Die Grossbazare und Massenzweiggeschäfte.* Berlin: Trowitzsch, 1899.

D'Espaigne, Dora. "The Lyceum Club for Ladies." *Lady's Realm* 16 (1904): 602–8.

Deutsch, Sarah. *Women and the City: Gender, Space, and Power in Boston, 1870–1940.* New York: Oxford University Press, 2000.

"Der deutsche Frauenkongress." *Der Tag,* no. 106, February 27, 1912.

Deutscher Lyceum-Club Berlin. *Aus der Geschichte des Deutschen Lyceum-Clubs in Berlin.* Berlin: Deutscher Lyceum-Club Berlin, 1973.

Deutscher Lyceum-Club: Offizielles Organ des Deutschen Lyceum-Clubs. Berlin, vol. 2 (1907) through vol. 29 (1934).

"Diplomingenieur Dieter." "Die Wohnung einer selbständigen Dame." *Daheim* 52, no. 32 (1916): 23–24.

Dollard, Catherine. "The *alte Jungfer* as New Deviant: Representation, Sex, and the Single Woman in Germany." *German Studies Review* 29, no. 1 (2006): 107–26.

Dölle, Gilla. *Die (un)heimliche Macht des Geldes: Finanzierungsstrategien der bürgerlichen Frauenbewegung in Deutschland zwichen 1865 und 1933.* Frankfurt am Main: dipa, 1997.

Dörhöfer, Kerstin. *Pionierinnen in der Architektur: Eine Baugeschichte der Moderne.* Berlin: Wasmuth, 2004.

Doughan, David, and Peter Gordon. *Women, Clubs and Associations in Britain.* London: Routledge, 2006.

Drews, Karl. "Weibliche Ingenieure: Ein Beitrag zur Frauenfrage." Published in 2 parts in *Die Umschau* 12 (1908), no. 4: 61–64; no. 5: 89–91.

Droste, Magdalena. "Lilly Reich: Her Career as an Artist." In Matilda McQuaid and Magdalena Droste, *Lilly Reich: Designer and Architect*, 47–59. New York: Museum of Modern Art, 1996.

———. "Women in the Arts and Crafts and in Industrial Design, 1890–1933." In *Women in Design: Careers and Life Histories since 1900*, ed. Angela Oedekoven-Gerischer, Andrea Scholtz, Edith Medek, and Petra Kurz, vol. 1, 174–202. Stuttgart: Design Center Stuttgart, 1989.

"D. W." "Momentbilder von der Frauenausstellung." *Vossische Zeitung*, no. 105, February 27, 1912.

"E. D." "Die Wohnungsinspektorin." *Daheim* 45, no. 11 (1908): 23.

"E. H." "Die Frau in Haus und Beruf." *Die Welt*, no. 24 (1912): 475–79.

Ehlert, Margarete. "Das Frauenbundhaus in Berlin." In *Jahrhundertwende, Jahrhundertmitte: Der Katholische Deutsche Frauenbund auf dem Wege, 1903–1953*, 24–25. Cologne: Zentrale des Katholischen Deutschen Frauenbundes, 1953.

Ehrenpreis, David. "Cyclists and Amazons: Representing the New Woman in Wilhelmine Germany." *Woman's Art Journal* 20, no. 1 (1999): 25–31.

Eichler, Elisabeth. "Die Frauenwohnung." *Daheim* 50, no. 24 (1914): 26–27.

Eifert, Christiane, and Susanne Rouette, eds. *Unter allen Umständen: Frauengeschichte(n) in Berlin.* Berlin: Rotation, 1986.

"Die Einweihung des Lehrerinnenheims." *Monatsblatt für Berliner Lehrerinnen* 6, no. 11 (1911): 215–19.

Eloesser, Arthur. *Die Strasse meiner Jugend: Berliner Skizzen.* 1919. Repr. Berlin: Arsenal, 1987.

"Else Oppler-Legband." In *Angewandte Kunst: Deutscher Lyceum-Club Berlin*, ed. Jarno Jessen. Berlin: Lipperheide, c. 1908.

"E. M. E." "What the Lyceum Club Is Doing." *Queen: The Lady's Newspaper* 116 (1904): 539.

Enke, Erich. *Private, genossenschaftliche und städtische Wohnungspolitik in Essen a/R. vom Anfang des 19. Jahrhunderts bis zur Gegenwart.* Stuttgart: Enke, 1912.

Enstam, Elizabeth York. *Women and the Creation of Urban Life: Dallas, Texas, 1843–1920.* College Station: Texas A&M University Press, c. 1998.

Enzelberger, Sabina. *Sozialgeschichte des Lehrerberufs: Gesellschaftliche Stellung und Professionalisierung von Lehrerinnen und Lehrern von den Anfängen bis zur Gegenwart.* Weinheim: Juventa, 2001.

Erdmann, Rhoda. "Berlins wissenschaftliche Anstalten." In *Was die Frau von Berlin wissen muss: Ein praktisches Frauenbuch für Einheimische und Fremde*, ed. Eliza Ichenhaeuser, 54–73. Berlin: Loesdau, 1913.

"Das erste Arbeiterinnenheim in Berlin." *Centralblatt des Bundes Deutscher Frauenvereine* 2, no. 6 (1900): 47.

"Die erste Genossenschaftsbank selbständiger Frauen." *Die deutsche Frau*, no. 28 (1911): 5–6.

"E. S." "Die Frau und die Wohnungskunst." *Bauwelt* 3, no. 16 (1912): 35–36.

Evans, Richard J. *The Coming of the Third Reich*. New York: Penguin, 2003.

———. *The Feminist Movement in Germany, 1894–1933*. Vol. 6 in Sage Studies in 20th Century History. London: Sage, 1976.

———. *Tales from the German Underworld: Crime and Punishment in the Nineteenth Century*. New Haven, Conn.: Yale University Press, 1998.

Falk, Erich. "Die rückständige Börsenordnung," parts I and II. *Frauenkapital—ein werdende Macht* (1914), no. 3: 1–2; no. 4: 1–2.

Faubel, Louise. "Das Viktoria-Studienhaus in Berlin." *Die deutsche Frau* 6, no. 24 (1916): 2–3.

"F. E." "Die Frau in Haus und Beruf." *Norddeutsche Allgemeine Zeitung* 51, no. 47, February 25, 1912.

Fechter, Paul. "Die Frau in der Kunst: Zur Ausstellung: 'Die Frau in Haus und Beruf.'" *Vossische Zeitung*, no. 109, February 29, 1912.

"Festkantate." *Deutscher Lyceum-Club* 8, 2a (1912): 71–72.

"Feuerbestattung und Virginität." *Die Frau im Osten* 6, no. 8 (1912): 64.

Flanagan, Maureen A. *Seeing with Their Hearts: Chicago Women and the Vision of the Good City, 1871–1933*. Princeton, N.J.: Princeton University Press, 2002.

Fleer, Ottilie. "Das Werden des ersten Studentinnenheims in Deutschland." *Nachrichtenblatt Haus Ottilie von Hansemann, Victoria-Studienhaus*, no. 26 (1940): 1–11.

Forty, Adrian. *Words and Buildings: A Vocabulary of Modern Architecture*. New York: Thames and Hudson, 2000.

Fout, John C., ed. *German Women in the Nineteenth Century*. New York: Holmes and Meyer, 1984.

"Fr." "Aerztliche Tagesfragen: Die Ausstellung 'Die Frau in Haus und Beruf.'" *Medizinische Klinik: Wochenschrift für praktische Ärzte Berlin* 8, no. 9 (1912): 382.

Frank, Ulrich [Ulla Wolff], ed. *Die Berlinerin*. Berlin: Concordia, 1897.

Franken, Else. "Die Tätigkeit einer Wohnungsinspektorin." *Die Welt der Frau*, no. 20 (1912): 326–27.

Franzoi, Barbara. *At the Very Least She Pays the Rent: Women and German Industrialization, 1871–1914*. Westport, Conn.: Greenwood, 1985.

"Frauen als Baumeister." *Illustrierte Frauenzeitung* 38, no. 2 (1910): 17.

"Frauen als Baumeisterinnen." *Frau und Gegenwart*, no. 14 (1926): 12.

"Frauenberufe." *Die Welt der Frau*, no. 23 (1918): 184.

"Frauenheimstätten." *Die Frauenwacht*, no. 23 (1913): 180–81.

"Frauenheimstätten." *P. F. H. II Zeitung* (July 1913): 8–10.

"Die Frauenheimstätten in Neu-Babelsberg-Nowaves." *Die deutsche Frau* 6, no. 32 (1916): 1–2.

"Die Frauen im Reichskanzlerpalais." *Hamburgischer Correspondent*, no. 115, March 3, 1912.

"Frauen in der Wohnungsinspektion." *Zeitschrift für Wohnungswesen* 10, no. 9 (1912): 135–36.

"Die Frauen und die Wohnungsaufsicht." *Die Frau* 21, no. 4 (1914): 246–47.

"Frau Hedwig Heyl Dead in Berlin, 83." *New York Times*, January 24, 1934, 17.

"Die Frau in der Wohnungspflege." *Kölner Frauen Zeitung* 20, no. 8 (1914): 6.

Die Frau in Haus und Beruf. Berlin: Rudolf Mosse, 1912.

"Die Frau in Haus und Beruf." *Simplicissimus* 16, no. 51 (1912): 891.

"Die Frau in Haus und Beruf." *Der Sturm* 3, no. 105 (1912): 2.

"Die Frau in Haus und Beruf." *Der Tag*, February 26, 1912.

"Die Frau in Haus und Beruf." *Vossische Zeitung*, no. 24, January 14, 1912.

"Die Frau in Haus und Beruf." *Die Woche* 14, no. 8 (1912): 322–29.

"'Die Frau in Haus und Beruf': Zur Eröffnung der Ausstellung." *Berliner Tageblatt*, no. 101, February 24, 1912.

Frevert, Ute. *Women in German History: From Bourgeois Emancipation to Sexual Liberty.* Trans. Stuart McKinnon-Evans. Oxford: Berg; and New York: St. Martin's, 1993.

Friedberg, Anne. *Window Shopping: Cinema and the Postmodern.* Berkeley: University of California Press, 1993.

Friedheim, A. "Aus unserer Bildermappe: Damenheime." *Der Bote für die christliche Frauenwelt* 2, no. 35 (1905): 357.

Friedlaender, Thekla. "Die Direktorin des 'Studentinnenheims des Viktoria-Studienhauses.'" *Deutscher Lyceum-Club* 13, no. 1 (1917): 13–14.

Friedman, Alice. "A Feminist Practice in Architectural History?" *Design Book Review* 25 (Summer 1992): 16–18.

———. *Women and the Making of the Modern House: A Social and Architectural History.* New York: Abrams, 1998.

Friedman, Alice, with Maristella Casciato. "Family Matters: The Schröder House, by Gerrit Rietveld and Truus Schröder." In Alice Friedman, *Women and the Making of the Modern House: A Social and Architectural History,* 64–91. New York: Abrams, 1998.

Fritzsche, Peter. *Reading Berlin 1900.* Cambridge, Mass.: Harvard University Press, 1996.

———. "Vagabond in the Fugitive City: Hans Ostwald, Imperial Berlin and the *Grossstadt-Dokumente.*" *Journal of Contemporary History* 29, no. 3 (1994): 385–402.

"F.-T." "Frauenindustrie." *Berliner Tageblatt*, no. 118, March 5, 1912.

Gélieu, Claudia von. *Frauengeschichte entdecken in Berlin.* Berlin: Elefanten, 1995.

"Die Genossenschaft 'Die Frauenwohnung' E.G.m.b.H." *Frauenkapital—eine werdende Macht*, no. 21 (1914): 18.

"Genossenschaft für Frauenheimstätten." *Die Frau* 20, no. 4 (1913): 248.

"Genossenschaft für Frauenheimstätten." *Die Lehrerin* 30, no. 1 (1913): 6–7.

"Genossenschaft für Frauenheimstätten." In *Was die Frau von Berlin wissen muss: Ein praktisches Frauenbuch für Einheimische und Fremde,* 279–80. 2nd ed. Berlin: Loesdau, 1932.

"Genossenschaft für Frauenheimstätten: Neubabelsberg-Nowawes, Heimdalstrasse." *Lehrerinnenhort* 19, nos. 21–22 (1914): 158–61.

"Genossenschaft für Frauenheimstätten: Sitz Berlin." *Frauenwirtschaft* 4, no. 2 (1913): 46–47.

Gerstenberger, Katharina. *Truth to Tell: German Women's Autobiographies and Turn-of-the-Century Culture.* Ann Arbor: University of Michigan Press, 2000.

"Geschäftsbericht für das Jahr 1913." *Monatsblatt für Berliner Lehrerinnen* 10, no. 1 (1914): 11–12.

Die gesundheitlichen Einrichtungen der Königl. Residenzstadt Charlottenburg: Festschrift gewidmet dem 3. internationalen Kongress für Säuglingsschutz in Berlin im September 1911. Berlin: Boil, 1911.

Gildemeister, H. "Das Einküchenhaus." *Die Welt der Frau*, no. 48 (1908): 753–54.

Glassie, Henry. *Vernacular Architecture.* Vol. 2 of Material Culture, ed. George Jevremović, William T. Sumner, and Henry Glassie. Philadelphia: Material Culture; and Bloomington: Indiana University Press, 2000.

Glinga, Werner. *Legacy of Empire: A Journey through British Society.* Trans. Stephan Paul Jost. Manchester: Manchester University Press, 1986.

Glock, E. "Die Dame im Restaurant." *Die deutsche Frau* 3, no. 13 (1913): 18.

Göckenjan, Gerd, and Angela Taeger. "Matrone, alte Jungfer, Tante: Das Bild der alten Frau in der bürgerlichen Welt des 19. Jahrhunderts." *Archiv für Sozialgeschichte* 30 (1990): 43–79.

Goldschmidt, Alfons. "Die Damenausstellung." *März* 6, no. 10 (1912): 394–96.

Gottberg, Margarete von. "Die Architektin." *Rheinische Blätter für Wohnungswesen und Bauberatung* 15, no. 11 (1919): 259–60.

———. "Die Wohnungsaufsicht in Bayern." *Kölner Frauen-Zeitung* 20, no. 7 (1914): 2–3.

Gottschalk, Johanna. "Bildungs- und Erziehungsfragen auf dem deutschen Frauenkongress in Berlin." *Frauenbildung* 11, no. 5 (1912): 225–30.

Greenhalgh, Paul. "Education, Entertainment and Politics: Lessons from the Great International Exhibitions." *The New Museology*, ed. Peter Vergo, 74–98. London: Reaktion, 1989.

———. *Ephemeral Vistas: The Expositions Universelles, Great Exhibitions and World's Fairs, 1851–1939.* Manchester: Manchester University Press, 1988.

Grever, Maria. "Reconstructing the Fatherland: Comparative Perspectives on Women and 19th Century Exhibitions." In *A Fatherland for Women: The 1898 "Nationale Tentoonstelling van Vrouwenarbeid" in Retrospect,* ed. Maria Grever and Fia Dieteren, 15–31. Amsterdam: Stichting beheer IISG, 2000.

Grever, Maria, and Fia Dieteren, eds. *A Fatherland for Women: The 1898 "Nationale Tentoonstelling van Vrouwenarbeid" in Retrospect.* Amsterdam: Stichting beheer IISG, 2000.

Grieser, Susanne. "Bürgerliche Frauenbewegung und Wohnungsaufsicht 1900 bis 1918: Zwischen praktischer Arbeit und politischer Einflussnahme in der Gemeinde." *Ariadne* 36 (1999): 22–29.

Grimm, Melitta. "Ein Studentinnenheim in Charlottenburg." *Frau und Gegenwart,* no. 18 (1926): 7–8.

Groddeck, Georg. *Hin zu Gottnatur.* 2nd ed. Leipzig: Hirzel, 1909.

Grube, Helene. "Rundgang durch die Ausstellung 'Die Frau im Haus und Beruf.'" *Die Wartburg* 11, no. 12 (1912): 115–16.

Grünert, Frieda. "Die Mode in Berlin." In *Was die Frau von Berlin wissen muss: Ein praktisches Frauenbuch für Einheimische und Fremde,* ed. Eliza Ichenhaeuser, 265–72. Berlin: Loesdau, 1913.

Gunga, Luise. *"Zimmer frei": Berliner Pensionswirtinnen im Kaiserreich.* Frankfurt: Campus, 1995.

Günther, Sonja. "International Pioneers." In *Women in Design: Careers and Life Histories since 1900,* vol. 1, ed. Angela Oedekoven-Gerischer, 22–147. Stuttgart: Landesgewerbeamts Baden-Württemberg and Design Center Stuttgart, 1989.

———. *Lilly Reich, 1885–1947: Innenarchitektin, Designerin, Ausstellungsgestalterin.* Stuttgart: Deutsche Verlags-Anstalt, 1988.

Günther, Sonja, Christine Jachmann, and Helga Schmidt-Thomsen, eds. *Architektinnenhistorie: Zur Geschichte der Architektinnen und Designerinnen im 20. Jahrhundert: Eine erste Zusammenstellung.* Berlin: Union Internationale des Femmes Architectes, 1984.

Gutman, Marta. "Adopted Homes for Yesterday's Children: Constructing Care in Oakland, California." Working Paper 32, Center for Working Families, University of California, Berkeley, 2002.

————. "Inside the Institution: The Art and Craft of Settlement Work at the Oakland New Century Club, 1895–1923." *Perspectives in Vernacular Architecture* 8 (2000): 248–79.

Haar, Sharon. "At Home in Public: The Hull House Settlement and the Study of the City." In *Embodied Utopias: Gender, Social Change, and the Modern Metropolis,* ed. Amy Bingaman, Lise Sanders, and Rebecca Zorach, 99–115. London: Routledge, 2002.

Habermas, Jürgen. *The Structural Transformation of the Public Sphere.* Trans. Thomas Burger. Cambridge, Mass.: MIT Press, 1989.

Haemmerling, Konrad. *Charlottenburg: Das Lebensbild einer Stadt, 1905–1955.* Berlin: Kulturbuch, 1955.

Hagen, H. von. "Zimmereinrichtungen von der Ausstellung 'Die Frau in Haus und Beruf.'" *Die Welt der Frau,* no. 45 (1912): 715–18.

Harder, Agnes. "Die Ausstellung 'Die Frau in Haus und Beruf.'" *Der Türmer* 14, no. 7 (1912): 52–56.

————. "Die Frau in Haus und Beruf." *Daheim* 48, no. 22 (1912): 23–24.

————. "Ein Heim für studierende Frauen in Berlin." *Die Welt der Frau,* no. 36 (1916): 563–66.

————. "Unsere Kunstgewerblerinnen." Published in 3 parts in *Die deutsche Frau* 3 (1913), no. 20: 6–8; no. 33: 9–11; no. 34: 5–8.

Haupt, Amalie. "Moderne Frauenwohnungen." *Die deutsche Frau* 1, no. 48 (1911): 11.

"Ein Haus der Frauen." *Kölner Frauen-Zeitung* 20, no. 17 (1914): n.p.

Haxthausen, Charles W. "'A New Beauty': Ernst Ludwig Kirchner's Images of Berlin." In *Berlin: Culture and Metropolis,* ed. Charles W. Haxthausen and Heidrun Suhr, 58–94. Minneapolis: University of Minnesota Press, 1990.

Haxthausen, Charles W., and Heidrun Suhr, eds. *Berlin: Culture and Metropolis.* Minneapolis: University of Minnesota Press, 1990.

Hayden, Dolores. *The Grand Domestic Revolution: A History of Feminist Designs for American Homes, Neighborhoods, and Cities.* Cambridge, Mass.: MIT Press, 1981.

Heeren, M. "Lehrerinnenheim in Berlin." *Deutsche Bauhütte* 16, no. 40 (1912): 330–32.

"Das Heim unsrer Studentinnen: Haus Ottilie von Hansemann, Berlin." *Daheim* 52, no. 47 (1916): 23–24.

Heller, Marie. "Die Frau in Beruf." *Die deutsche Frau* 2, no. 14 (1912): 1–3.

H[eller], M[arie]. "Noch einmal die Wohnungsinspektorin." *Daheim* 46, no. 19 (1910): 25.

Helly, Dorothy O., and Susan M. Reverby, eds. *Gendered Domains: Rethinking Public and Private in Women's History: Essays from the 7th Berkshire Conference on the History of Women.* Ithaca, N.Y.: Cornell University Press, 1992.

Henderson, Susan R. "Bachelor Culture in the Work of Adolf Loos." *Journal of Architectural Education* 55, no. 3 (2002): 125–35.

————. "A Revolution in the Woman's Sphere: Grete Lihotzky and the Frankfurt Kitchen." In *Architecture and Feminism,* ed. Debra Coleman, Elizabeth Danze, and Carol Henderson, 221–53. New York: Princeton Architectural Press, 1996.

Herminghouse, Patricia, and Magda Mueller. *Gender and Germanness: Cultural Productions of Nation*. Providence, R.I.: Berghahn, 1997.

Herzog, Elsa. "Arbeiterinnenheime." *Die praktische Berlinerin*, no. 16 (1906): 281–82.

Hessberger, Maria. "Wohnungswesen in Berlin." In *Was die Frau von Berlin wissen muss: Ein praktisches Frauenbuch für Einheimische und Fremde*, 224–28. 2nd ed. Berlin: Loesdau, 1932.

Heuss, Theodor. "Die Frauenausstellung in Berlin." *Die Hilfe* 18, no. 11 (1912): 170–71.

Heyer, P. "'Lehrerinnenheim.'" *Monatsblatt für Berliner Lehrerinnen* 6, no. 1 (1910): 11–13.

Heyl, Hedwig. *Aus meinem Leben*. Berlin: Schwetschke, 1925.

———. "Die Ausstellung: Die Frau in Haus und Beruf." *Frauenwirtschaft* 2, nos. 11–12 (1912): 262–64.

———. "Die Ausstellung 'Die Frau in Haus und Beruf.'" *Die Woche* 14, no. 4 (1912): 129–31.

———. "Hausfrauenarbeit als Berufsarbeit." In *Was die Frau von Berlin wissen muss: Ein praktisches Frauenbuch für Einheimische und Fremde*, 184–87. 2nd ed. Berlin: Loesdau, 1932.

Heynen, Hilde, and Gülsüm Baydar, eds. *Negotiating Domesticity: Spatial Productions of Gender in Modern Architecture*. London: Routledge, 2005.

Hirsch, Rahel. "Was Berlin für seine Kranken tut." In *Was die Frau von Berlin wissen muss: Ein praktisches Frauenbuch für Einheimische und Fremde*, ed. Eliza Ichenhaeuser, 147–60. Berlin: Loesdau, 1913.

Hirschfeld, Käthe. "Die Ausstellung 'Die Frau in Haus und Beruf' in Berlin: Fortsetzung." *Deutsche Frauen-Zeitung* 25, no. 30 (1912): 314–15.

Hirschfeld, Käthe, Emma Böhmer, and Marie Böhmer. "Die Ausstellung 'Die Frau in Haus und Beruf' in Berlin." Published in 4 parts in *Deutsche Frauen-Zeitung* 25 (1912), no. 27: 283–84; no. 30: 314–15; no. 31: 325–26; no. 34: 358.

Hoesch, Kristin. *Ärztinnen für Frauen: Kliniken in Berlin, 1877–1914*. Stuttgart: Metzler, 1995.

Hong, Young Sun. "Femininity as Vocation: Gender and Class Conflict in the Professionalization of German Social Work." In *German Professions, 1800–1950*, ed. Geoffrey Cocks and Konrad H. Jarausch, 232–51. New York: Oxford University Press, 1990.

Hopffgarten, Elise von. "Die Ausstellung: Die Frau in Haus und Beruf." In *Hedwig Heyl: Ein Gedenkblatt zu ihrem 70. Geburtstage dem 5. Mai 1920*, ed. Hopffgarten, 112–16. Berlin: Reimer, 1920.

———, ed. *Hedwig Heyl: Ein Gedenkblatt zu ihrem 70. Geburtstage dem 5. Mai 1920*. Berlin: Reimer, 1920.

Horowitz, Helen Lefkowitz. *Alma Mater: Design and Experience in the Women's Colleges from Their Nineteenth-Century Beginnings to 1930*. 2nd ed. Amherst: University of Massachusetts Press, 1993.

Horwitz, Georg. "Frauen an der Börse." *Frauenkapital—ein werdende Macht*, no. 3 (1914): 2–4.

Huerkamp, Claudia. *Bildungsbürgerinnen: Frauen im Studium und in akademischen Berufen 1900–1945*. Göttingen: Vandenhoeck and Ruprecht, 1996.

Hughes, Francesca, ed. *The Architect: Reconstructing Her Practice*. Cambridge, Mass.: MIT Press, 1998.

Ichenhaeuser, Eliza. "Berliner Ausflüge und Spaziergänge." In *Was die Frau von Berlin wissen muss: Ein praktisches Frauenbuch für Einheimische und Fremde*, ed. Eliza Ichenhaeuser, 288–92. Berlin: Loesdau, 1913.

———. "Einleitung." In *Was die Frau von Berlin wissen muss*, ed. Eliza Ichenhaeuser, 11–12. Berlin: Loesdau, 1913.

———. "Frauenklubs." *Die Welt der Frau*, no. 46 (1911): 727–29.

———. "Vorwort." In *Was die Frau von Berlin wissen muss: Ein praktisches Frauenbuch für Einheimische und Fremde*, ed. Eliza Ichenhaeuser, 7. Berlin: Loesdau, 1913.

———, ed. *Was die Frau von Berlin wissen muss: Ein praktisches Frauenbuch für Einheimische und Fremde*. Berlin: Loesdau, 1913.

———. "Weibliche Arzte [*sic*] und Frauenkrankenhäuser unter Leitung weiblicher Ärzte." *Die Welt der Frau*, no. 39 (1910): 611–14.

"Im Lyzeumklub." *Berliner Tageblatt*, no. 565, November 5, 1905.

Irmer, Anna. "Zur Wohnungsfrage der Studentinnen." *Die Studentin* 5, no. 2 (1916): 9–11.

1 Jahr Studentinnen-Tagesheim (Helene-Lange-Heim), 1928–1929. Foreword by Marie-Elisabeth Lüders. Berlin: Studentenwerk, c. 1930.

James, Kathleen. "From Messel to Mendelsohn: German Department Store Architecture in Defence of Urban and Economic Change." In *Cathedrals of Consumption: The European Department Store, 1850–1939*, ed. Geoffrey Crossick and Serge Jaumain, 252–78. Aldershot: Ashgate, 1999.

Jarzombek, Mark. "The Discourses of a Bourgeois Utopia, 1904–1908, and the Founding of the Werkbund." In *Imagining Modern German Culture: 1889–1910*, ed. Françoise Forster-Hahn, 126–45. Vol. 53 of Studies in the History of Art. Washington, D.C.: National Gallery of Art, 1996.

———. "The *Kunstgewerbe*, the *Werkbund*, and the Aesthetics of Culture in the Wilhelmine Period." *Journal of the Society of Architectural Historians* 53, no. 1 (1994): 7–19.

Jecker, Maria. "Aufbau und Aufgaben des Reichsverbandes Deutscher Hausfrauenvereine." In *Was die Frau von Berlin wissen muss: Ein praktisches Frauenbuch für Einheimische und Fremde*, 149–53. 2nd ed. Berlin: Loesdau, 1932.

Jefferies, Matthew. *Politics and Culture in Wilhelmine Germany: The Case of Industrial Architecture*. Oxford: Berg, 1995.

Jelavich, Peter. *Berlin Cabaret*. Cambridge, Mass.: Harvard University Press, 1993.

Jessen, Jarno [Anna Michaelson], ed. *Angewandte Kunst: Deutscher Lyceum Club Berlin*. Berlin: Lipperheide, c. 1908.

———. "Der Deutsche Lyzeumklub und seine bildenden Künstlerinnen." *Westermanns Monatshefte* 120, no. 716 (1916): 165–78.

———. "Das Kunstgewerbe in Berlin." In *Was die Frau von Berlin wissen muss: Ein praktisches Frauenbuch für Einheimische und Fremde*, ed. Eliza Ichenhaeuser, 44–53. Berlin: Loesdau, 1913.

———. "Der Lyceumklub." *Daheim* 42, no. 41 (1905): 23.

———. "Das Reich der Frau: XIII: Die Frau in Haus und Beruf und Deutscher Frauenkongress." *Westermanns Monatshefte* 56, no. 9 (1912): 413–22.

Johnson, Eric A. *Urbanization and Crime: Germany 1871–1914*. Cambridge: Cambridge University Press, 1995.

Jordan, Hedwig. "Im Studentinnenheim." *Die Woche* 11, no. 8 (1909): 334–37.

Kaplan, Marion A. *The Making of the Jewish Middle Class: Women, Family, and Identity in Imperial Germany*. New York: Oxford University Press, 1991.

Katscher, Leopold [Spectator, pseud.]. *Berliner Klubs.* Vol. 25 of Die Grossstadt Dokumente, ed. Hans Ostwald. Berlin: Seemann, 1906.

Kay, Joseph. *The Social Condition and Education of the People in England and Europe.* 2 vols. London: Longman, Brown, Green, and Longmans, 1850.

Kerber, Linda. *Toward an Intellectual History of Women: Essays by Linda K. Kerber.* Chapel Hill: University of North Carolina Press, 1997.

Kester-Conrad, Else. "Weibliche Wohnungsinspektion." *Die Frau im Osten* 5, no. 9 (1911): 71–73.

"K. H." "Unser Lehrerinnenheim." *Monatsblatt für Berliner Lehrerinnen* 6, no. 4 (1910): 68.

Kickbusch, Ilona, and Barbara Riedmüller, eds. *Die armen Frauen: Frauen und Sozialpolitik.* Frankfurt: Suhrkamp, 1984.

Kiehm, Johanna. "Das Wohnungsproblem der Studentin." *Die Frau* 23, no. 10 (1916): 604–5.

Kirschner, Mathilde. "Ein Heim für Arbeiterinnen." *Die Welt der Frau,* no. 2 (1912): 28–31.

Kissel, Mary. "Gymnastik und Sport in der Reichshauptstadt." In *Was die Frau von Berlin wissen muss: Ein praktisches Frauenbuch für Einheimische und Fremde,* ed. Eliza Ichenhaeuser, 275–81. Berlin: Loesdau, 1913.

Klinkott, Manfred. "Martin Gropius und die Berliner Schule." Doctoral dissertation, Technical University Berlin, 1971.

Klopfer, Paul. "Die Frau und das Kunstgewerbe." *Kunstwart* 24, no. 15 (1911): 215–18.

"Kongress für 'Wohnungsaufsicht und Wohnungspflege.'" *Zeitschrift für Wohnungswesen* 12, no. 6 (1913): 93–100.

Koonz, Claudia. *Mothers in the Fatherland: Women, the Family, and Nazi Politics.* New York: St. Martin's, 1981.

Koschwitz-Newby, Heidi. "Hedwig Heyl—die beste Hausfrau Berlins." In *Unter allen Umständen: Frauengeschichte(n) in Berlin,* ed. Christiane Eifert and Susanne Rouette, 60–79. Berlin: Rotation, 1986.

Kraus, Karl. "Mir schwirrt der Kopf." *Die Fackel* 13, nos. 345–46 (1912): 1–4.

Krempel, Ulrich, and Susanne Meyer-Büser, eds. *Garten der Frauen: Wegbereiterinnen der Moderne in Deutschland, 1900–1914.* Hannover: Sprengel Museum, 1996.

Kröhne, Marie. "Ehrenamtliche Wohnungsfürsorge." *Neue Bahnen* 49, no. 15 (1914): 114–16.

———. "Eindrücke vom Wohnungskongress in Berlin." *Blätter für soziale Arbeit* 6, no. 1 (1914): 1–2.

———. "Wohnungsaufsicht." *Frauenberuf und -erwerb,* no. 13 (1912): n.p.

Krukenberg, Elsbeth. *Die Frau in der Familie.* Die Kulturaufgaben der Frau, ed. Jakob Wychgram. Leipzig: Amelangs, 1910.

Kuhn, Bärbel. *Familienstand ledig: Ehelose Frauen und Männer im Bürgertum, 1850–1914.* Cologne: Böhlau, 2002.

"Das Kultusministerium und die Hansemann-Stiftung." *Frauen-Fortschritt* 1 (May 5, 1910): 3.

"L." "Bürgerliche Innen-Räume." *Innen-Dekoration* 23 (1912): 218–24.

Ladd, Brian. *The Ghosts of Berlin: Confronting German History in the Urban Landscape.* Chicago: University of Chicago Press, 1998.

———. *Urban Planning and Civic Order in Germany, 1860–1914.* Cambridge, Mass.: Harvard University Press, 1990.

Lamping, Marie. "Ein Frauenhotel in Neuyork." *Die deutsche Frau* 3, no. 44 (1913): 13.

Lane, Barbara Miller. *Architecture and Politics in Germany, 1918–1945.* 1968; Cambridge, Mass.: Harvard University Press, 1985.

—————. *National Romanticism and Modern Architecture in Germany and the Scandinavian Countries.* Cambridge: Cambridge University Press, 2000.

Lange, Auguste. "Die Frau in der Wohnungsinpektion." Published in 2 parts in *Die Frauenwacht* 4 (1916), nos. 11 and 12: 41–43; nos. 13 and 14: 49–51.

Lange, Helene. "Ausstellung und Kongress 'Die Frau in Haus und Beruf.'" *Die Frau* 19, no. 5 (1912): 300–303.

—————. "Das Berliner Victoria-Studienhaus." *Die Frau* 23, no. 6 (1916): 339–42.

"L. D." "Architektin E. Winkelmann." *Innen-Dekoration* 20 (1909): 154.

Lees, Andrew. *Cities, Sin, and Social Reform in Imperial Germany.* Ann Arbor: University of Michigan Press, 2002.

Lehmann, Henni. "Die 'Damenausstellung': Ein Wort der Abwehr." *Centralblatt des Bundes Deutscher Frauenvereine* 14, no. 2 (1912): 9–10.

Lehr de Waal, Annie. "Die Wohlfahrtspflege in Berlin." In *Was die Frau von Berlin wissen muss: Ein praktisches Frauenbuch für Einheimische und Fremde,* ed. Eliza Ichenhaeuser, 129–46. Berlin: Loesdau, 1913.

"'Lehrerinnenheim,' Bau- und Sparverein." *Monatsblatt für Berliner Lehrerinnen* 6, no. 6 (1910): 111–12.

"Das Lehrerinnenheim des Vereins Berliner Volkschullehrerinnen." *Monatsblatt für Berliner Lehrerinnen* 6, no. 3 (1910): 54.

Lejeune, Anthony. *The Gentlemen's Clubs of London.* New York: Mayflower, 1979.

Lengefeld, Cecilia. *Der Maler des glücklichen Heims: Zur Rezeption Carl Larssons im wilhelminischen Deutschland.* Heidelberg: Universitäts Verlag C. Winter, 1993.

Levy-Rathenau, Josephine. *Die deutsche Frau im Beruf: Praktische Ratschläge zur Berufswahl.* Berlin: Moeser, 1912.

—————. "Soziale Berufsarbeit in der öffentlichen und privaten Wohlfahrtspflege." *Die deutsche Frau* 1, no. 1 (1911): 8–9.

—————. "Unsre deutschen Frauenklubs und ihre Leistungen." *Frauen-Fortschritt* 1 (March 10, 1910): 3.

Lewis, Beth Irwin. *Art for All? The Collision of Modern Art and the Public in Late-Nineteenth-Century Germany.* Princeton, N.J.: Princeton University Press, 2003.

Lindenberg, Paul. *Pracht-Album photographischer Aufnahmen der Berliner Gewerbe-Ausstellung 1896.* Berlin: Werner, 1896.

Linton, Eliza Lynn. *The New Woman in Haste and at Leisure.* New York: Merrian, 1895.

Lister, Ruth. *Citizenship: Feminist Perspectives.* New York: New York University Press, 1997.

Loewe, Emma. "Die Frau im Architektenberuf." *Frauenberuf und -erwerb,* no. 6 (1920).

Lorm, J. "'Die Frau in Haus und Beruf': Ein Rundgang durch die Ausstellung." *Berliner Lokal-Anzeiger,* no. 100, February 24, 1912.

Lüders, Marie-Elisabeth. "Der Entwurf zum Berliner Wohnungsamt." *Centralblatt des Bundes Deutscher Frauenvereine* 14, no. 23 (1913): 177–78.

—————. *Fürchte Dich Nicht: Persönliches und Politisches aus mehr als 80 Jahren, 1878–1962.* Cologne: Westdeutscher, 1963.

———. "Probleme der städtischen Wohnungspflege und die weibliche Wohnungsinspektion." *Die Frau* 21, no. 3 (1913): 129–37.

"The Lyceum Club of London: An Organization of Women Engaged in Literary, Artistic, and Scientific Pursuits." *Critic* 46, no. 2 (1905): 132–37.

"Der Lyzeumklub." *Die Frau* 12, no. 12 (1905): 752–55.

Maasberg, Ute, and Regina Prinz. *Die Neuen kommen! Weibliche Avantgarde in der Architektur der zwanziger Jahre.* Hamburg: Junius 2004.

Maier, Dr. "Begleitworte des Vorsitzenden des Kuratoriums Oberpräsidenten i. R. Dr. Maier." *Nachrichtenblatt Haus Ottilie von Hansemann, Victoria-Studienhaus*, no. 26 (1940): 14–15.

Maier-Dependorf, Albertine. "Constance Smedley." In *Lyceum Club.* Hamburg: Association Internationale des Lyceum Clubs, 1986.

Marcus, Sharon. *Apartment Stories: City and Home in Nineteenth-Century Paris and London.* Berkeley: University of California Press, 1999.

Marelle, Luise. "Berliner Frauenklubs." In *Was die Frau von Berlin wissen muss: Ein praktisches Frauenbuch für Einheimische und Fremde*, 162–66. 2nd ed. Berlin: Loesdau, 1932.

———. *Die Geschichte des Deutschen Lyceum-Clubs.* Berlin: Deutscher Lyceum-Club, 1933.

Marg., P. "Feuerbestattung und Virginität." *Die Flamme* 29, no. 3 (1912): 33.

Martin, Dora. "Heim der Genossenschaft für Frauenheimstätten." *Frau und Gegenwart*, no. 40 (1926): 9–10.

Masur, Gerhard. *Imperial Berlin.* New York: Dorset, 1970.

Maurenbrecher, Hulda. "Warum gedeiht das Einküchenhaus nicht?" Published in 2 parts in *Die Frauenbewegung* 17 (1911), no. 8: 60–61; no. 9: 71.

Mazohl-Wallnig, Brigitte, ed. *Bürgerliche Frauenkultur im 19. Jahrhundert.* Vienna: Bölhau, 1995.

Mazón, Patricia M. *Gender and the Modern Research University: The Admission of Women to German Higher Education, 1865–1914.* Stanford, Calif.: Stanford University Press, 2003.

McClelland, Charles E. *State, Society, and University in Germany 1700–1914.* Cambridge: Cambridge University Press, 1980.

McQuaid, Matilda, and Magdalena Droste. *Lilly Reich: Designer and Architect.* New York: Museum of Modern Art, 1996.

Mebes, Paul. *Um 1800: Architektur und Handwerk im letzten Jahrhundert ihrer traditionellen Entwicklung.* Munich: Bruckmann, 1908.

Meckel, Anne, ed. *Das Pestalozzi-Fröbel-Haus: Entwicklung eines Frauenberufs.* Berlin: Arbeitsgruppe "Geschichte des Pestalozzi-Fröbel-Hauses," 1991.

Meehan, Johanna, ed. *Feminists Read Habermas: Gendering the Subject of Discourse.* New York: Routledge, 1995.

Melton, James Van Horn. *The Rise of the Public in Enlightenment Europe.* Cambridge: Cambridge University Press, 2001.

Mensch, Ella. "An Damen wird nicht vermietet." *Die deutsche Frau* 2, no. 37 (1912): 7–8.

———. "Das Haus in der Sonne." *Frauenkapital—eine werdende Macht*, no. 24 (1914): 18–19.

Mentner, Regina. "Bürgerliche Frauenbewegung und Arbeiterinnenheime." *Ariadne*, no. 36 (1999): 31–35.

———. "Lebensräume für Frauen zwischen Fremdbestimmung und Selbstverwirklichung: Zur Engagement der deutschen Frauenbewegung in der Wohnungspolitik, 1871–1933."

Unpublished report. Feministische Organisation von Planerinnen und Architektinnen, Dortmund, 1995.

Meskimmon, Marsha. *We Weren't Modern Enough: Women Artists and the Limits of German Modernism.* Berkeley: University of California Press, 1999.

Meyer, Edina. *Paul Mebes: Miethausbau in Berlin 1906–1938.* Berlin: Seitz, 1972.

Meyer, Günter. "Auf der Suche nach den historischen Stätten des 'Vereins der Berliner Künstlerinnen.'" In *Profession ohne Tradition: 125 Jahre Verein der Berliner Künstlerinnen,* 291–98. Berlin: Berlinische Galerie, 1992.

Miller, Cristanne. *Cultures of Modernism: Marianne Moore, Mina Loy, and Else Lasker-Schüler.* Ann Arbor: University of Michigan, 2007.

"Mitglieder der Heimgenossenschaft für Frauen." *Die deutsche Frau* 2, no. 44 (1912): 3.

"Mitteilung, betreffend die Vorarbeiten zur Gründung einer Heimgenossenschaft für aus dem Beruf geschiedene gebildete Frauen." *P. F. H. II Zeitung,* "Probenummer" issue (July 1912): 23–24.

"Die Mitwirkung der Frau in der Wohnungspflege und Wohnungsaufsicht." *Frauenberuf* 17, no. 21 (1914): 113–14.

Mommsen, Wolfgang J. *Imperial Germany, 1867–1918: Politics, Culture, and Society in an Authoritarian State.* Trans. Richard Deveson. London: Arnold, 1995.

Monsterberg, Elimar von. "Die Frau in Haus und Beruf." *Hamburgischer Correspondent,* no. 119, March 5, 1912.

Mühsam-Werther, Charlotte. "Was muss die Hausfrau von Berlin wissen?" In *Was die Frau von Berlin wissen muss: Ein praktisches Frauenbuch für Einheimische und Fremde,* 153–58. 2nd ed. Berlin: Loesdau, 1932.

Müller, Lise. "Berlin als Musik- und Konzertstadt." In *Was die Frau von Berlin wissen muss: Ein praktisches Frauenbuch für Einheimische und Fremde,* ed. Eliza Ichenhaeuser, 112–28. Berlin: Loesdau, 1913.

Müller, Renate. "Die Kunst, in Berlin prominent zu sein." In *Was die Frau von Berlin wissen muss: Ein praktisches Frauenbuch für Einheimische und Fremde,* 202–8. 2nd ed. Berlin: Loesdau, 1932.

Müller, Wilhelm. "Die amerikanischen Frauenklubs." *Dokumente des Fortschritts* 7, nos. 6–7 (1914): 330–36.

Münsterberg, E., ed. *Die Anstaltsfürsorge in Deutschland.* Leipzig: Duncker and Humblot, 1910.

Muthesius, Hans, ed. *Alice Salomon: Die Begründerin des sozialen Frauenberufs in Deutschland: Ihr Leben und Ihr Werk.* Schriften des Deutschen Vereins für öffentliche und private Fürsorge. Cologne: Heymanns, 1958.

Muthesius, Hermann. "Die Bedeutung des Kunstgewerbes." *Dekorative Kunst* 10, no. 5 (1907): 177–92.

———. *Style-Architecture and Building-Art: Transformations of Architecture in the Nineteenth Century and Its Present Condition.* Trans. Stanford Anderson. Santa Monica: Getty Center for the History of Art and the Humanities, 1994.

National Council of Women of Great Britain. *Women as Sanitary Inspectors.* London: P. S. King and Son, 1902.

"Ein neues Arbeiterinnenheim in Berlin." *Blätter für soziale Arbeit* 4, no. 7 (1912): 49.

Nevill, Ralph. *London Clubs: Their History and Treasures.* London: Chatto and Windus, 1911.

"A New Club for Women Workers: Opening of 'The Lyceum.'" *Sketch* (June 29, 1904): 382–83.

Nieritz, Gustav. *Mutterliebe und Brudertreu; oder: Die Gefahren einer grossen Stadt.* 4th ed. Düsseldorf: Felix Bagel, 1880.

"Nochmals die 'möblierte Dame.'" *Die Welt der Frau*, no. 39 (1913): 628.

Noever, Peter ed. *Die Frankfurter Küche von Margarete Schütte-Lihotzky.* Berlin: Ernst and Sohn, 1992.

Nolan, Mary. *Visions of Modernity: American Business and the Modernization of Germany.* New York: Oxford University Press, 1994.

Nord, Deborah Epstein. *Walking the Victorian Streets: Women, Representation, and the City.* Ithaca, N.Y.: Cornell University Press, 1995.

Norden, Max, ed. *Frauen-Führer: Auskunftsbuch über Vereine, Ausbildungsgelegenheiten und Wohlfahrtseinrichtungen in Berlin.* 6th ed. Berlin: Habel, 1907.

Oedekoven-Gerischer, Angela, Andrea Scholtz, Edith Medek, and Petra Kurz, eds. *Women in Design: Careers and Life Histories since 1900.* 2 vols. Stuttgart: Design Center Stuttgart, 1989.

Ohlert, Annie. "Das Lehrerinnenheim in Hamburg." *Frauen-Rundschau* 13, no. 11 (1912): 238–39.

"Orte der Mütterlichkeit: Tiergartenviertel." In *Immer den Frauen nach! Spaziergang am Landwehrkanal zur Berliner Frauengeschichte*, ed. Cornelia Carstens and Margret Luikenga, 130–34. Berlin: Berliner Geschichtswerkstatt, 1993.

Osborn, Max. "Frauenarbeit in Kunst und Kunstgewerbe." *Berliner Morgenpost*, no. 55, February 25, 1912.

Ostwald, Hans. *Berlin und die Berlinerin: Eine Kultur- und Sittengeschichte.* Berlin: Basch, 1911.

———. *Dunkle Winkel in Berlin.* 3rd ed. 1904. Vol. 1 of Die Grossstadt-Dokumente, ed. Hans Ostwald. Berlin: Seemann, 1904–8.

———. *Prostitutionsmärkte.* Vol. 6 of *Das Berliner Dirnentum*, 10 vols., ed. Hans Ostwald. Leipzig: Fiedler, 1907.

"O. T. Sch." "Die Frau in Haus und Beruf: Eröffnung der Ausstellung im Zoologischen Garten." *Vossische Zeitung*, no. 100, February 24, 1912.

Otto, Rose. "Die Frau in der Wohnungsinspektion." *Centralblatt des Bundes Deutscher Frauenvereine* 14, no. 24 (1913): 187–89.

Pappritz, Anna. "Feuerbestattung und Virginität." *Centralblatt des Bundes Deutscher Frauenvereine* 13, no. 19 (1912): 146–47.

Parsons, Deborah L. *Streetwalking the Metropolis: Women, the City and Modernity.* Oxford: Oxford University Press, 2000.

"P. B." "Die Frau in Haus und Beruf: Zur Eröffnung der Ausstellung." *Berliner Tageblatt*, no. 100, February 24, 1912.

Pearson, Lynn. *The Architectural and Social History of Cooperative Living.* New York: St. Martin's, 1988.

Peiss, Kathy. *Cheap Amusements: Working Women and Leisure in Turn-of-the-Century New York.* Philadelphia: Temple University Press, 1986.

Petro, Patrice. *Joyless Streets: Women and Melodramatic Representation in Weimar Germany.* Princeton, N.J.: Princeton University Press, 1989.

Peyser, Dora. "Alice Salomon: Ein Lebensbild." In *Alice Salomon: Die Begründerin des sozialen Frauenberufs in Deutschland: Ihr Leben und Ihr Werk,* ed. Hans Muthesius, 9–121. Schriften des Deutschen Vereins für öffentliche und private Fürsorge. Cologne: Heymanns, 1958.

Pick, Margarete. *Zur Berufswahl der Frauen: Ratgeber für 35 Berufe.* Breslau: Allegro, 1909.

Planert, Ute. *Antifeminismus im Kaiserreich: Diskurs, soziale Formation und politische Mentalität.* Vol. 124 of Kritische Studien zur Geschichtswissenschaft. Göttingen: Vandenhoeck and Ruprecht, 1998.

———, ed. *Nation, Politik und Geschlecht: Frauenbewegungen und Nationalismus in der Moderne.* Frankfurt: Campus, 2000.

Plothow, Anna. "Die Ausstellung die Frau in Haus und Beruf." *Berliner Tageblatt,* no. 100, February 24, 1912, Frauen-Rundschau section.

———. "Die Ausstellung 'Die Frau in Haus und Beruf' I." *Frauenwirtschaft* 3, no. 2 (1912): 25–32.

———. "Berliner Frauenklubs." *Neues Frauenleben* 15, no. 11 (1903): 16–19.

———. "Der deutsche Frauenkongress in Berlin vom 27. Februar bis 2. März 1912." *Frauenwirtschaft* 3, no. 3 (1912): 53–59.

———. "Frauenbewegung und Frauenvereine." In *Was die Frau von Berlin wissen muss: Ein praktisches Frauenbuch für Einheimische und Fremde,* ed. Eliza Ichenhaeuser, 161–88. Berlin: Loesdau, 1913.

———. "Rundgang durch die Ausstellung." *Deutscher Lyceum-Club* 8 (1912), no. 2a: 86–90; no. 3: 113–16.

Pochhammer, Margarete. "Berliner Wohnungsverhältnisse." In *Was die Frau von Berlin wissen muss: Ein praktisches Frauenbuch für Einheimische und Fremde,* ed. Eliza Ichenhaeuser, 231–38. Berlin: Loesdau, 1913.

Posener, Julius. *Berlin auf dem Wege zu einer neuen Architektur: Das Zeitalter Wilhelms II.* Munich: Prestel, 1979.

Profession ohne Tradition: 125 Jahre Verein der Berliner Künstlerinnen. Berlin: Berlinische Galerie, 1992.

"Protest preussischer Frauen gegen die Ausführungsbestimmungen zum preussischen Feuerbestattungsgesetz." *Die Flamme* 29, no. 1 (1912): 2–4.

"Die 'purpurne Revolution' der Suffragetten." *Der Tag,* no. 114, March 2, 1912.

Radel, Frieda. "Von der Berliner Ausstellung 'Die Frau in Haus und Beruf.'" *Hamburger Fremdenblatt,* no. 48, February 27, 1912.

Rappaport, Erika Diane. *Shopping for Pleasure: Women in the Making of London's West End.* Princeton, N.J.: Princeton University Press, 2000.

Ratzka-Ernst, Clara. "Die Ausstellung 'Die Frau in Haus und Beruf.'" *Neue Bahnen* 47, no. 6 (1912): 37–40.

Reagin, Nancy R. *A German Women's Movement: Class and Gender in Hanover, 1880–1933.* Chapel Hill: University of North Carolina Press, 1995.

Reicke, Ilse. *Das tätige Herz: Ein Lebensbild Hedwig Heyls.* Leipzig: Eichblatt, 1938.

Rendell, Jane. *The Pursuit of Pleasure: Gender, Space and Architecture in Regency London.* New Brunswick, N.J.: Rutgers University Press, 2002.

Rendell, Jane, Barbara Penner, and Iain Borden, eds. *Gender, Space, Architecture: An Interdisciplinary Introduction.* London: Routledge, 2000.

Reuter, Gabriele. "Ein Frauenwerk." *Der Tag,* no. 571, November 16, 1905.

———. *From a Good Family.* Trans. Lynne Tatlock. Rochester, N.Y.: Camden House, 1999. Original German ed., 1895.

———. "Ein Klubhaus für Frauen in Berlin: Zur Gründung des Lyzeum-Klubs." *Der Montag,* no. 546, November 21, 1904.

Richards, Anna. "Sense and Sentimentality? Margarete Böhme's *Tagebuch einer Verlorenen* in Context." In *Commodities of Desire: The Prostitute in Modern German Literature,* ed. Christiane Schönfeld, 98–109. Rochester, N.Y.: Camden House, 2000.

Riemann, Ilka. "Die Rolle der Frauenvereine in der Sozialpolitik: Vaterländischer Frauenverein und gemässigter Flügel der Frauenbewegung zwischen 1865 und 1918." In *Die armen Frauen: Frauen und Sozialpolitik,* ed. Ilona Kickbusch and Barbara Riedmüller, 201–24. Frankfurt: Suhrkamp, 1984.

Riess, Margot. "Schaffende Frauen: Die Frau als Architektin." *Frau und Gegenwart* 28, no. 2 (1931): 36–37.

Ritter, Erich. "Das Cecilienhaus des Vaterländischen Frauenvereins Charlottenburg." *Daheim* 47, no. 19 (1911): 26–27.

Roberts, Mary Louise. *Disruptive Acts: The New Woman in Fin-de-Siècle France.* Chicago: University of Chicago Press, 2002.

Roerdansz, Käte von. "Die Frau als Architekt." *Berliner Tageblatt,* no. 133, March 13, 1908, Frauen-Rundschau section.

Roloff, Katarina. "Rat an alleinstehende Frauen." *Die Welt der Frau* 25, no. 12 (1906): 177–78.

Roth, A. "Das Arbeiterinnenheim in der Greifswalder Strasse als Zufluchtsstätte." *Die Welt der Frau,* no. 13 (1915): 201.

Rowe, Dorothy. *Representing Berlin: Sexuality and the City in Imperial and Weimar Germany.* Aldershot: Ashgate, 2003.

Ryan, Jenny. "Women, Modernity, and the City." *Theory, Culture, and Society* 11 (1994): 35–63.

Ryan, Mary P. "Gender and Public Access: Women's Politics in Nineteenth Century America." In *Habermas and the Public Sphere,* ed. Craig Calhoun, 143–63. Cambridge, Mass.: MIT Press, 1992.

———. *Women in Public: Between Banners and Ballots, 1825–1880.* Baltimore, Md.: Johns Hopkins University Press, 1990.

Sachsse, Christoph. *Mütterlichkeit als Beruf: Sozialarbeit, Sozialreform und Frauenbewegung, 1871–1929.* Frankfurt am Main: Suhrkamp, 1986.

Salomon, Alice. "Ein Arbeiterinnen-Klub in Berlin." *Soziale Praxis* 12, no. 87 (1903): 994–96.

———. *Character Is Destiny: The Autobiography of Alice Salomon.* Ed. Andrew Lees. Ann Arbor: University of Michigan Press, 2004.

———. *Frauenemanzipation und soziale Verantwortung: Ausgewählte Schriften.* Vol. 1 (1896–1908). Ed. Adriane Feustel. Berlin: Luchterhand, 1997.

———. "Frauenklubs." *Centralblatt des Bundes Deutscher Frauenvereine* 1, no. 16 (1899): 124–26.

———. "Das Frauenstudium und die wissenschaftlichen Frauenberufe." In *Was die Frau von Berlin wissen muss: Ein praktisches Frauenbuch für Einheimische und Fremde,* ed. Eliza Ichenhaeuser, 198–203. Berlin: Loesdau, 1913.

———. "Das Frauenstudium und die wissenschaftlichen Frauenberufe." In *Was die Frau von Berlin wissen muss: Ein praktisches Frauenbuch für Einheimische und Fremde*, 2nd ed., 171–78. Berlin: Loesdau, 1932.

———. "Rückblick auf den Frauenkongress." *Der Tag*, no. 58, March 9, 1912.

———. "Soziale Frauenarbeit in Berlin." In *Was die Frau von Berlin wissen muss: Ein praktisches Frauenbuch für Einheimische und Fremde*, ed. Eliza Ichenhaeuser, 204–7. Berlin: Loesdau, 1913.

———. "Zehn Jahre Arbeiterinnenheime." *Centralblatt des Bundes Deutscher Frauenvereine* 10, no. 17 (1908): 132–33.

———. "Zur Eröffnung der Ausstellung 'Die Frau in Haus und Beruf.'" *Centralblatt des Bundes Deutscher Frauenvereine* 13, no. 22 (1912): 173–75, Beilage.

———. "Zur Eröffnung der Ausstellung 'Die Frau in Haus und Beruf.'" *Der Tag*, no. 46, February 24, 1912.

———. "Zur Eröffnung der Sozialen Frauenschule." *Die Frau* 16, no. 2 (1908): 103–7.

———. *Zwanzig Jahre soziale Hilfsarbeit: Anlässlich des zwanzigjährigen Bestehens der "Mädchen- und Frauengruppen für soziale Hilfsarbeit" in Berlin*. Karlsruhe: Braun, 1913.

Sauer, Birgit. "Den Zusammenhang zwischen der Frauenfrage und der sozialen Frage begreifen: Die 'Frauen- und Mädchengruppen für soziale Hilfsarbeit' (1893–1908)." In *Unter allen Umständen: Frauengeschichte(n) in Berlin*, ed. Christiane Eifert and Susanne Rouette, 80–98. Berlin: Rotation, 1986.

Scheffler, Karl. *Die Architektur der Grossstadt*. Berlin: Cassirer, 1913.

———. *Berlin—ein Stadtschicksal* [1910]. Vol. 3 of Berliner Texte, ed. Detlef Bluhm. Berlin: Fannei and Walz, 1989.

———. *Die Frau und die Kunst*. Berlin: Bard, 1908.

Schirmacher, Käthe. "Berufsarbeit und Einküchenhaus." *Die Frau im Osten* 1, no. 2 (1909): 10–11.

Schlör, Joachim. *Nights in the Big City: Paris, Berlin, London, 1840–1930*. Trans. Pierre Gottfried Imhof and Dafydd Rees Roberts. London: Reaktion, 1998.

"Schlusssitzung des Frauenkongresses." *Der Tag*, no. 114, March 2, 1912.

Schmidt, Ada von. "Die 'möblierte Dame.'" *Die Welt der Frau*, no. 27 (1913): 432–33.

Schmidt-Thomsen, Helga. "Frauen in der Architektur: Neue Berufswege seit der Jahrhundertwende." In *Architektinnenhistorie: Zur Geschichte der Architektinnen und Designerinnen im 20. Jahrhundert: Eine erste Zusammenstellung*, ed. Sonja Günther, Christine Jachmann, and Helga Schmidt-Thomsen, 15–30. Berlin: Union Internationale des Femmes Architectes, 1984.

Scholtz, Alfred. "Die Frau in Haus und Beruf." *Die Welt am Montag*, no. 10, March 4, 1912.

Schönfeld, Christiane, ed. *Commodities of Desire: The Prostitute in Modern German Literature*. Rochester, N.Y.: Camden House, 2000.

Schrey, Käthe. "Soziale Berufe: Die Wohnungsinspektorin." *Deutsche Frauen-Zeitung* 26, no. 107 (1913).

———. "Die Wohnungsfrage der alleinstehenden Berufsfrau." *Deutsche Frauen-Zeitung* 25, no. 148 (1912): n.p.

Schröder, Iris. "Soziale Frauenarbeit als bürgerliches Projekt: Differenz, Gleicheit und weiblicher Bürgersinn in der Frauenbewegung um 1900." In *Wege zur Geschichte des Bürgertums*, ed. Klaus Tenfelde and Hans-Ulrich Wehler, 209–30. Göttigen: Vandenhoeck and Ruprecht, 1994.

Schulze, Marie. "Das Haus in der Sonne." *P. F. H. II Zeitung* (October 1914): 8–9.

Schulze, Otto. "Wohnungsaufsicht: Die Frau in der Wohnungsinspektion." *Zeitschrift für Wohnungswesen* 12, no. 17 (1914): 260–61.

Schulze-Brück, Louise. "Die Budenfrage." *Die deutsche Frau* 3, no. 31 (1913): 3–5.

Schwartz, Frederic J. *The Werkbund: Design Theory and Mass Culture before the First World War.* New Haven, Conn.: Yale University Press, 1996.

Schwarzer, Mitchell. *German Architectural Theory and the Search for Modern Identity.* Cambridge: Cambridge University Press, 1995.

Scott, Joan Wallach. *Gender and the Politics of History.* Gender and Culture, ed. Carolyn G. Heilbrun and Nancy K. Miller. New York: Columbia University Press, 1988.

Sembach, Klaus-Jürgen, et al. *1910: Halbzeit der Moderne: Van de Velde, Behrens, Hoffmann und die Anderen.* Stuttgart: Hatje, 1992.

"Eine Sensation im Berliner Tiergarten: Vier Damen im Hosenrock." *Die Welt* 23, no. 1 (1911): 5.

Seton Veitch, Chairman. "London Lyceum Club: 1904–1985." In *Lyceum Club,* 49–53. Hamburg: Association Internationale des Lyceum Clubs, 1986.

Seydel. *Das Charlottenburger Wohnungsamt: Seine Entstehung und seine Organisation.* Berlin: Boll, 1911.

Showalter, Elaine. *Sexual Anarchy: Gender and Culture at the Fin de Siècle.* London: Bloomsbury, 1991.

Siebenmorgen, Antje. *Die Geschichte des Internationalen Lyceum-Clubs Berlin e.V., 1905–1995: Zum 90 jährigen Bestehen.* Berlin, 1995.

Simmel, Georg. *Simmel on Culture: Selected Writings.* Ed. David Frisby and Mike Featherstone. London: Sage, 1997.

———. *Soziologie: Untersuchungen über die Formen der Vergesellschaftung.* Leipzig: Duncker, 1908.

Simmons, Sherwin. "Ernst Kirchner's Streetwalkers: Art, Luxury, and Immorality in Berlin, 1913-16." *Art Bulletin* 82, no. 1 (2000): 117–48.

Sinha, Mrinalini. "Britishness, Clubbability, and the Colonial Public Sphere: The Genealogy of an Imperial Institution in Colonial India." *Journal of British Studies* 40, no. 4 (2001): 489–521.

Skladny, Gertrud. "Genossenschaft für Frauenheimstätten E.G.m.b.H.: Bericht über die erste ordentliche Generalversammlung." *Lehrerinnenhort* 18, no. 13 (1913): 101–2.

Smedley, Constance. *Crusaders.* London: Duckworth, 1929.

Sneeringer, Julia. *Winning Women's Votes: Propaganda and Politics in Weimar Germany.* Chapel Hill: University of North Carolina, 2002.

Soden, Eugenie von, ed. *Frauenberufe und -Ausbildungsstätten.* Vol. 1 of Das Frauenbuch. Stuttgart: Franckh'sche, 1913.

Sonnenschein, Carl. *Wie Studenten Wohnen.* Flugschriften des Sekretariats Sozialer Studentenarbeit, no. 2. Mönchengladbach: Volksvereins-Druckerei, 1911.

Spain, Daphne. *How Women Saved the City.* Minneapolis: University of Minnesota Press, 2001.

Spencer-Wood, Suzanne M. "Utopian Visions and Architectural Designs of Turn-of-the-Century Social Settlements." In *Embodied Utopias: Gender, Social Change, and the Modern Metropolis,* ed. Amy Bingaman, Lise Sanders, and Rebecca Zorach, 116–32. London: Routledge, 2002.

Spickernagel, Ellen. "Wohnkultur und Frauenrolle im Biedermeier." In *"The Wise Woman*

Buildeth Her House": Architecture, History and Women's Studies, ed. Margrith Wilke, Vrouwen-studies Letteren Groningen, vol. 1, 26–31. Groningen: University of Groningen, 1992.

Spiekermann, Uwe. "Theft and Thieves in German Department Stores, 1895–1930: A Discourse on Morality, Crime and Gender." In *Cathedrals of Consumption: The European Department Store, 1850–1939,* ed. Geoffrey Crossick and Serge Jaumain, 135–59. Aldershot: Ashgate, 1999.

Spitzer, Barbara. "Zwei Veranstaltungen, ein Zeitpunkt: Gewerbeausstellung und internationaler Frauenkongress in Berlin 1896." In *Die verhinderte Weltausstellung: Beiträge zur Berliner Gewerbeausstellung 1896,* 167–74. Berlin: Berliner Debatte, 1996.

Sprengel, Auguste. "Die Frau in Haus und Beruf." *Lehrerinnenhort* 17, no. 5 (1912): 33–35.

———. "'Die Frau in Haus und Beruf': Heime für alleinstehende Frauen." *Lehrerinnenhort* 17, no. 6 (1912): 49–52.

Statistik der Frauenorganisationen im Deutschen Reich. Berlin: Heymanns, 1909.

Stephani-Hahn, Elisabeth von. *Schaufenster Kunst.* Berlin: Schottlaender, 1926.

Stimpson, Catharine, ed. *Women and the Making of the American City.* Chicago: University of Chicago Press, 1980.

Stöcker, Helene. "Ein Nachwort zum Berliner Frauenkongress." *Die Gegenwart* 41, no. 11 (1912): 164–68.

Stoehr, Irene. "Neue Frau und Alte Bewegung? Zum Generationenkonflikt in der Frauenbewegung der Weimarer Republik." In *Frauenmacht in der Geschichte: Beiträge des Historikerinnentreffens 1985 zur Frauengeschichtsforschung,* ed. Jutta Dalhoff, Uschi Frey, and Ingrid Schöll, 390–402. Düsseldorf: Schwann, 1986.

Stoeving, Curt. "Ausstellung des Londoner Lyceum-Club in Berlin." *Deutsche Kunst und Dekoration* 16 (1905): 509–16.

Stratigakos, Despina. "Architects in Skirts: The Public Image of Women Architects in Wilhelmine Germany." *Journal of Architectural Education* 55, no. 2 (2001): 90–100.

———. "'I Myself Want to Build': Women, Architectural Education, and the Integration of Germany's Technical Colleges." *Paedagogica Historica* 43, no. 6 (2007): 727–56.

———. "The Professional Spoils of War: German Women Architects and World War I." *Journal of the Society of Architectural Historians* 66, no. 4 (2007): 464–75.

———. *Skirts and Scaffolding: Women Architects, Gender, and Design in Wilhelmine Germany.* Ann Arbor, Mich.: University Microfilms, 1999.

———. "The Uncanny Architect: Fears of Lesbian Builders and Deviant Homes in Modern Germany." In *Negotiating Domesticity: Spatial Productions of Gender in Modern Architecture,* ed. Hilde Heynen and Gülsüm Baydar, 145–61. London: Routledge, 2005.

———. "Women and the Werkbund: Gender Politics and German Design Reform, 1907–14." *Journal of the Society of Architectural Historians* 62, no. 4 (2003): 490–511.

Stratz, C. H. "Die Vermännlichung der Frau." *Die Welt der Frau,* no. 13 (1911): 193–95.

Streich, Wolfgang Jürgen. "Franz Heinrich Schwechten." In *Baumeister, Architekten, Stadtplaner: Biographien zur baulichen Entwicklung Berlins,* ed. Wolfgang Ribbe and Wolfgang Schäche, 257–76. Berlin: Stapp, 1987.

Stropp, Emma. "Die Ausstellung 'Die Frau in Haus und Beruf.'" *Die deutsche Frau* 2, no. 13 (1912): 1–4.

———. "Die Ausstellung 'Die Frau in Haus und Beruf.'" *Illustrirte Zeitung* 138, no. 3584 (1912): 447–50.

———. "Berliner Frauenklubs." In *Was die Frau von Berlin wissen muss: Ein praktisches Frauenbuch für Einheimische und Fremde*, ed. Eliza Ichenhaeuser, 256–64. Berlin: Loesdau, 1913.

———. "Die Frau in Haus und Beruf: Die Ausstellung des Deutschen Lyzeum-Klubs: Kunstgewerbe, bildende Kunst, Architektur." *Die deutsche Frau* 2, no. 11 (1912): 1–4.

———. "Die Wohnungsnot der gebildeten Frau." *Die Welt der Frau*, no. 36 (1918): 286.

"Ein Studentinnenheim in Charlottenburg." *Frau und Gegenwart*, no. 18 (1926): 7–8.

"Das Studentinnenheim in der Berliner Strasse." *Die Frau* 23, no. 3 (1915): 183.

Süchting-Hänger, Andrea. "'Gleichgrosse mut'ge Helferinnen' in der weiblichen Gegenwelt: Der Vaterländische Frauenverein und die Politisierung konservativer Frauen 1890–1914." In *Nation, Politik und Geschlecht: Frauenbewegungen und Nationalismus in der Moderne*, ed. Ute Plantert, 131–46. Frankfurt: Campus, 2000.

Sykora, Katharina, Annette Dorgerloh, Doris Noell-Rumpeltes, and Ada Raev, eds. *Die Neue Frau: Herausforderung für Bildmedien der Zwanziger Jahre.* Marburg: Jonas, 1993.

Szczesny-Heyl, Rose H. "Die Ausstellung: 'Die Frau in Haus und Beruf.'" *Die Welt der Frau*, no. 5 (1912): 65–66.

Tartar, Maria. *Lustmord: Sexual Murder in Weimar Germany.* Princeton, N.J.: Princeton University Press, 1995.

Temming, Theodor. *Sturmfreie Buden: Eine Denkschrift für alle, denen das Wohl unserer studierenden Jugend und unseres Volkes am Herzen liegt.* Essen: Fredebeul and Koenen, 1913.

Tenfelde, Klaus, and Hans-Ulrich Wehler. *Wege zur Geschichte des Bürgertums.* Göttigen: Vandenhoeck and Ruprecht, 1994.

Terlinden, Ulla, Susanne Grieser, and Bettina Ross. *Wohnungspolitik in der alten Frauenbewegung.* Arbeitsberichte des Fachbereichs Stadtplanung, Landschaftsplanung, no. A 137. Kassel: University of Kassel, 1999.

Terlinden, Ulla, and Suzanna von Oertzen. *Die Wohnungsfrage ist Frauensache! Frauenbewegung und Wohnreform, 1870–1933.* Berlin: Reimer, 2006.

Teuteberg, Hans J., and Clemens Wischerman. *Wohnalltag in Deutschland 1850–1914: Bilder, Daten, Dokumente.* Münster: Coppenrath, 1985.

Thoma, Eduard. "Zur Ausstellung: 'Die Frau in Haus und Beruf.'" *Die Gegenwart* 41, no. 10 (1912): 158.

Tiersten, Lisa. "Marianne in the Department Store: Gender and the Politics of Consumption in Turn-of-the-Century Paris." In *Cathedrals of Consumption: The European Department Store, 1850–1939*, ed. Geoffrey Crossick and Serge Jaumain, 116–34. Aldershot: Ashgate, 1999.

"Tietz und Wertheim." *Die Zukunft* 32 (29 September 1900): 537–45.

Trost, Klara. "Die Frau als Architektin." *Die Frauenfachschule*, no. 28 (1919): 569–72.

Trott, Magda. "Die Wohnungsfrage eine brennende Frauenfrage." *Die Frau der Gegenwart* 9, no. 19 (1915): 139–40.

Uhlig, Günther. *Kollektivmodell "Einküchenhaus": Wohnreform und Architekturdebatte zwischen Frauenbewegung und Funktionalismus 1900–1933.* Werkbund-Archiv 6. Giessen: Anabas, 1981.

Urbach, Rosa. "Bilder aus der Ausstellung." *Die Frau im Osten* 6, no. 12 (1912): 93–94.

————. "Die Frau in Haus und Beruf." *Die Frau im Osten* 6, no. 11 (1912): 83–84.

Urban, Gisela. "Die Frau als Architektin." *Der Bazar* 74, no. 9 (1928): 16–17.

Velsen, Ruth von. "Die Wohnungsverhältnisse der Studentinnen." *Die Studentin* 2, no. 11 (1913).

"Die Vereinigung für Frauenwohnungen." *Frauenkapital—eine werdende Macht*, no. 5 (1914): 20.

"Eine 'Vereinigung für moderne Frauenwohnungen.'" *Die Frau im Osten* 5, no. 22 (1911): 188.

"Die Vereinigung für moderne Frauenwohnungen." *Die deutsche Frau* 1, no. 30 (1911): 7.

"Die Vereinigung für Frauenwohnungen." *Die deutsche Frau* 1, no. 43 (1911): 3.

"Vereinigung für moderne Frauenwohnungen." *Frauen-Rundschau* 12, no. 17 (1911): 402.

Vicinus, Martha. *Independent Women: Work and Community for Single Women, 1850–1920.* Women in Culture and Society, ed. Catharine R. Stimpson. Chicago: University of Chicago Press, 1985.

Vickery, Margaret Birney. *Buildings for Bluestockings: The Architecture and Social History of Women's Colleges in Late Victorian England.* Newark: University of Delaware Press, 1999.

"Victoria-Studienhaus." *Die Studentin* 4, no. 4 (1915): 38–39.

"Vom Victoria-Studienhaus." *Die Frau* 42, no. 1 (1934): 43–44.

"Von der Ausstellung." *Vossische Zeitung*, no. 102, February 25, 1912, Aus der Frauenwelt section.

"Vorträge im Viktoria-Studienhaus." *Die Studentin* 5, no. 1 (1916): 2–3.

Voss-Zietz, Martha. "Die Arbeit der Frau in der Wohnungsfürsorge." *Frauenkapital—eine werdende Macht*, no. 8 (1914): 9–11.

Walkowitz, Judith R. *City of Dreadful Delight: Narratives of Sexual Danger in Late-Victorian London.* Chicago: University of Chicago, 1992.

Walter, Leopold. "Berliner Klubs." *Elegante Welt*, no. 3 (1912): 4–6.

Was die Frau von Berlin wissen muss: Ein praktisches Frauenbuch für Einheimische und Fremde. 2nd ed. Berlin: Loesdau, 1932.

Watkin, David, and Tilman Mellinghoff. *German Architecture and the Classical Ideal.* Cambridge, Mass.: MIT Press, 1987.

Weber, Adelheid. "Die alte Jungfer von einst und das reife Mädchen von heut." *Die Welt der Frau*, no. 39 (1906): 609–10.

Weedon, Chris. *Gender, Feminism, and Fiction in Germany, 1840–1914.* Vol. 5 of Gender, Sexuality, Culture, ed. William J. Spurlin. New York: Peter Lang, 2006.

"Weibliche Gesundheitsinspektoren." *Neue Bahnen* 29, no. 4 (1894): 28.

"Weibliche Sanitätsinspektion in England." *Die Frau* 13, no. 10 (1906): 625–29.

Weinberg, Margarete. "Ein neues Frauenheim." *Frau und Gegenwart* 5, no. 18 (1928): 9.

Weintraub, Jeff. "The Theory and Politics of the Public/Private Distinction." In *Public and Private in Thought and Practice: Perspectives on a Grand Dichotomy*, ed. Jeff Weintraub and Krishan Kumar, 1–42. Chicago: University of Chicago Press, 1997.

Weintraub, Jeff, and Krishan Kumar, eds. *Public and Private in Thought and Practice: Perspectives on a Grand Dichotomy.* Chicago: University of Chicago Press, 1997.

Weiss, Penny A., and Marilyn Friedman, eds. *Feminism and Community.* Philadelphia: Temple University Press, 1995.

Welsch, Sabine. *Ein Ausstieg aus dem Korsett: Reformkleidung um 1900.* Darmstadt: Häusser, 1996.

Wentscher. "Die Frau als Architekt." *Welt der Frau*, no. 27 (1912): 431–32.

"Das Werden des ersten Studentinnenheims in Deutschland." *Nachrichtenblatt Haus Ottilie von Hansemann, Victoria-Studienhaus*, no. 26 (1940): 1–17.

Westheim, Paul. "Berlin: Ausstellung 'Die Frau in Haus und Beruf.'" *Kunstgewerbeblatt* 23, no. 7 (1912): 142–43.

————. "Die Frauenausstellung." *Kunst und Handwerk*, no. 9 (1912): 268–75.

————. "Von der Frauen-Ausstellung-Berlin." *Deutsche Kunst und Dekoration* 15, no. 8 (1912): 88–89.

Wiese, Edda. "Inneneinrichtung des neuen Hauses." *Deutscher Lyceum-Club* 10, no. 7 (1914): 275–76.

Wigley, Mark. *White Walls, Designer Dresses: The Fashioning of Modern Architecture.* Cambridge, Mass.: MIT Press, 1995.

Wilbrandt, Robert, and Lisbeth Wilbrandt. *Die deutsche Frau im Beruf.* Vol. 4 of Handbuch der Frauenbewegung, ed. Helene Lange and Gertrud Bäumer. Berlin: Moeser, 1902.

Wildenthal, Lora. *German Women for Empire, 1884–1945.* Durham, N.C.: Duke University Press, 2001.

Wilhelmy-Dollinger, Petra. *Die Berliner Salons: Mit historisch-literarischen Spaziergängen.* Berlin: Walter de Gruyter, 2000.

Wilke, Margrith, ed. *"The Wise Woman Buildeth Her House": Architecture, History and Women's Studies.* Vol. 1 of Vrouwenstudies Letteren Groningen. Groningen: University of Groningen, 1992.

Williams, Rosalind H. *Dream Worlds: Mass Consumption in Late Nineteenth-Century France.* Berkeley: University of California Press, 1982.

Wilson, Elizabeth. *The Contradictions of Culture: Cities, Culture, Women.* Theory, Culture and Society, ed. Mike Featherstone. London: Sage, 2001.

————. *The Sphinx in the City: Urban Life, the Control of Disorder, and Women.* Berkeley: University of California Press, 1991.

Wininger, S. *Grosse jüdische National-Biographie.* Vol. 3. Chernivtsi, Ukraine: Orient, 1928.

Winkelmann, Emilie. "Die Architektin und die Ingenieurin." In *Frauenberufe und -Ausbildungsstätten.* Vol. 1 of Das Frauenbuch, ed. Eugenie von Soden, 108–9. Stuttgart: Franckh'sche, 1913.

Wirz, Wilhelm. "Frau und Qualität." *Wohlfahrt und Wirtschaft* 1, no. 4 (1914): 196–200.

Wischerman, Clemens. *Wohnalltag in Deutschland 1850–1914: Bilder, Daten, Dokumente.* Münster: Coppenrath, 1985.

"Wohungsaufsicht: Ausbau der Wohnungsaufsicht und Wohnungspflege in Bayern. (Schluss)." *Zeitschrift für Wohungswesen* 10, no. 20 (1912): 284–86.

"Wohnungsaufsicht: Die Frau in der Wohnungsinspektion." *Zeitschrift für Wohnungswesen* 12, no. 4 (1913): 76.

"Wohnungsbeaufsichtigung: Die Frau in der Wohnungsinspektion." *Zeitschrift für Wohnungswesen* 11, no. 10 (1913): 162–63.

Wolff, Irma. "Die Frau als Kunstgewerblerin." *Neue Bahnen* 49, no. 7 (1914): 51–54.

Wolff, Janet. *Feminine Sentences: Essays on Women and Culture.* Cambridge, U.K.: Polity, 1990.

"Woman's Work in Many Fields." *New York Times,* February 25, 1912, C2.

"Women's Bank a Failure." *New York Times,* April 25, 1915.

"Women's Club in London." *New York Times*, June 26, 1904.

"Women's Financial Daily." *New York Times*, January 15, 1914.

"Women Would Join the Boerse." *New York Times*, February 8, 1914.

"W. T." "Die Frau in Haus und Beruf." *Königsberger Tageblatt*, no. 49, February 28, 1912.

Zepler, Margarete. "Frauenheime." *Die Welt der Frau*, no. 14 (1905): 211–15.

———. "Heimstätten für Arbeiterinnen." *Die Welt der Frau*, no. 43 (1905): 683–85.

Zunk, Johanna. "Die Töchter der Alma mater." *Illustrierte Frauenzeitung* 38, no. 7 (1911): 55–56.

Zwaka, Petra, et al. *"Ich bin meine eigene Frauenbewegung": Frauen-Ansichten aus der Geschichte einer Grossstadt*. Berlin: Hentrich, 1991.

"Das Zweite Arbeiterinnenheim in Berlin." *Centralblatt des Bundes Deutscher Frauenvereine*, no. 15 (1903): 119.

Archival Sources

Alice-Salomon-Archiv, Alice Salomon Fachhochschule, Berlin

Amt für Denkmalpflege, Potsdam

Archiv, Bau- und Wohnungsaufsichtsamt, Bezirksamt Charlottenburg-Wilmersdorf

Archiv, Deutscher Staatsbürgerinnen-Verband, Berlin

Archiv, Pestalozzi-Fröbel-Haus, Berlin

Bauaktenarchiv, Bezirksamt Tempelhof-Schöneberg

Bildarchiv Preussischer Kulturbesitz, Berlin

Geheimes Staatsarchiv Preussischer Kulturbesitz, Berlin

Heimatmuseum Charlottenburg-Wilmersdorf

Helene-Lange-Archiv, Landesarchiv Berlin

Landesarchiv Berlin

Pankow Bauaktenarchiv

Staatsarchiv Hamburg

Werkbund-Archiv, Berlin

Zentrum für Berlin-Studien, Zentral- und Landesbibliothek Berlin

INDEX

Despina Stratigakos is assistant professor of architecture at the University at Buffalo, State University of New York.